D1288130

Grosse Pointe, Jan 26. 2012

To Nooush & Jean,
Picasso is coming
YAY!
Thought that, in his honor,
you might want to do
some reading before!!
Love You,
Me

PICASSO'S WORLD

JOHN FINLAY

METRO BOOKS
NEW YORK

Contents

Previous Page
Nude, Green Leaves, and Bust *1932*
Oil on canvas, 164.4 x 132 cm (64.7 x 51.9 in).
Private collection.

This work is one of a series of paintings that Picasso executed in 1932, and where a plaster bust gazes upon the artist's sleeping/dreaming lover – the blonde Marie-Thérèse Walter. The fruit and the philodendron plant sprouting from her naked body not only suggest fecundity and fertility – her body as a ripe vessel – but are also strongly reminiscent of the foliage and iconography in Picasso's famous sculpture *Woman in a Garden* of 1929–30 (see Chapter 16, p. 146).

METRO BOOKS
New York

An Imprint of Sterling Publishing
387 Park Avenue South
New York, NY 10016

METRO BOOKS and the distinctive Metro Books logo are trademarks of Sterling Publishing Co., Inc.

This 2011 edition published by Metro Books by arrangement with Carlton Publishing Group

ISBN 978-1-4351-3580-2

For information about custom editions, special sales, and premium and corporate purchases, please contact Sterling Special Sales at 800-805-5489 or specialsales@sterlingpublishing.com.

Manufactured in China

1 2 3 4 5 6 7 8 9 10

www.sterlingpublishing.com

Introduction

Pablo Picasso (1881–1973) remains one of the most important artists of the twentieth-century. A brilliant draughtsman, painter, printer, sculptor and theatrical designer, he was the creator of Cubism – along with Georges Braque (1882–1963) – and remained at the forefront of the *avant-garde* for many years. Consistently upholding and defying traditional methods of representation, Picasso produced many unusual and groundbreaking works of art and, in doing so, made a most original contribution to twentieth-century culture.

Hailed and reviled at different times, Picasso has been seen as a prodigy, bohemian, agent provocateur, conformist, classicist, primitivist, shaman, *surréaliste*, dissident, matador, poet, communist, counterfeiter and even a *pasticher* of his own art. The list is almost endless, but is perhaps the most logical way of observing the artist's *oeuvre*, as a means of analyzing the apparent discontinuity of styles that exists within it as a whole. Picasso's paradoxical method of challenging artistic canons and referring back to his earlier inventions may appear incongruous to the viewer or art historian, but it undoubtedly led the artist to interpret the world around him in diverse ways and, as observers, we are all the richer for his rather obscure approach to making and documenting art.

Another way of interpreting Picasso's life and work would be to follow the development of his art chronologically and to investigate the artists, characters, friends and collaborators who profoundly shaped his art. Picasso's work can also be situated within the context of the various idioms or art movements, as well as the social and political conditions that shaped the different strands of Modernism of the twentieth century: Post-Impressionism, Primitivism, Cubism, Futurism, Classicism and Surrealism.

One of the other defining characteristics of Picasso's art was that of rendering and expressing the human condition by means of multitudinous forms, guises, rituals and highly theatrical gestures. His work could be imaginative, humorous, erotic, the stuff of dreams or nightmares, full of apparent abstractions (but never entirely abstract), biographical and esoteric in content and nature. His imagery was sometimes androgynous, phallic, surreal, cruel, violent, destructive and, as we shall see, even sadistic.

Yet his art could also express deep love, philosophical or political ideas, transient, fraternal, mystical or magical themes, or, as was usually the case with Picasso, all of these things at once. For Picasso, the body was the definitive subject and artistic mediator, and finding alternative methods to recreate radical forms – human or otherwise – became the ultimate motivation behind the inventive character of his greatest artworks. This is evidenced by the diffuseness of his drawings, paintings, prints and sculptures throughout his life.

In looking at all these genres and in appraising Picasso's artistic expression and development, we must recognize that theatre and ballet were major catalysts of his creative process. These have often been marginalized in the context of various histories and theories debating his art. Consequently, such narratives have superseded what are undoubtedly sustained theatrical influences running through the artist's work. Historians have overlooked or found difficulty in placing the theatre and the performative character of his work within the wider context of his *oeuvre*. So theatre remains something of an uncultivated area within Picasso scholarship, especially in the context of the artist's Cubism.

This book will follow Picasso, the man and his artistic experiments, discoveries and achievements, bringing them under one umbrella and presenting his work in a more cohesive, intelligible and new way. Picasso was a man who believed in the power of magic to transform the imagination, and it is to be hoped that *Picasso's World* will also inspire readers' imaginations, by giving a fresh insight into the creativity, mythology and mystery of a truly unique artist, whose work was as boundless as it was beguiling.

By the late 1890s, Picasso had mastered many of the nineteenth century's realist and modernist styles of art, which the artist encountered in Spain and Paris, where he settled permanently in 1904. Between 1901 and 1905, Picasso's work evolved from phases of Spanish Symbolism and French Impressionism through to the so-called Blue and Rose Periods. Picasso's powerful sense of visual expression and restless imagination also led him to explore primitive art, culminating in his masterpiece *Les Demoiselles d'Avignon* (1907), which proved something of an epiphany in twentieth century modern art. *Les Demoiselles*, like much of Picasso's art from this period, incorporates stylistic elements derived from tribal artefacts of Africa and Oceanic cultures.

1

Section 1: 1881–1907

Chapter 1

Pigeons, Bullfights and Sacred Subjects: Picasso's Origins and Youth, 1881–98

Whether it is a true story or the product of a vivid imagination, Picasso claimed to have been born of fire and smoke when his uncle, Dr Salvador Ruiz Blasco, blew the fumes from his burning cigar into the face of what was presumed to be a stillborn infant on 25 October 1881. The story, which is reminiscent of the deity Vulcan's impossible survival, his supernatural manipulation of fire and transformative powers, was often repeated by his biographers. Roland Penrose follows Picasso's rather picturesque tradition of romanticizing his birth, and succumbs to the artist's mythologizing in his description of how death, so omnipresent at birth, "lurked in Picasso's imagination throughout his life".[1] Most of what we know about Picasso's early life and work comes from the book *Picasso: Portraits et Souvenirs* (1949), by Jaime Sabartès, who was the artist's loyal friend and his private secretary from 1935 onwards. However, as John Richardson astutely points out, many of Sabartès's comments come from Picasso. Although Picasso's memory was astounding; in certain areas, particularly childhood, we have to allow for a degree of grandiloquence or fictitiousness.

Picasso was born into a poor, working-class family from Málaga in Andalusia, and his father, Don José Ruiz Blasco, was a teacher and a painter who was best known for his academic representations of pigeons. Picasso would pay homage to his father in the Cubist painting *Still Life with Pigeons* (1912), and adopt Don José's *columbofila* as an icon of peace in the 1950s, exercising the right to "have repaid him in pigeons".[2] Contrary to Picasso's assertion that his father "never left the house" except to teach and "amuse himself painting",[3] Don José made efforts to establish himself in the community. He courted local collectors, exhibited his paintings and attained a position as a professor at the Instituto da Guarda in La Coruña, where his son would also study. Later, he became a founding member of the Real Academia Gallega de Bellas Artes, where he took on teaching and secretarial responsibilities to earn money. He was known as an avid café frequenter, a wonderful conservationalist and, most notably, a lifelong *aficionado* of the bullfight: traits that his son inherited.

Picasso's mother, Doña María, an individual with high levels of energy and focus, was more conventional in terms of her religious devotion to a lay sisterhood in Málaga. Although no more pious than was to be expected from a woman living in a Catholic country, Doña María had prayed hard to be given a son and was rewarded for her dedication to *La Virgin de la Merced*. As we shall see, in the late 1890s, Picasso would go on to paint sacred subjects based on what his father deemed to be more lucrative, religious art forms, depicting scenes drawn from the Catholic faith.

Far from being a gifted adolescent prodigy, Picasso's early drawings show that he had to work hard to improve his competence, let alone achieve the mastery he claimed to possess from an early age on receiving the paints and brushes handed to him by his father. According to myth, after giving his son his materials, Picasso's father never painted again, but research has revealed that Don José continued to paint pigeons for many years. Tales of self-denial perpetuated by the artist even led him to claim that he had produced a real drawing of a statue of Hercules in his father's house.

The drawing in question was executed in November 1890, when Picasso was aged nine (see page 7), and is similar to the type of sketching that one would expect from a boy of his age. Picasso's first surviving works depicting a bullfighting scene (see page 37) and a picador on horseback also demonstrate the typical perception of a juvenile. Even the pigeons around the edges of this sketch are probably copies of his father's own work. In fact, the painting of a picador and drawing depicting a matador tossed by a bull are far more interesting for their iconography than for any artistry. These works show Picasso's enthusiasm for a subject that would dominate a large portion of his output: bullfighting. This would become an obsession, culminating in his great painting *Guernica* (see Chapter 17), which would continue to occupy him well into his eighties. As Robert Otero explains, Don José was an *aficionado* of the bullfight and his father took his son to the bullfighting ring from an early age. Picasso

---

1 Roland Penrose, *Picasso: His Life and Work*, Victor Gollancz Ltd, London, Chapter I, "Origins and Youth", 1958, p. 23.
2 John Richardson, A Life of Picasso. Volume I: 1881–1906, with Marilyn McCully, Pimlico, London, 1992, p. 52.
3 Jaime Sabartès, *Picasso: Portraits et souvenirs*, Louis Carré et Maximilien Vox, Paris, 1946, p. 9. Translated as *Picasso: An Intimate Portrait*, W. H. Allen, London, 1949.

recalled: "I must have been ten years old when my father took me to see El Lagartijo fight".[4]

Surprisingly little work survives from Picasso's early youth, although family members always claimed that he drew endlessly. The artist's talents extended to creating *papiers découpes*, cut-out silhouettes of flowers, animals and groups of people, using his aunt Eloísa's embroidery scissors, as a form of entertainment to please his mother and his sister Conchita. "Do us a portrait of Tola Calderon's Newfoundland dog," they would insist.[5] It is well known that Picasso loved animals and he was hardly ever without a pet throughout his life. Two *papiers découpes* (cut-out silhouettes) of a *Dove/Colombe* (see page 7), and a *Dog* of 1890, both in the Museu Picasso, Barcelona, offer surviving examples of the dexterity employed by a nine-year-old boy when executing paper cut-outs.

The artist would put this artistry to great use in making his Synthetic Cubist collages of 1912–14 (namely the well-known cardboard *Guitar*, see Chapter 8), and when employing cut-out techniques for his sheet-metal sculptures, such as *Woman*, in the 1960s (see Chapter 19). The language of Picasso's *papiers collés* (pasted paper collages) clearly depended on the dressmaking technique, which he had acquired as a child under the watchful gaze of female family members such as his sister Lola.

When the family moved to La Coruña in 1891, Picasso was enrolled the following year in Don José's drawing class at the Instituto da Guarda. The young artist seems to have willingly submitted himself to the role of a diligent student. He progressed so quickly that in a short time he was producing competent drawings from antique plaster casts or from plates in books, such as those of Charles Bargue's *Cours de dessin* of 1868. These works were, however, a long way off from his boast that he could, in adolescence, draw like Raphael. Picasso's first oil paintings, dating from between 1894 and 1895, were mainly realistic portraits, or idealized subjects, such as *Beggar in a Cap* and *Girl with Bare Feet* (see page 8).

The latter work, with its hieratic pose and sculptural mass anticipates the heavily set and highly primitivized female nudes Picasso would create in 1905–06, and the neo-classical figure compositions he would make during the "call to order" period after the First World War (see Chapter 13). A reviewer for *La Voz de Galicia* wrote in an article published on 21 February 1895 that if Picasso continued painting in the same manner: "There is no doubt that he has days of glory and a brilliant future ahead of him".[6]

In September 1895, Don José accepted a teaching position at the prestigious La Llotja art school in Barcelona, where Picasso's newly acquired skills and precocious talent impressed his classmates, including his lifelong friend Manuel Pallarès. As he later recalled, Picasso appeared to be way ahead of the other students. Pallarès also suggests that the young Spaniard had an air of superiority about him, but he never got carried away with his own self-importance, nor had the "character [and] the behaviour of a boy of his age".[7]

Don José may have been a mediocre and rather unsuccessful painter, but he was determined to learn from his own disappointments and did everything he could to steer Picasso's artistic career in a way that he thought was right and proper: in the direction of sacred or allegorical subjects. Don José seems to have dictated the subjects of the *First Communion* (see page 9) and *Science and Charity* (see page 6), since he was well aware that sentimental genre scenes like these were popular in Spain and France, and more likely to make Picasso's name. These works were therefore collaborative undertakings, and Don José intelligently thought that the pious Roman Catholic ceremony depicting a female child about to receive the First Holy Communion – the body and blood of Christ – to be within easy reach of his son's adolescent sensibility.

Don José prepared the canvas and posed as the father figure for *Science and Charity*. The painting was carefully planned by means of preparatory drawings based on the subject of an innocent communicant reciting prayers before an altar. The realism of certain details, including a clumsy-looking boy about to topple a vase of flowers, lit candles, the garland and elaborate dress of the young girl, along with the theatrical organization, suggests great intelligence for a boy of Picasso's age. Moreover, the artist's work, if somewhat stilted, had all the ingredients of a successful genre painting devoted to God and the Catholic faith. The work was exhibited at the Exposición de Bellas Artes y Industrias Artísticas in Barcelona in April 1896, and a review in the *Diario de Barcelona* (25 May 1896) describes the picture as "the work of a novice in which one perceives sensibility in the principal figures".[8]

The endeavour of *First Communion* most likely derived from Picasso's teachers at La Llotja, especially José Ramón Garnelo Alda, who was a specialist in these idealized, pious subjects. Don José naturally arranged for his son to work under the auspices of this established Andalusian painter, who had been a colleague of his at La Llotja between 1895 and 1899. Picasso's paintings of altar-boys and first communions were highly reminiscent of José Ramón Garnelo Alda's subjects and typical of the School of Málaga in general. Picasso could not, however, resist suggesting an amorous relationship between the male and female protagonists, and therefore harnessing his sexuality to the painting. The diagonal line joining both adolescent figures, the flowers and strewn petals, as well as the two snuffed-out candles, which intimate the transience of life and a loss of innocence, could be an anecdotal suggestion that the altar-boy has a future connection with the young and virtuous bride of Christ.

John Richardson, on the other hand, claims that the candles and rose petals are symbolic of two deaths in the Ruiz Blasco family – souls who died in innocence. Two of the candles are aflame but two have been snuffed out, and something that perhaps indicates a symbolic rather than an anecdotal touch in Picasso's *First Communion*. Richardson reminds us that a census of 1885 records the Ruiz Blascos as having a second son, José, who, presumably, died early on. The candles could symbolize two surviving and two deceased children. Emblems of mortality are found in the petals scattered on the altar steps, which act as a *memento mori* device commemorating the departed Conchita and thriving Lola.

By the age of sixteen, Picasso had shrugged off his father's attempts to mould him into a traditional painter of religious subjects. He had been enrolled in the prestigious art school at the Academia Real de San Fernando, but soon rebelled and stopped attending classes, preferring to draw whenever pleased him. When he returned to Barcelona in 1899, he flatly refused to resume his studies at the Academia. This was Picasso's message to his father that his five years of art school training were over, as far as the ambitious painter was concerned. After recovering from a severe bout of scarlet fever, he appears to have grown in confidence. Self-portraits of the time depict him as mustachioed and looking straight at the viewer. As if re-born, the young artist rebelliously signed himself "Picasso", occasionally adding the prefix "Yo" ("I") to his signature, and intimating a newfound ego and identity.

The artist returned to Barcelona after a brief spell painting in the abstract style of *japonisant* (a type of Art Nouveau) while recuperating from his bout of scarlet fever on Pallarès's family farm in Horta de Sant Joan, in the mountains between Catalonia and Aragon. As he later told Sabartés, "all I know, I learned in [that] village".[9] Soon Picasso began associating with the artistic circle that gathered at the *modernista* Els Quatre Gats (The Four Cats) café. He brought with him the academic disciplines of drawing, which would be central to his painting and sculptural practice, and crucial to his entire *oeuvre*.

4 Robert Otero, *Forever Picasso*, trans., Elaine Kerrigan, Abrams, New York, 1974, p. 43-44.
5 Jaime Sabartès, *Picasso: Documents Iconographiques*, Geneva, Pierre Cailler, 1954, p. 305.
6 *Picasso: The Early Years, 1892–1906*, edited by Marilyn McCully, Yale University Press, New Haven and London, 1997, "Chronology" p. 23.
7 Pierre Cabanne, *Picasso: His Life and Times*, William Morrow and Company, New York, 1977, Chapter II, "The Apprentice Years" (1895–1901), p. 33.
8 M. McCully, *Picasso The Early Years*, p. 25.
9 Picasso to Jaime Sabartès, 1949, p. 43.

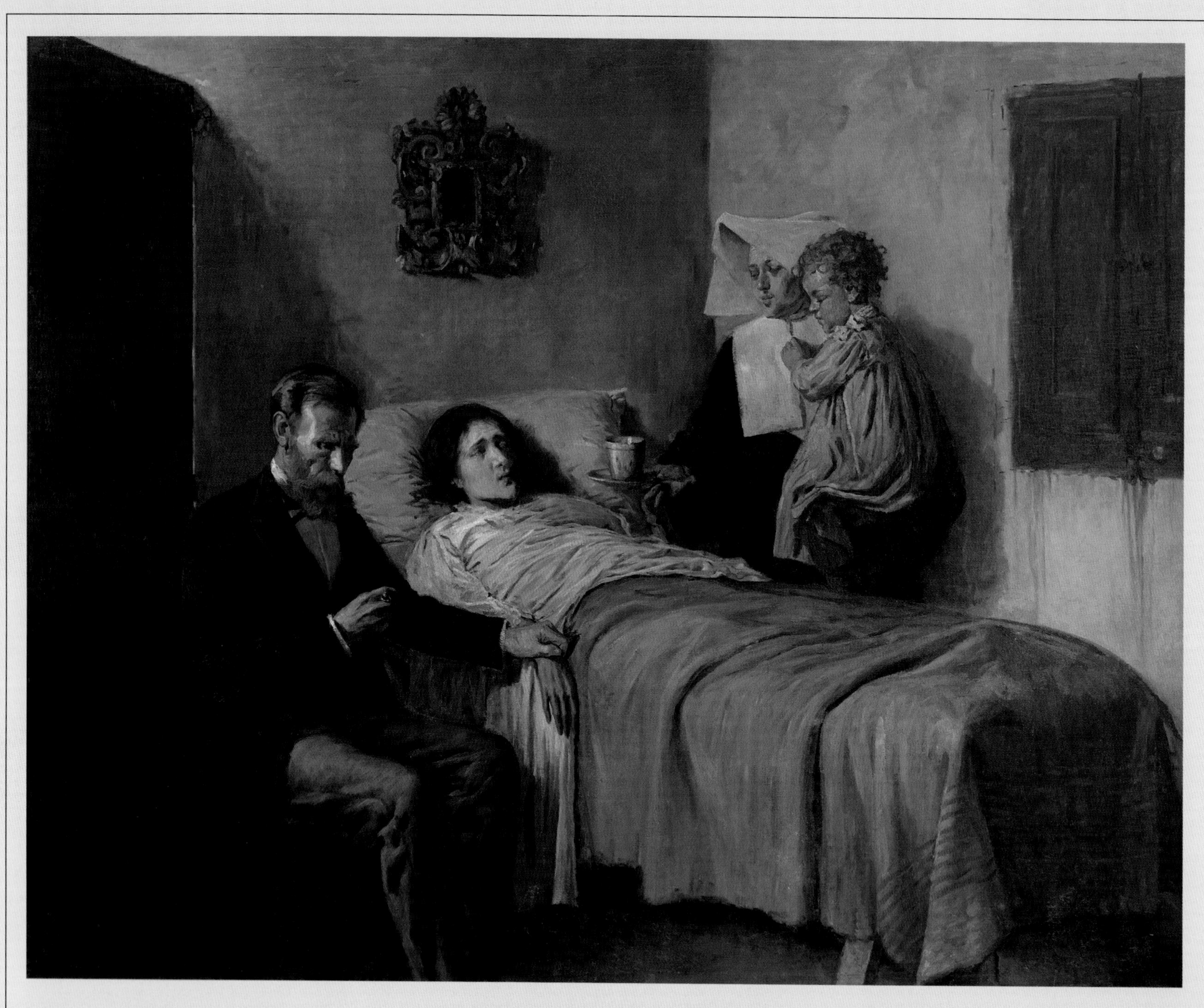

Science and Charity, *1897*

Oil on canvas, 197 x 249.5 cm (77.5 x 98 in). Museu Picasso, Barcelona

Science and Charity of 1897 was a large allegorical painting that received an honourable mention when exhibited at the Exposición General de Bellas Artes in Madrid and a gold medal at the Exposición Provincial de Málaga. To celebrate, the Málaga painter Joaquin Martínez de la Vega (1846–1905) poured champagne over Picasso's head in an exuberant gesture of his great triumph. The success was an immense achievement in the eyes of his family. The painting was given to Picasso's uncle Salvador, a medical doctor, who perhaps saw the image of his brother Don José as a portrait of himself and, later, as a reflection of his own qualities.

As he had done in *First Communion*, Don José outlined the subject matter and title of this quasi-devotional work, prepared the canvas and served as one of its principal guides. However, as one Madrid critic wrote about the limp and gangrenous-looking hand of the stricken woman, "I am sorry to laugh callously at such grief, but I cannot help it, for surely the doctor is feeling the pulse of a glove."[10] Moralistic, theatrical and anecdotal genre subjects, such as *Science and Charity*, were popular in late nineteenth-century Europe. At the time, the genre painting *The Doctor*, by Luke Fildes, garnered a great deal of attention when exhibited at the Royal Academy of Arts, London, in 1891, and may have drawn Picasso and his father's attention as a subject for *Science and Charity*. Surely it is not a coincidence that Don José, who poses as the doctor, looks remarkably similar to the physician in Fildes's painting. Picasso worked on this vast canvas in a tiny studio on Carrer de la Plata. The cramped conditions of the worksite may be observed in the painting's claustrophobic setting, in which the bedridden invalid and other protagonists are compressed into the tiny space of the maudlin sickroom. According to the artist's biographer John Richardson, the death of Picasso's younger sister Conchita was the catalyst for a work based on the celebrated Castilian artist Enrique Paternina's painting *The Mother's Visit* of 1896, which depicts a nun observing a mother at the hospital bedside of her sick-looking child. Picasso, however, manipulates the viewer by removing almost all feeling of solace (apart from the doctor checking his patient's pulse) and by endowing the figure with a deathly ill countenance and filling the scene with doom so as to recapitulate the conditions of Conchita's mortal illness.

10 Marilyn McCully, *A Picasso Anthology*, Princeton, 1981, p. 21.

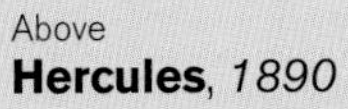

Above
Hercules, *1890*
Pencil on paper, 49.6 x 32 cm (19.3 x 12.5 in). Museu Picasso, Barcelona

A pencil sketch showing Picasso's skill as a young draughtsman, which despite the artist's claims to have been able to draw like Raphael, or to have never drawn like a child, shows nothing more than competence for a nine-year-old boy.

Above
Dove/Colombe, *1890–91*
Paper cut-out, 5 x 8.5 cm (2 x 3.5 in). Museu Picasso, Barcelona

Picasso was skilled at making paper cut-outs and this image of a small dove was probably done for the entertainment of family members. This type of work anticipates Picasso's famous paper and cardboard constructions and his late sheet metal sculpture.

Left

Girl with Bare Feet, *1895*

Oil on canvas, 75 x 50 cm (29.5 x 19.5 in). Musée Picasso, Paris

This is an arresting image of a young and wild-looking peasant girl, who was only a few years younger than Picasso, and whom his father hired as a model. The hieratic stature of the young female and her rather large feet anticipate, to a degree, the style and subject of the pseudo-classical female figures that Picasso would paint in the early 1920s.

Opposite

First Communion, *1896*

Oil on canvas, 166 x 118 cm (65.5 x 46.5 in). Museu Picasso, Barcelona

This was Picasso's first foray into the area of religious subjects, a popular theme in Spain and France during the period, which launched the fourteen-year-old Picasso's career as a painter.

Chapter 2

Modernisme at Els Quatre Gats Café and Picasso's First Visit to Paris, 1899–1901

Els Quatre Gats (The Four Cats) was advertised as a beer hall cum tavern/inn, but doubled as a showroom for local arts and crafts, and its walls were not only covered with paintings and drawings (mostly of the clientele), but also ceramics and trophies. Additionally, the café entertained puppet shows, musical evenings, poetry readings, theatrical productions, regular art exhibitions and other light entertainment. Catalan *modernisme*, as a prominent literary and artistic movement, attracted many dramatists and writers to the café, and a number of the clientele seem to have held strong anarchist or political sympathies, as well as displaying an obsessive interest in the work of the German writer Friedrich Nietzsche. For a generation of young artists, writers and intellectuals at Els Quatre Gats, Nietzsche represented a heroic individualism and a struggle against anachronistic values and cultural ideals. Els Quatre Gats, as a focal point for the avant-garde in Barcelona, would certainly have allowed Picasso to learn all about the latest developments in art, literature, music, poetry, politics and philosophy, especially the ideas of Nietzsche, Oscar Wilde, Paul-Marie Verlaine, Richard Wagner and the political theorist and anarchist Peter Kropotkin. These were just some of the important writers and thinkers discussed among the young and would-be intellectuals at the café. However, as Robert Lubar argues, despite there being expansive ideas concerning poverty, suffering and social alienation in the work of Picasso and his contemporaries (notably in that of Santiago Rusiñol and Ramon Casas), these images "[fall] far short of a partisan statement"[1], let alone signalling the young artist's allegiance to any specific political cause or anarchist group. Lubar explains that Picasso's representations of prostitution, beggars and destitute family groups depict universal social types in generalized settings as opposed to specific individuals: types very much in opposition to anarchist imagery of the era, and generally illustrating the divisions between underclass marginalization and bourgeois society.

Hence Picasso's poster design for a retirement fund for workers portrays a mother enveloping her children in a long, flowing cloak, and making an allegorical or psychological statement about protection, poverty and social wrongs rather than declaring any specific political stance. Picasso's image also adopts the symbolist sensibilities and imagery of contemporary artists such as Edvard Munch. A self-portrait of 1900 (see page 42), with expressive charcoal lines and a gaunt countenance revealing jet black eyes staring straight out at the viewer, is also undeniably Munchian in style. Furthermore, Picasso absorbs the influence of El Greco's expressive manner, creating a pastiche of this in a number of contemporary sketches and oils, such as his *Portrait of Casagemas*. Interestingly, in *El Liberal* on 24 March 1904, Picasso's friend Carles Junyer Vidal describes the artist's work as a pure expression of the psychological forces in his art rather than resorting to political ideology or social anarchism.

In October 1900, Picasso travelled to Paris with his poet-painter friend Carles Casagemas. Picasso had met the intelligent and prepossessing Casagemas in the spring of 1899, at the age of seventeen. Casagemas was a poet, painter and striving decadente, but also appears to have been a self-destructive, needy and volatile individual, tragically addicted to alcohol and morphine. Eighteen months later, Casagemas committed suicide, and the event would greatly affect Picasso and his blue period work (see Chapter 3).

The artist's painting *Last Moments* was to be hung in the Exposition Universelle in Paris, and Picasso was keen to see his work on display in the Décennale exhibition of contemporary art at the Grand Palais. We have no record of what this painting looked like because Picasso later used the canvas for his *La Vie* composition (see Chapter 3), but judging from the surviving sketches, we can imagine that it displayed comparable qualities to the moribund symbolism of Rusiñol's *The Morphine Drug Addict* (1894) and despair of Munch's lithograph *Death in the Sickroom*, published in *La Plume* in 1897 (see page 14). Picasso and Casagemas stayed in Paris for three months, taking over the vacated studio of their Spanish compatriot Isidre Nonell at 48 rue Gabrielle in Montmartre, and making contact with other members of the large Catalan community residing in the Parisian quarter. Picasso and Casagemas visited the vibrant café scene on the Boulevard de Clichy, sampling the delights of cabarets, theatres, dance halls and brothels. Marilyn McCully, a specialist in Picasso's early career, points out that besides seeing his own show and the painting sections at the fair, the artist may have visited the other special exhibitions including electrical displays; spectacles from around the world, plaster moulds from Africa, South America and Asia, as well as demonstrations of X-rays, wireless telegraphy, films and other visual entertainment and

1 Robert S. Lubar, "Barcelona Blues", in Marilyn McCully, *Picasso: The Early Years*, p. 93.

performances by the Japanese dancer Sada Yacco (Picasso later made a drawing of Yacco) or the hugely popular veil dancer Loïe Fuller.

Picasso appears to have drawn inspiration from some of these spectacles when depicting the liberal atmosphere of *Le Moulin de la Galette* in 1900 (see pages 16–17). The opportunity to paint the latter was his principal motive for visiting Paris, and the trip also gave him the chance to absorb modernist developments in French art. The Exposition Universelle was international in outlook and scope, and the adjoining Décannale exhibition allowed for an extensive study of French painting from between 1800 and 1889. Subsequently, creating *Le Moulin de la Galette* seems to have triggered Picasso's determination to understand these radical forms in painting. In a resolute attempt to shrug off the vestiges of symbolism in works such as *Last Moments*, he threw himself into conveying the everyday subject matter of couples dancing, flirting or holding intimate conversations among the vice-like, seedy and swirling atmosphere of Paris's famous nightspot. At the time, perhaps the best-known painting of *Le Moulin de la Galette* was Pierre-Auguste Renoir's work of 1876, illustrating joyous couples and happy family members amusing themselves and socializing in the dappled, impressionistic sunlight. As Elizabeth Cowling emphasizes, Picasso undoubtedly adapted Renoir's style, subject matter and highly optimistic mood in favour of a more bohemian setting. Picasso replaces day-time surroundings with a distinct night-time aura so as to transform Renoir's idyllic setting into a scene of hedonism, sensuality and city vice. In Picasso's painting, the women become cocottes and his men well-dressed debauchees, while smooching pairs of women undoubtedly suggest lesbianism and the general raunchiness of the time.

Picasso had also visited the Moulin Rouge with Casagemas, another popular nightspot for painters such as Henri de Toulouse-Lautrec (see page 14), who depicted comparable satirical figures with horribly made-up, haunted-looking faces and bodies pressed together in the hectic atmosphere of the dance hall. The works of Picasso's Spanish compatriots (Casas, Rusiñol, Utrillo et al), must have looked rather tame and mimetic besides Toulouse-Lautrec's strange physiognomies, experimental use of swirling colour and grand-scale compositions, demonstrating his irresistible bravado and dazzling painterly techniques. Through his assimilation of these influences and development of his expressionist style, Picasso achieved great success in his approach towards French Modernism. This can be observed in the fact that *Le Moulin de la Galette* was immediately sold to the French newspaper publisher Arthur Huc, who was a patron of a number of contemporary artists, including Toulouse-Lautrec.

Apart from a few, brief interludes in Málaga and Madrid, during which Picasso's new painting *Lady in Blue* (see page 13) took on a distinctly Spanish flavour under the influence of Diego Velázquez's portrait of *Queen Mariana of Austria* (1652–53), the artist was soon back in Paris to work on a show of paintings for Ambroise Vollard's gallery on 6 rue Laffitte, held from 25 June until 14 July 1901. Judging by the sheer range of subjects on display and by a review of the show, Picasso appears to have been out to prove that he too was "a passionate lover of modern life"[2], and that he could tackle subjects such as the Boulevard de Clichy, just as Camille Pissarro and other French painters had done before him. As Picasso's friend the poet Max Jacob, whom he met through the dealer of modern Spanish art Pere Mañach, later recalled: "[Picasso] was accused of imitating Steinlen, Lautrec, Vuillard, van Gogh etc., but everyone recognized that he had fire. A real brilliance, a painter's eye".[3]

Picasso did indeed start to imitate, and even make pastiches of works by other modern artists, such as Édouard Manet and Paul Gauguin. Most notably, in 1901, the artist looked towards the expressive style, thickly impastoed surfaces and intense colour ranges of Vincent van Gogh, and appropriated them in his painting *Death of Casagemas* (see page 15). Here the burning flame and wilting candle exorcise the ghost of Casagemas and evoke the memory and sufferings of both men, by reminding the viewer that an absence can be traced. Casegemas had pursued Germaine Gargallo with desperate letters of betrothal, but was eventually rejected and, over diner at L'Hippodrome (now the Palace Clichy) in Montmatre, with her and other friends, the Spaniard shot himself in the temple. Picasso was certainly haunted by Casagemas's death and by regrets about deserting him to return to Paris to bolster his career, as well as his guilt over an affair with the very woman who had been at the centre of his friend's suicide. The death of his great friend Casagemas seems to have gradually precipitated the artist's tragic world-view of human misery, and would surely have necessitated a longing for the painter to immerse himself in the nostalgia of Catalan culture, both past and present. In contemplating the death of Casagemas, Picasso's palette slowly changed, and he began to paint almost entirely in shades of blue, leading to what Jaime Sabartès would call "Les Bleus de Barcelone" ("Barcelona Blues").

---

2 Elizabeth Cowling, *Picasso: Style and Meaning*, Phaidon Press, London, 2002, Chapter 2, p. 77.
3 Marilyn McCully, *A Picasso Anthology*, p. 3.

Portrait of Angel Fernández de Soto, *1899*

Oil on canvas, 69.7 x 55.2 cm (27.4 x 21.7 in). Private Collection

Picasso returned to Barcelona to live with his family in 1899 and, no longer an art student, began contributing drawings to journals and providing illustrations for Pere Romeu's café-cabaret Els Quatre Gats (The Four Cats), which was frequented by some of the most progressive literary and artistic figures in Barcelona. The concept of a *modernista* movement stemmed from the rebirth of Catalan nationalism, whose followers sought to restore the language, cultural values and traditions of the region, while at the same time promoting and expanding links with European Modernism, culture and industry. Influenced in every way by the flamboyant cultural character of Paris, the burgeoning Catalan community looked towards the artistic trends of the thriving bohemian quarter of Montmartre. Els Quatre Gats was therefore modelled on the free-spirited meeting place Le Chat Noir (The Black Cat) in Montmartre, and soon became popular with Catalan artists and writers whom the Barcelona press labelled *decadentes* or *modernistas*, and who were influenced by a love affair with French art, in particular, Art Nouveau.

Two influential journals were also published at the tavern, *Quatre Gats* and *Pel & Ploma*, and it held many exhibitions, puppet shows, plays and other theatrical spectacles. Many key figures of the art world joined its vibrant *modernista* circle, and they soon numbered among Picasso's best friends. Among them were important writers, poets and artists, such as Jaime Sabartès, Ramon Pichot, Carles Casagemas, Josep and Joan Cardona, Isidre Nonell, Francisco de Asís Soler, Carles and Sebatià Junyer Vidal. They participated alongside senior figures such as Ramon Casas, Miguel Utrillo and Santiago Rusiñol, who had founded the tavern and were successful portraitists in their own right. On joining this group, Picasso was soon taken up as something of a prodigy and artistic outsider, and was commissioned by Romeu to create graphic designs advertising the café, including the poster design for the puppet play, *Dramas Criollos*, as well as the menu card for Els Quatre Gats itself.

With these works, Picasso followed the *moderniste* idiom earmarked by Casas and Utrillo for their own designs, and used the bold, flat colours favoured by French artists such as Henri de Toulouse-Lautrec to define the contours, shapes or silhouettes of objects and figures. Picasso's *Portrait of Angel Fernández de Soto* (see right) also shows him absorbing the painterly techniques of Casas and Rusiñol in his use of rapid, sketch-like brushwork to imitate their more loosely expressive, melancholy portraits – which were characteristic of both *fin de siècle* and *modernista* styles, as well as symbolist art in general. Besides alluding directly to the portraiture of Casas and Rusiñol, Picasso also makes rather subtle references to the Spanish master El Greco, giving *Fernandez de Soto* the air of nobility and fashionable guise of the non-conformist *flâneur*. Picasso also exhibited many portraits of his friends, supporters and admirers for a solo exhibition at Els Quatre Gats in February 1900. The show was fundamentally a response to Casas's portrait, displayed at the Sala Parés of Barcelona in October 1899. Casagemas, Pallarès, Sabartès and the de Soto brothers thought that their young prodigy could produce far better work than Casas's "Barcelona iconography", as one local critic described his works. This was Picasso's first important exhibition and it incorporated the *fin de siècle* painting *Last Moments*, which clearly demonstrated the influence of the Barcelona group of Els Quatre Gats upon the artist's practice. As one critic caustically remarked, "One cannot deny that Señor Picasso has talent and a feeling for art [but] the exhibition reveals in the painter, as in many others who have preceded him [that they] are madly in love with the *modernista* school, a lamentable confusion of artistic sensibility and a mistaken concept of art." [4]

4 Sebastià Trullol i Plana, Diario de Barcelona, 7 February, 1900, Cited in Marilyn McCully, *Picasso: The Early Years*, p. 30.

Above
Lady in Blue, *1901*
Oil on canvas, 113 x 101 cm (44.5 x 40 in). Museo Nacional Centro de Arte Reina Sofia, Madrid

Picasso's *Lady in Blue* is more than likely to have been a reference to the state portraits of courtesans by the Spanish artist Diego Velázquez in the Prado, Madrid, but whose jewels, fashions and fabrics suggest opulence in a contemporary urban society.

Top

Death in the Sickroom, *c.1895, Edvard Munch*

Oil on canvas, 134.5 x 160 cm (53 x 63 in). Munch Museum, Oslo

Edvard Munch's painting was probably one of the sources of inspiration for Picasso's no longer extant *Last Moments*, and the theme of a lonely figure prostrate and dying on a bed was one of the subjects he was best known for at the time.

Above

At the Moulin Rouge, *1892–3, Henri de Toulouse-Lautrec*

Oil on canvas, 116 x 150 cm (45.5 x 59 in). Philadelphia Museum of Art

Henri de Toulouse-Lautrec's painting depicts the Moulin Rouge, a popular nightspot with many great French artists of the era. The trend to paint scenes of gaiety and vice would probably have attracted Picasso.

Above
Death of Casagemas, *1901*
Oil on panel, 27 x 35 cm (10.5 x 14 in). Musée Picasso, Paris

The influence of Vincent van Gogh can clearly been seen in this work. The thick encrusted surfaces, stippled brushwork, intense colour and use of dark outlines bear the hallmarks of the fated artist's work. Picasso's painting undoubtedly connected both artists' sad lives and violent ends, caused as a result of fatal and self-inflicted gunshot wounds.

Left

Le Moulin de la Galette, *1900*

Oil on canvas, 88.2 x 115.5 cm (34.7 x 45.5 in). Solomon Guggenheim Museum, New York

One of the most important paintings created by Picasso during his trip to Paris, showing *cocottes* (sarcastically known as "les horizontals") and depicting the bohemianism of *Le demi-monde* (the half world) of the Parisian café-cabaret scene. The popular nightspot that is depicted here attracted countless artists at the turn of the twentieth century.

Chapter 3

"Les Blues de Barcelona", 1902–03

Typical of Picasso's work in 1901–02 are paintings of lonely figures absorbed in thought or a mother protecting a child. *Woman and a Child by the Sea* (see page 21) depicts a female holding a tiny infant in one hand and a bright red flower in another, standing by the water's edge upon which an eerie boat floats towards two isolated, sickly-looking figures. As John Richardson notes, the flower may be a traditional emblem worn by prostitutes to warn of illness or menstruation, and *Woman at a Bidet* (see page 22), showing a naked female gazing at her own blood in the water, perhaps evidences Picasso's less overt reference to a red flower in *Woman and a Child by the Sea*. According to Picasso, he visited Saint-Lazare earlier in 1901, and made contact with Dr Louis Jullien, a well-known venereologist, in order to paint the women in the prison-hospital. Later, Picasso gave *Woman and a Child by the Sea* to the gynaecologist Josep Fontbona, perhaps as part of an agreement allowing the artist to depict the women of Saint-Lazare, or, even, in return for medical services relating to a female in his company. The painting was thus associated in Picasso's mind with a form of dilemma or physical illness. The boat most probably refers to death's boatman – the mythical figure Charon – who ferries the damned in his bark across the River Styx (or Acheron), towards fire and brimstone. A dark island, which alludes to hell, can be seen in the distance across the murky blue waters, whereas the luminous red flower, and the scene of wandering figures waiting for the arrival of the boat, recollects the lines from Dante's *Inferno*: "Charon, his eyes red like a burning brand, thumps with his oar the lingerers that delay, and rounds them up, and beckons with his hand".[1]

Seated Woman and Child is a slightly earlier painting of a lonely mother, bending protectively over her child. The woman is draped in a shawl and wearing a white Phrygian bonnet, signifying that she is a syphilitic prostitute who has lost her way in the world. However, the women portrayed in *Seated Woman and Child*, *Two Sisters* or *Woman and a Child by the Sea* are not so modern; they represent archetypal figures lost in their own melancholy, symbolic of universal alienation. The weary women resting themselves against their sickly children recall, once more, fourteenth-century medieval figures, such as those on the *Visitation* altar-front from Lluça in the Museu Episcopal in Vich. Notably, Picasso's stylized, female Blue Period figures call to mind the religiosity of the medieval Romanesque frescoes on display, among 1,800 ancient Catalan works exhibited at the Palau de Bellas Artes in Barcelona in the autumn of 1902. This suggests that they rekindled the painter's fascination with ancient Spanish art.

Picasso would also have had the opportunity to see the paintings of El Greco at this exhibition in Barcelona, especially his famous *Saint John the Evangelist* of c.1604, which influenced many of Picasso's paintings of this period, including the highly ambitious *La Vie* of 1903. As in his earlier Blue Period works, Picasso referred to the Spanish master in his use of simple religious signs, seen in the delicate arrangement, slender character and symbolic gestures intimated by the hands and fingers, the oddly stretched anatomies and, most obviously, a melancholy mix of blue, white and cream shades. It is worth noting that *La Vie* originated at a time of real crisis in the artist's life and career, when he was so demoralized and penniless that he even resorted to recycling the canvas of the outmoded *Last Moments* (see Chapter 2) to create this masterpiece of his Blue Period. Studies for the composition suggest that the artist initially envisaged himself standing to the left, with a bearded figure holding a palette on the right. However, as the work progressed, Picasso painted in the features of his dead friend Carles Casagemas, and the face of Germaine Gargallo (with whom the artist had a brief affair), removing the older male figure and introducing a typical Blue Period mother and child. There has been much debate over the sophisticated iconography of *La Vie*, but little consensus by scholars of Picasso's art. The complex interrelationships of the figures in the painting and the preparatory drawings of other related works, such as *The Embrace* (see page 22), demonstrate that Picasso struggled at first to decide on the narrative of the painting. He considered desperate lovers/parents desiring or rejecting an infant; the tragedy of an infant's last moments (the child looks terribly frail, as do many of the infants in his paintings at this time); Oedipal conflicts, alluding to his painter-father Don José; a companion piece to Gustave Courbet's *The Painter's Studio* (1855); the discord between parenthood and sexual desire, as well as other autobiographical and esoteric subjects. Indeed, *La Vie* may have been influenced by Max Jacob's

1 *The Comedy of Dante Alighieri: Cantica I, Hell (L' Inferno)*, Translated by Dorothy L. Sayers, Penguin Books, Harmondsworth, Middlesex, England, 1949 [1951], "Passage of Acheron – The Damned: Charon", Canto III, 109, p. 88.

knowledge of the Tarot, in particular the magician card. The symbolism of this card was familiar to anyone with knowledge concerning occult iconography and practices, and those in Picasso's circle, Jacob especially, would have easily recognized the famous upward and downward gesture contained in the *Tabula Smaragdina* (*The Emerald Tablet*), and attributed to the renowned and magical character of Hermes Trismegistus. Jacob, as an amateur Cartomancer, undoubtedly associated this gesture with the Magician in the Tarot pack, and representing the artistic traits of will power, creativity, individuality and duplicity. Jacob would in all likelihood, then, have identified the Magician card with Picasso, which is also linked with the magical character of Harlequin Trismegistus.

Picasso's fascination with magic and the occult probably took hold in the winter of 1902, when the artist moved in with the poet Max Jacob on the Boulevard Voltaire. Jacob was eccentric, to say the least and, according to Fernande Olivier, he was addicted to ether and henbane (two highly poisonous narcotics), which apparently stimulated his powers as a soothsayer. Picasso's stay with Max Jacob must surely have exacerbated the artist's already superstitious nature, and, in the likelihood of *La Vie*'s connection with the death of Casagemas, he would have undoubtedly attached great significance to Jacob's predictions, for he had taught the artist the fundamentals of astrology, chiromancy and the Tarot. According to Fernande Olivier, Jacob cast horoscopes, read palms and astrological signs for those in the *bande à Picasso*, which they clung to with "apprehension or hope".[2] We should not underestimate Picasso's omnipotence of thought and we know from Fernande Olivier that Jacob was deeply involved with the mysticism of palmistry, the Tarot and the magical arts. It was at this time, that Jacob appears to have attained a certain notoriety as a reader of Tarot cards for his neighbours and friends, and became something of an amateur astrologer, fortune-teller and clairvoyant, as well as creating lucky charms and talismen decorated with strange designs, hieroglyphics and cabalistic figurations (etched using a hatpin Fernande had given him). Whether these were fantastic creations of Jacob's own imagination – he claimed to know Hebrew – those in Picasso's circle were superstitious enough to guard these items jealously, and out of fear of loss or bad luck. Fernande claims that she always carried one of Max's charms with her in her handbag, and that it was made from a heavy, two-inch long piece of copper, decorated with cabalistic signs.

Richardson's interpretation is plausible, since we now know that magic, mysticism and the occult would fascinate the artist and punctuate his oeuvre, culminating in his great painting *La Cuisine* (see Chapter 18). It is supported by the fact that *La Vie* does not show a credible narrative depicting a real event, but appears "interesting and provocative", as one commentator stated in June 1904 in *El Liberal*.[3] Consequently, *La Vie* allows the spectator to imaginatively reconstruct its story and dialogue, a strategy that would be key to the multiple, fluctuating readings of later Cubist works, which has much in common with symbolist doctrine. "To name an object," Stéphane Mallarmé famously remarked in an interview in 1891, was "to suppress… the enjoyment of the poem. To suggest it, that is the dream".[4] The idea that *La Vie* and Picasso's other Blue Period paintings, such as the Ascetic, *The Old Guitarist* and *The Blind Man's Meal* (see page 23) are influenced purely by literary symbolism is, however, problematic. As Peter Read observes, the latter characters, like Picasso's other unfortunates, have just as much in common with "the 'outsiders' who populate Charles Baudelaire's prose poems or the urban poor of naturalist novels".[5] In fact, the later blue paintings that Picasso executed in the summer of 1903 depart from this Mallarméan symbolism, and revert to the simple formula of using El Greco-esque mannerisms and the religiosity of *Two Sisters*, *Seated Woman and Child* and *Woman and a Child by the Sea*. The philosophical musings in these, and other works of the period, were inherent in *fin de siècle* painting circles in Barcelona. As Picasso later told Jaime Sabartès, the artist held a pessimistic a view of art and believed that it emanated from sadness and pain.

La Vie fuses various styles to create a delicate balancing act, which juxtaposes naturalism with Spanish mysticism, the magical arts of the Tarot and the occult, as well as the religiosity of Gothic art. This simultaneous use of styles would become fundamental to the kinds of disruptions and inconsistencies that Picasso would employ in his later works, such as *Family of the Saltimbanques* and, most notably, *Les Demoiselles d'Avignon* (see Chapters 4 and 5). Picasso would go on to use all of these conceits and strategies when searching for a new type of iconography beyond the Spanish borders. When Picasso left his homeland to reside permanently in Paris, he would seek out and discover new players from French romantic literature: circus performers, itinerant groups, harlequins, actors and other extraordinary characters, born out of the magical arts of poetry and illusion.

---

2 Fernande Olivier, *Loving Picasso: The Private Journals of Fernande Olivier*, translated from the French by Christine Baker and Michael Raeburn, Foreword and notes by Marilyn McCully and an Epilogue by John Richardson, Harry N. Abrams, Inc., Publishers, New York, 2001, p. 267–268 [p.220].

3 Probably written by Carles Junyer Vidal and cited in John Richardson, *Life of Picasso, Volume I*, p. 276.

4 Stéphane Mallarmé's response to Jules Huret's *Enqête sur evolution littéraire (Survey of Literary Development)*, 1891. Quoted in John House, "The Legacy of Impressionism in France", Post Impressionism: Cross Currents in European Painting, London, Royal Academy of Arts, 1979–80, p. 17.

5 Peter Read. "Au Rendez-vous des Poètes: Picasso, French Poetry, and Theatre", 1900-1906, in Marilyn McCully, *Picasso: The Early Years*, p. 212.

Two Sisters, *1902*

Oil on wood, 152 x 100 cm (60 x 39.5 in). State Hermitage Museum, St Petersburg

When Picasso returned to Barcelona in January 1902, he was almost penniless, living back with his parents and surrounded, if one is to believe his paintings, by wretchedness, poverty and disease. Paintings of modern life and decadentes, *modernistas* or *flâneurs* no longer suited Picasso. The artist's new pictures of whores, beggars, blind men, minstrels, street sellers, harlequins, wanderers, loners, mothers and children, focused on the sorrow, suffering and inherent alienation of human life. Through the ages, itinerants, outcasts and society's unfortunates have been the subject of endless romantic, yet compassionate, sources for painters and sculptors, and Picasso's down-at-heel circumstances – coupled with his constant travelling from city to city, place to place and studio to studio – perhaps triggered the melancholic outlook and atmosphere of his work during his time spent in Barcelona. Picasso began in earnest by executing a series of crouching women and other scenes of deprivation, including *Two Women at a Bar*, *Woman and a Child by the Sea* and, most notably, *Two Sisters* (see right). In a letter to Max Jacob, Picasso complains about how his contemporaries thought his new painting had "too much soul and no form" and that he was planning "a picture of a Saint-Lazare whore and a mother".[6]

The painting in question, *Two Sisters*, is probably the most fascinating of the Saint-Lazare images, and was carried out about a year after Picasso had visited the women's prison there to paint its inmates in the summer or autumn of 1901. The artist took great care over the execution of this picture, painting it soon after his return to the Catalan city, and the work is a culmination of pictures representing prostitutes and mothers with children, made in Paris the previous year. *Two Sisters* also coincides with his good friend Isidre Nonell's exhibition at the Sala Parés, depicting gypsies and unkempt, lost figures ostracized in doorways or forced into ghettos on the outskirts of Barcelona. Nonell's somewhat romantic depictions of destitution and degradation in the slums of the city were adored by his friends from Els Quatre Gats, but found little favour with the Barcelona bourgeoisie. Nevertheless, Picasso must have absorbed these images and been determined to create works depicting individuals and groups haunted by the ghosts of misery, waste or disillusionment. Barcelona was at this time in the grip of social unrest, with riots, strikes and fighting in the streets initiating a state of emergency.

Picasso was no political activist but he, and the intelligentsia who associated with Els Quatre Gats, undoubtedly sided with the workers and the downtrodden. The tragic plight of ordinary folks in the slums of Barcelona must have evoked empathy in Picasso, as would the unfortunates incarcerated (many with children) in the Saint-Lazare prison. Yet Picasso's painting of *Two Sisters* universalizes and obfuscates the political, social and industrial problems of his age: difficulties that may well have inspired the artist to paint images of degradation, misery and injustice. The white Phrygian bonnet of the whore on the left is symptomatic of prostitutes suffering from syphilis in Saint-Lazare. If *Two Sisters* appears comparable to an altarpiece it is, as John Richardson suggests, because the painting was probably influenced by El Greco's *Visitation* (1607–14), which was created for the Capilla Obale in San Vicente in Toledo and represents similarly clothed figures reciprocating caring gestures in front of a doorway and a niche. Elizabeth Cowling recognizes that the expressive countenance, placement of feet and the gesticulation of the figures in Picasso's painting is highly reminiscent of the twelfth-century frescoes of *The Virgin and St John the Evangelist* in the Museum of Catalan Art in Barcelona. If Picasso drew on the traditional iconography of a holy visitation or annunciation for *Two Sisters*, it was a blasphemous reference to the noblesse and worship of nuns and Madonnas living in an ancient house of ill repute, sickness, suffering and death.

6 Marilyn McCully, *A Picasso Anthology*, p. 38.

Above

Woman and a Child by the Sea, *1902*

Oil on canvas, 81.5 x 60 cm (32 x 23.5 in). Private Collection, Japan

The image of a single and lonely female down on her luck or suffering from a form of venereal disease is typical of Picasso's paintings in 1901–02, and shows the mother protecting or mourning her child. The subject of the prison-hospital of Saint-Lazare in Paris recurs around this period. It is possible that Picasso needed treatment for a similar condition from Dr Louis Jullien, who worked at the hospital.

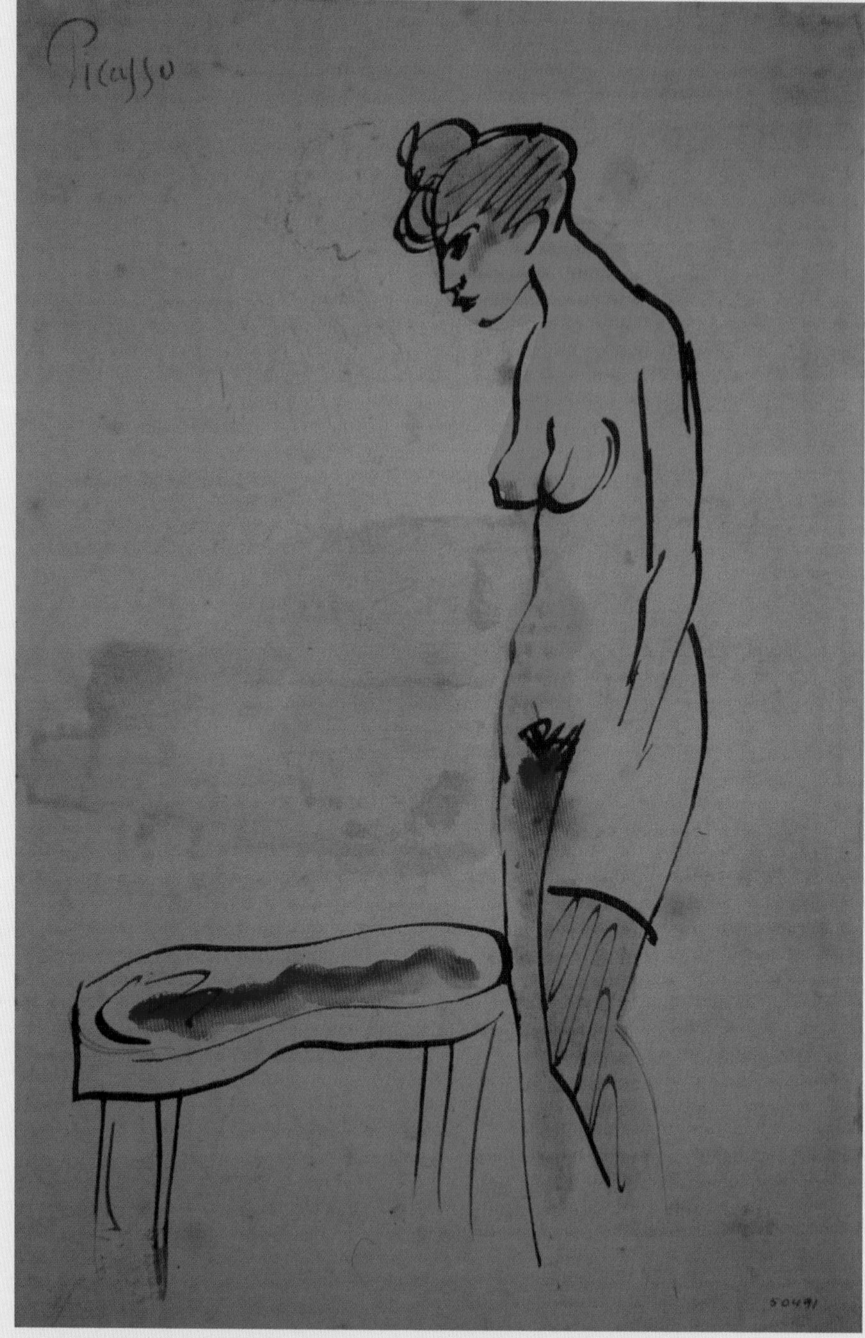

Above left
The Embrace, *1903*
Pastel on paper, 98 x 57 cm (38.5 x 22.5 in).
Musée de l'Orangerie, Paris

Here a pregnant woman weeps into the arms of her despairing companion. Her tragic mood suggests that the child is about to be born into an uncertain future. The painting's huddled figures evoke the story of Adam and Eve after the Fall, as they confront a world of sadness and pain.

Above right
Woman at a Bidet, *1902–03*
Pen and watercolour on paper, 20 x 13 cm (8 x 5 in).
Museu Picasso, Barcelona

This sketch is an important work manifesting the subject of menstruation and possibly a warning of illness in relation to the Blue Period. The painting is reminiscent of Picasso's *Le Tub* (*The Blue Room*) of 1901, depicting a female sponging herself in a hip-bath, and a popular example of contemporary scenes of domestic hygiene.

Left
La Vie, *1903*
Oil on canvas, 197 x 127.5 cm (77.5 x 50 in).
Cleveland Museum of Art

This is undoubtedly the most ambitious and most important work of Picasso's Blue Period. It creates a tense and ambiguous relationship between the three main protagonists. Images of suffering women in the background heighten the mystery and intensity of feeling in this masterly painting.

Above right
The Blind Man's Meal, *1903*
Oil on canvas, 95.3 x 94.6 cm (37.5 x 37.2 in). Metropolitan Museum of Modern Art, New York

Picasso's blind man tentatively reaches out to touch a vase with his right hand and, in the other, clutches a piece of bread. The painting illustrates a simple story of poverty, humility and abstinence, among other traditional themes associated with representations of religious martyrs and saints.

Chapter 4

Circus Figures and Harlequins, 1903–05

When Picasso arrived in Paris in April 1904, he immediately began looking for a new subject, whose iconography was timeless, steeped in mythology and moved away from the Spanish religiosity associated with the *fin de siècle* and *modernista* painting of Catalonian artists, such as Santiago Rusiñol and Ramón Casas in Barcelona. Picasso was searching for a theme with French and classical motifs, but without academic connotations, and he found this in the iconography of travelling street entertainers and circus players. Acrobats, performers, jesters and harlequins, accompanied by favourite animals, playing musicians and actors, became heroes for the young, ambitious Spaniard.

These were semi-tragic characters from folklore, such as the *Seated Harlequin* (see page 28) and the *commedia dell'arte* (comedy of craft), but they were distant enough from the quasi-religious figures of Picasso's Spanish Blue Period paintings, so they suited him perfectly. There were a number of other reasons for Picasso's choice of subject matter. These popular and old-fashioned characters had an air of questioning and a timeless appeal about them, and a number of important French artists, including Daumier, Degas, Toulouse-Lautrec and Seurat, had been drawn to these antiquated yet contemporary street performers. They were often depicted as figures estranged from modern society, yet could still be seen performing on the streets of Paris in makeshift theatres and dwellings, as seen in Honoré Daumier's watercolour of *Saltimbanques at a Fair* of 1865–69. Picasso and his contemporaries were drawn to Parisian circus figures and itinerant characters precisely because they were traditionally viewed as outsiders, as Picasso must have seen himself at this time. As a Spaniard newly settled in Paris, and with his French (according to Fernande Olivier) relatively poor at the time, Picasso would perhaps have identified with the tribal authenticity, itinerancy and social isolation associated with such groups. These groups were imagined to be more poetic and, with the dawn of a new century, their world was disappearing fast, as more popular forms of entertainment and other spectacles started to occupy the domain of indoor theatres. Thus, these itinerants were associated with romantic notions of street players plying their trades, as we can see in mid-nineteenth century paintings such as Édouard Manet's *The Old Musician* (1862).

Picasso's decision to return to Paris seems to have been triggered by a desire to transcend the limitations of his life and work in Barcelona, although this did not happen immediately because the artist was not willing to give up the Blue Period styles completely. But as his palette warmed, diversified and his symbolist melancholy began to fade in paintings such as *Meditation* (see page 27), the iconography of the *saltimbanques*, itinerant entertainers and other characters from the circus, fairground and theatre increasingly began to infiltrate Picasso's art from around 1905. This was partly due to a change in his personal circumstances that included a new woman in his life, Fernande Olivier, and an extended family, along with influential groups of French friends, such as Guillaume Apollinaire, as well as many other poets and writers. Picasso rented a studio in the Bateau-Lavoir (see page 44), a floating laundry so-called because it was filthy, creaky and located on a hill, which his compatriot Paco Durio had given up in April 1904. The rundown building, with neither electricity or gas, at 13 rue Ravignan in Montmarte, became an ideal residence for an artist looking to settle into a new artistic milieu in Paris, for it had the distinction of being extremely cheap and almost overflowing with bohemian artists.

The squalid yet vibrant Bateau-Lavoir also stood in close proximity to the Théâtre de Montmartre, a few minutes' walk from Picasso's studio on the rue Ravignon, and the Médrano Circus, near Pigalle, which proved crucial to his artistic transformation. Cultivating the anti-naturalist ethos that was essential to the aesthetic development of Picasso's great friend Guillaume Apollinaire, these laboratories fostered an unhindered creativity, which would drive Picasso's *saltimbanque* phase and shape the revolutionary *Les Demoiselles d'Avignon* (see Chapter 5). Apollinaire's influence on Picasso at this time was immense and the poet and painter's initial meeting first took place around mid-February 1905, when Max Jacob, who had known Picasso since 1901, played the role of a catalyst for their shared friendship. Jacob always insisted that Austin's café on the rue d'Amsterdam was the start of a "triple friendship that lasted up until about the War in which we separated neither for work, nor for eating, nor for pleasure".[1] Circuses and *saltimbanques* were naturally shared subjects of Picasso and Apollinaire between 1904 and 1905, and both painter and poet frequently combined circus, fairground and theatrical imagery in their works. Picasso's circus works of this time, and his monumental canvas *Family of the Saltimbanques*, coincide with two draft poems

1 Max Jacob, "Souvenirs sur Guillaume Apollinaire", 1937. *Le Flâneur des deux rives 6*, June 1955, p. 2–6 [p. 3]. Cited and translated in Peter Read, *Picasso and Apollinaire: The Persistence of Memory*, University of California Press, Berkeley, Los Angeles and London, 2008, p. 10.

entitled "Spectacle" ("Performance") and "Les Saltimbanques" ("The Acrobats"), which Apollinaire penned for Picasso on 1 November 1905, and featured travelling circus groups, fairground and theatrical imagery of itinerant players of various kinds. Apollinaire later revised "Spectacle" under the title of "Crépuscule" ("Twilight") – which was published in *Alcools* in 1913 – by reworking the last stanza of the poem that he originally gave to Picasso in 1905 to include a reference to Harlequin Trismegistus. The verses that the poet wrote for his friend in 1905, "Spectacle" and "Les Saltimbanques", have since become two of the most popular poems of the twentieth century.

Peter Read perceives the iconography of Apollinaire's poems as intimately bound up with the imagery of Picasso's *Family of the Saltimbanques* painting, and therefore as a symbol of the poet's and painter's creative collaboration. Apollinaire's references to itinerancy and circus acts and creative individuals, whose identity is defined by art, skill, and knowledge, were intrinsic to both his and Picasso's "fraternal complicity", and a key characteristic of early European Modernism. Thus, as Read conceives, Picasso forever kept his great friend's postcard (see page 45) inside a 1905 sketchbook: a sketchbook filled with images of harlequins, *saltimbanques* and other itinerant players, and underpinning both the poet and painter's creative partisanship. These were poems that Picasso secretly guarded throughout his life, celebrating Harlequin but based on the great mythological character Hermes, and conflating Harlequin Trismégiste with the magical figure Hermes Trismegistus (Thrice Great), keeper of the underworld, god of fertility and author of the occult treatise and creation myth *The Emerald Tablet*, which was adopted as a seminal text by European alchemists.

As Marilyn McCully observes, the poems "Spectacle" and "Les Saltimbanques", sent to Picasso by Apollinaire in 1905, take the arts of magic and illusion as their main themes. Furthermore, as John Richardson suggests, these poems eulogize Picasso as the magical, demonic figure Harlequin Trismegistus. For the poet was well aware of old Walloon legends regarding "her-lequin" – a soul departed from hell. In "Spectacle", Harlequin (Picasso) is identified as a sorcerer whose magical power over nature helps him to bind heaven and earth with the supernatural act of unhooking a star. Meanwhile, the hanged man, who gives Harlequin his theatrical cue to begin the performance, takes the symbol of a traditional Tarot card. In "Les Saltimbanques", however, Picasso is portrayed as Harlequin Trismegistus the alchemist, who transforms the "doors of grey inns" into a scene of "drums and gilded hoops", so as to draw a poetic analogy between art and alchemy.

This imagery also held a personal meaning for Picasso and, as the artist told Josep Palau i Fabre, depictions of circus performers first began to appear in his work after he happened upon a troupe of wandering acrobats on the Place des Invalides, traditionally a site for *fêtes foraines* (fun fairs) in Paris. Apollinaire, nevertheless, took the credit for sowing the seed of the circus "in Picasso's soul… whence it grew into marvellous works of art".[2] We know from Fernande Olivier and Picasso's other friends that the artist loved visiting the Cirque Médrano, mingling with acrobats and clowns in the circus bar, and listening to the tales of the Spanish owner "Boum-Boum" (Géronimo Médrano), as well as other compatriots on the road. Henri de Toulouse-Lautrec and Georges Seurat had earlier depicted the same circus (then called Cirque Fernando), but, whereas their paintings show performers and the audience in a ring or beneath canvas, Picasso preferred to highlight their itinerant, gypsy-like qualities by placing them outside.

The theme of the stone cube, or the classical representation of a figure seated on a drum, appears throughout Picasso's sketchbooks of 1904–05, but is fully expressed in the large painting *Acrobat on a Ball* (see page 27), whose composition sprang out of drawings with a similar theme. The strongman figure recalls Apollinaire's acrobats, who hold "heavy weights, round or square", while the little girl, balancing with such dexterity on a ball, may have been derived from ancient Greco-Roman vases, and is highly evocative of the circus acts in Apollinaire poems. The significance of the subject is not only poetic, but has a fundamental bearing on the driving forces behind the opposing values of Picasso's later Synthetic Cubism, especially seen in the processes of his assemblage sculpture. A group of six ink drawings from the famous *Saltimbanques* sketchbook of a *Seated Boy on a Stone Cube*, depicting a slender youth in front, back and three-quarters views, impels the onlooker to study these drawings as if they were a sculpture in-the-round, thus profiting from being a creative individual whose goal is the construction of separate profiles into a single, sculptural whole. The painting, like the earlier studies of *Seated Boy on a Stone Cube*, depicts a muscular young man (a strongman) in a three-quarters position, sitting on a stone cube, opposite an androgynous acrobat, balanced perfectly on a ball. Both figures are also set at a diagonal to the picture plane (from right to left) to emphasize a specific relationship of opposing values. The muscular, powerfully built figure that sits so squarely is a reflection of the bulk and mass of the stone cube on which he is seated. In juxtaposition, the graceful acrobat assumes a contrasting poise of balance and dexterity. Together, they establish a model for the relationship between solid structures and finely balanced elements seen in the artist's later work.

If Fernande Olivier remembers correctly, the group of acrobats and a child attempting to balance on a ball that she saw in Picasso's studio undoubtedly provided the subject of the *Harlequin's Family with an Ape* (see page 29) of 1905. When Olivier refers to the artist's protracted method in saying that Picasso was permanently unsatisfied with his efforts and "is constantly reworking his pictures",[3] we can deduct that the watercolour provided the basic elements for the large *Family of the Saltimbanques*. Picasso would soon go on to use similar working processes to forge ambitious and aesthetic changes in his work, and expand on the inherent sculptural possibilities of drawings and paintings at this time.

---

2 Guillaume Apollinaire, *Oeuvres complètes*, 4 vols (ed.) Michel Décaudin, iconography by Pierre-Marcel Adéma, Paris, Balland et Lecat, 1966, p. 895. Cited and trans in Peter Read, *Picasso and Apollinaire*, p. 22.

3 Fernande Olivier, *Loving Picasso*, p. 162.

Family of the Saltimbanques, *1905*

Oil on canvas, 212.8 x 229.6 cm (83.8 x 90.4 in). National Gallery of Art, Washington, DC

Family of the Saltimbanques (see right) has a fairytale atmosphere, exhibiting a hazy, carnivalesque colour scheme that matches the poems Guillaume Apollinaire sent to Picasso on 2 November 1905 – poems that the artist would keep among a sketchbook filled with drawings of harlequins, *saltimbanques* (acrobats) and travellers. Notably, the sketchbook also contained a coloured pencil drawing of a *Jester Holding a Child*, which Picasso gave to Apollinaire in the same year, indicating a shared interest in the circus that seems to have cemented their friendship. In her private journals, Fernande Olivier clearly describes the subjects that Picasso was painting in the autumn of 1905, and that he was re-working a number of old canvases. The blue figures, Fernande claims, that were highly reminiscent of the works of El Greco, were painted over with images of acrobats and harlequins. She specifically describes a large painting of a red harlequin wearing a pointed cap replacing the image of an "old cripple with a basket flowers", as well as large canvas depicting acrobats practicing by their caravan; an acrobat on a ball and others performing "leaps in a haunting, deserted landscape", painted in "pale, matt, pastel shades.[4]"

The monumental *Family of the Saltimbanques*, which Picasso began in the spring and completed in the autumn of 1905, was his greatest painting to date. The sheer size of the canvas suggests that Picasso was totally committed to painting a work of epic grandeur, with six life-size characters representing an itinerant circus troupe, at a time when the artist could barely make ends meet as a painter. The characters include Harlequin (with Picasso holding the role of paterfamilias), an obese clown in a red outfit, two young male acrobats and a little girl wearing a ballerina's costume and holding Harlequin's hand. To the right, another young woman is seated next to an earthenware jar. The fingers of Harlequin indicate that this is a close-knit troupe of players, whereas the lone female implies that they are a related yet independent group of individuals. As studies demonstrate, Picasso removed any audience or anecdotal content so the setting, of barren hills against cloudy blue skies, makes for a timeless, dream-like composition that sacrifices his previous Spanish religious symbolism for a masterpiece that is as poetic and mysterious as the figures it represents. Naturally, scholars have attempted to identify the figures with Picasso's friends, lovers and close associates, but such literal and autobiographical interpretations have often proved to be entirely inaccurate, or missing the deeply allegorical nature of the painting itself.

Peter Read explains in *Picasso and Apollinaire: The Persistence of Memory*, 2008, that the *Family of the Saltimbanques* were created allegorically to

intimate Picasso, Apollinaire, and their group, brought together to stand resolute in the twentieth century, yet without a "map, rule book, or clear paths to guide them.[5]" Paradoxically, they each stand alone, but are together, and Picasso's painting appears to show himself at the precise moment deciding on which new direction he should take.[6] Moreover, Picasso's identification with the *commedia dell'arte* character of Harlequin, and his brilliantly patterned costume, extracted from his predecessors Watteau, Daumier, Cézanne, Toulouse-Lautrec and Seurat, would reappear constantly as one of the artist's favourite acts of guile and transformation in his oeuvre.

4 Fernande Olivier, *Loving Picasso*, p. 162.
5 Peter Read, *Picasso and Apollinaire*, Chapter 3, "Circuses and Saltimbanques", p. 23–24.

Left
Acrobat on a Ball, *1905*
Oil on canvas, 147 x 95 cm (58 x 37.5 in). Pushkin Museum of Fine Arts, Moscow

Circus performers and acrobats began to appear as a separate, heroic subject matter during the spring of 1905. They derived from an earlier sketch entitled *The Circus Family*, which showed an itinerant group of performers practising their skills in the open air within a mystical landscape. Here themes of balance, as seen in the figure on a ball, are juxtaposed with those of solidity (a strongman seated on a cube). The arrangement prefigures the conceits and opposing values in Picasso's later sculptural work.

Above right
Meditation, *1904*
Watercolour and pen on paper, 36.8 x 27 cm (14.5 x 10.6 in). The Museum of Modern Art, New York

This is one of two watercolours from the winter of 1904–05, depicting Picasso's lover Fernande Olivier asleep, this time, being gazed upon by the artist himself. The theme was explored time and again in Picasso's later works, where the sleeper is watched or, perhaps, dreaming of her lover.

Opposite
Seated Harlequin, *1905*
Watercolour and Indian ink on cardboard, 57.2 x 41.2 cm (22.5 x 16 in). Staatliche Museen zu Berlin, Nationalgalerie, Museum Berggruen

Heralding a move from Picasso's Spanish Blue Period to the French Rose Period, this work belongs to a group of *Saltimbanques*: tragic-looking wandering players and circus figures.

Above
Harlequin's Family with an Ape, *1905*
Gouache, watercolour, ink and pastel on paper, 104 x 75 cm (41 x 29.5 in). Göteborg Museum of Art

Ordered and symmetrical, Picasso's harlequin group adopt the classicizing style and structural formation of many Italian Renaissance subjects depicting the holy family, though infused with a low-life theme and touched by Picasso's familiar melancholy.

Chapter 5

Tradition, Modernism and Regression: *Les Demoiselles d'Avignon*, 1906–07

The first compositional study for *Les Demoiselles d'Avignon* (see page 34) in Picasso's winter sketchbook of 1906–07 identifies seven figures including two males: a medical student carrying a book (previously holding a skull as an emblem of the transience of life or a *memento mori*) and the seated figure of a sailor, who has in front of him a Spanish drinking flask (*porrón*), some watermelon slices and a vase of flowers, and who appears to look in the direction of the young doctor. Five nude females or prostitutes accompany the sailor. One enters through the curtain on the right as two stand behind, one with arms raised above her head, while another female with crossed legs sits on a chair and a further woman squats down. Picasso eventually decided to transform the standing male physician into another prostitute, remove the seated female and finally the sailor as well. Although the assembled cast was the final choice for Picasso's brothel painting, the previous set of characters would become part of the artist's composition for around five months and their omission was ultimately a last-minute decision. The question is why?

Another pencil sketch made in the winter of 1906–07 (see page 51) shows the *demoiselle* squatting when seen from behind. The woman is entirely naked, with her legs spread apart, while she sits on a cushion, stool or maybe even a bowl. Sometimes, she simply squats as if carrying out her ablutions in front of the other females. That this was Picasso's initial intention is perhaps confirmed by studying three side-view drawings of a bowl, executed from May until June 1907, accompanied by what might be a mirror or a plan view of the bowl itself, with detailed scallop shapes around the edges or on the handles. Some of these sketches also show female figures with raised arms carrying a bowl or a vessel of some kind above their head. These may well have been extracted from Picasso's collection of Edmond Fortier's ethnographic collotypes, depicting Malinké women from West Africa in 1906. Here, the females are seen posing, standing and squatting on the ground with bowls at their feet. Although the themes and composition of Picasso's painting may have been derived from Titian's *Diana and Actaeon* and Rubens's *The Judgement of Paris*, the latter drawings shed light on Picasso's original intentions: the squatting figure in Picasso's *Les Demoiselles* could, in fact, be an iconoclastic jibe and a reference to the traditional image of "Venus at her Toilette", attended to by a number of handmaidens.

Les Demoiselles hints at this mythological figure of a beautiful woman at her toilette, gazing at her own image in a mirror, which has been depicted in paintings through the ages. These include Giorgione's *Venus of Urbino* (c.1538), Giovanni Bellini's *Naked Young Woman in Front of the Mirror* (1515), Rubens's *Venus at a Mirror* (c.1515–16), Velázquez's *Rokeby Venus* (c.1649–51), and, most famously of all, Botticelli's *The Birth of Venus* (c.1483–5, see page 34). Picasso knew the Venus myth and imagery intimately because he had painted the subject of *La Toilette* in the summer of 1906 (see page 35). According to the eighth-century BC Greek oral poet Hesiod, Venus was born of the sea's foam and floated ashore with the aid of a scallop shell, carried on the gentle winds of Zephyr and Chloris and eventually fetching up on the sands of Paphos in Cyprus. The figure of Venus in Botticelli's work at the Uffizi, Florence, is based on the fabled classical artist Apelles's vanished painting of the goddess rising from the briny waters and airing out her hair. This mythological tale is intimately connected with the subject of the Three Graces, or Venus's handmaidens, Aglaia, Euphrosyne and Thalia, dancing a roundel against a flower-strewn orchard in Botticelli's *Primavera* (c.1478), which looks at the earthly contemplation of divine beauty. Picasso had previously painted a witty statuesque parody of the much-studied Hellenistic statue of the *Three Graces* (an ancient Roman copy in Siena Cathedral) in his *Three Dutch Girls* of 1905 (see page 35), and was familiar with the classical concepts of Venus and the Three Graces as representations of pagan and humanist ideals of chastity, beauty and love.

Flowers have appeared as a love motif through the ages. It is worth remembering that Chloris flees from Zephyr in Botticelli's *The Birth of Venus*, and as he embraces her she is transformed into the goddess of flowers. In Manet's *Olympia* of 1863, a black servant hands a wrapped bouquet of flowers to the prostitute in an image and symbol no doubt borrowed from Rubens's *Venus at a Mirror*. Picasso's painting bears similarities, but the motif is distorted to further extremes, in that his Venus ostensibly proffers excreta to her handmaidens to carry instead of a sweet-smelling bunch of flowers. It is hardly a coincidence that Manet's painting – itself a scandalous plagiarism of Titian's *Venus of Urbino* (1538) – was hung in the Louvre in 1907, alongside Ingres's *La Grande Odalisque* (1814), and throughout the entire process of Picasso creating his philosophical brothel painting. The dog lying on the bed next to Titian's Venus was originally intended as a motif in Picasso's *Les Demoiselles* composition too, and is perhaps inspired by the numerous sketches of his Afghan hound Kazbek suckling its young and possibly a rather moralistic reference to wanton whorishness, fallen behaviour and the cause of solicitation. John Richardson also suggests that one of Picasso's maidens is a "dog-faced *demoiselle*"[1] and, in this context, gives new meaning to the bestial nature of men and women in *Les Demoiselles*.

Picasso's painting also opposes the aggrandizements of Courbet's *The Painter's Studio* (1855), which demonstrates heroic self-promotion and a manifesto of the idealized modern artist (with a similar attendant and semi-naked model) at work in the studio. The artist's claustrophobic setting in *Les Demoiselles*, which violently projects its figures forwards, compresses the pictorial space and obfuscates meaning, is a kind of retort and parody of the grandiloquent compositions of artistic life in many Salon paintings. The black humour regarding Picasso's flagrant usurping of classical models, seen in Venus excreting toilet water rather than wringing the billows from her hair, is topical and highly seditious in the context of the academic tradition of morally pure and idealized representations of beauty. Indeed, the image of the flying figures of Zephyr and Chloris in Botticelli's painting was actually taken from Lorenzo de Medici's most prized possession, the second-century BC Hellenistic *Tazza Farnese*, a carved semi-precious stone bowl acquired in Rome in 1471, and Picasso may also have parodied the use of this ornate and valuable object for a simple toilet bowl. Whatever the precise reference, the artist's squatting Venus, who turns her supposed sexual immorality and mirrored gaze towards the male viewer, delivers perhaps Picasso's greatest insult to those who first viewed the painting.

Memento mori themes are also intrinsic to Picasso's *Les Demoiselles*, as we can see in the drawings of the medical student holding a skull, as well as the image of forbidden fruits on a table in the centre of the composition. The emblematic still-life subject depicting a crescent-shaped slice of melon, a pear, a soft round peach and a bunch of grapes become carnal metaphors when juxtaposed with the sexual charge and "thanatophobia" or morbid fear of death suffusing the atmosphere of what was originally entitled *Le Bordel philosophique*. The term "philosophical brothel" appears to have been invented by Guillaume Apollinaire, himself a notorious pornographer, and could be a veiled reference to the Marquis de Sade's text *La Philosophie dans le Boudoir* of 1795. Apollinaire – a great admirer of the writer – introduced Picasso to the "cult" of the Marquis de Sade, and this is probably where *Les Demoiselles* acquired its genesis: from a brothel in Barcelona supposedly called Les Filles d'Avignon, as a colloquial expression for "fille de joie", another French term for prostitution.

Of course, Picasso banished all the explicit references to prostitution in the final composition, leaving only traces in the nakedness, gestures and postures of *Les Demoiselles*, which in reality had nothing to do with real women in brothels, who generally did not sit about unclothed, waiting for clients. In fact, the exact opposite is true if we are to believe Henri de Toulouse-Lautrec, an ardent frequenter and painter of the modern Parisian brothel, whose relatively straightforward pastel drawing treats the subject from a sensitive perspective. Picasso's *Les Demoiselles* was nothing like Toulouse-Lautrec's Baudelairean images of modern life, but focused instead on the friction between the pledge of uninhibited sex and fear of sickness, as well as death and madness from the effects of venereal disease.

With his *Les Demoiselles* Picasso was perhaps trying to distance himself from the Parisian vanguard artist Henri Matisse; in particular, his controversial masterpiece *Bonheur de Vivre* (see page 36), exhibited at the Salon des Indépendants in 1906. Matisse's glowing landscape, strewn with naked females in an uncritical state of supposed "primitive" nature, mentality and joyful abandon, must have irritated Picasso in the extreme, just as much as the avant-garde leader perceived *Les Demoiselles* as "an outrage, an attempt to ridicule the modern movement" and an "audacious hoax"[2]. In later life, Picasso always took the stance of denying any connection between *Les Demoiselles* and tribal art, but as his preparatory studies for the painting reveal, its relationship with primitivism and *l'art nègre* is irrefutable. The shock and force of experiencing tribal artefacts amassed from Oceania and Africa in the Musée d'Ethnographie had an effect akin to a supernatural encounter, and Picasso later described this momentous discovery to André Malraux in 1937. It was only then that he acknowledged the debt that he owed to such objects, in recalling the impact that these "magical masks", "intercessors" and "spirits" had on his painting: "*Les Demoiselles d'Avignon* must have come to me that day; not because of the forms but because it was my first exorcizing picture, yes".[3]

Although not exhibited until 1916, *Les Demoiselles* was nevertheless reproduced and discussed in passing in an article entitled "The Wild Men of Paris", written for the New York journal *The Architectural Record* in 1910. The title was a reference to Picasso and other artists' use of tribal art in their paintings and the effrontery, decadence and "crimes" of the modern artists who create the following: "Monstrous, monolithic women, creatures like Alaskan totem poles, hacked out of solid, brutal colours, frightful, appalling!"[4] Picasso's reference to the primitivism of *l'art nègre* therefore clearly affected the conception of *Les Demoiselles d'Avignon*, as well as changing the formal structure of his Cubism in general. It is under these circumstances that we can begin to understand his references to tribal sculpture, masks and fetishes.

---

1 John Richardson, *A Life of Picasso, Volume II: A Painter of Modern Life, 1907–1917*, Random House, New York, 1996, p. 33.
2 Roland Penrose, *Picasso: His Life and Work*, 1958, p. 125.
3 André Malraux, *La Tête d'Obsidienne*, Paris Gallimard, 1974, p. 17–19.
4 Gellet Burgess, "The Wild Men of Paris", *The Architectural Record*, New York, 1910.

Les Demoiselles d'Avignon, *1907*

Oil on canvas, 244 x 233.5 cm (96 x 92 in). The Museum of Modern Art, New York

Historians of Picasso have argued that the artist's *Les Demoiselles d'Avignon* (1907), although not a Cubist painting in itself, nevertheless allowed for the dramatic break that made Cubism possible. *Les Demoiselles* has been at the centre of debate in twentieth-century critical theory for some decades; with its huge inconsistencies in style, strident ugliness and intentionally shocking subject matter, the work has drawn more attention than any other painting in the history of Modernism. *Les Demoiselles* is now seen as the first real twentieth-century painting that encompasses complex discussions, including personal traumas (desire and death), anarchist sympathies and colonialism relating to Picasso's appropriation of non-western, and particularly Iberian statuary, African masks and Egyptian hieroglyphs. The adaptation of spatial solidity, seen in the work of the Post-Impressionist painter Paul Cézanne, has been regarded as a key component in the creation of *Les Demoiselles*.

The Cubist facets that appear on some of the women's breasts and among the crumpled drapery, have been linked to the attempts of Braque and Picasso to create sculptures through means of painting. The work portrays five nude females, prostitutes in a bordello, tightly packed into a shallow space and standing on a narrow platform, leaning back against a pair of bulky curtains that act like huge stage flanks. While two masked females burst on to the scene through a background set of curtains, their forward-facing companions threaten the spectator with menacing and disconcerting gazes. The references to prostitution often appeared in the work of modern artists, such as Henri de Toulouse-Lautrec and Edgar Degas, and Picasso is known to have produced his own erotica for the salacious entertainment of himself and his friends. Picasso's attitude towards women is difficult to characterize in the context of his work (female subjects could include virgins, mothers, lovers, whores and screaming maenads), but given the content of *Les Demoiselles* – 'primitivised' faces and female bodies in connection with debased sexuality, prostitution and brothel life – Picasso manipulates or fosters stereotypes linking white and non-white women with coarse sexual displays and supposed instinctual vitality and potency.

Although the artist was inspired to paint *Les Demoiselles* on seeing Manet's *Olympia* (1863), depicting a prostitute attended to by a maid, and Ingres's *La Grande Odalisque* (1814), he also drew inspiration from traditional mythological themes of works such as Rubens's *The Judgement of Paris* (c.1633) and Titian's Diana and Actaeon (1559).

Understandably, history thus records the bewilderment of Picasso's contemporaries at a work shunning classical beauty, coherence or completeness. When foisted upon a group of surprised visitors, the painting led them to experience something akin to a physical attack. Georges Braque felt like he had been forced to drink gasoline and spit fire, whereas André Derain was so shocked by the work that he predicted that the artist would one day be found "hanged from a rope behind his big painting".[5] The art dealer Daniel-Henry Kahnweiler summed up the general reactions to the work at the time when stating, "The picture he had painted seemed to everyone mad or monstrous."[6] Research suggests that preliminary studies for *Les Demoiselles* reveal Picasso had originally conceived that a medical student or a doctor should enter the stage on the left, through a curtain while holding a book or a board, presumably to carry out a medical inspection of some kind, which was standard practice in French brothels. Picasso's decision to eliminate the male figure (and a sailor who also appeared early on) in favour of his five female protagonists was a stroke of genius designed to centre their gaze outwards, to rest upon the audience. As Elizabeth Cowling has remarked, Picasso's intention was to draw focus away from the drama of the female figures and shift it on to the spectator, who therefore becomes a lead in the "psychological and spatial structure of the picture."[7] *Les Demoiselles d'Avignon* stayed under wraps in Picasso's studio and was not exhibited until 1916. It was later bought – on the advice of the leader of the Surrealists, André Breton – by the couturier Jacques Doucet in 1924, and despite being written about in the New York journal *The Architectural Record* in 1910, the painting was not well known until after 1937.

5 Daniel-Henry Kahnweiler, in William Rubin, Hélène Seckel, Judith Cousins, *Les Demoiselles d'Avignon*, MOMA, New York, 1994, p. 234.

6 Daniel-Henry Kahnweiler with Francis Crémieux, *My Galleries and Painters*, trans Helen Weaver, Thames and Hudson, London, 1971, p. 38.

7 Elizabeth Cowling, *Picasso: Style and Meaning*, p. 163.

Opposite top
Study for Les Demoiselles d'Avignon, *1907*
Pencil and pastel on paper, 47.5 x 63.5 cm (18.5 x 25 in). Öffentliche Kunstsammlung, Kupferstichkabinett, Basel

Picasso's study for *Les Demoiselles* shows naked whores grouped around a male figure, entering from the left and carrying a notebook (sometimes a skull), suggesting the presence of a medical doctor. The artist would later substitute the physician for a *demoiselle* to remove the allegorical and moralizing content in this early study for his large painting.

Opposite bottom
The Birth of Venus, Botticelli, *c.1483–5*
Tempera on panel, 172.5 x 278 cm (69 x 109.5 in). Uffizi, Florence

Picasso's *Les Demoiselles* was partly a reaction to the repetition of mythological and classical subjects such as *The Birth of Venus*, which conveyed ideas of perfection, beauty, chastity and other expressions regarding morally pure or idealized beauty.

Below left
La Toilette, *1906*
Oil on canvas, 151.1 x 99.1 cm (59.5 x 39 in). Albright-Knox Art Gallery, Buffalo

A mysterious painting that appears to show a clothed Fernande Olivier holding a mirror up to a voluptuous female beauty. The subject illustrates the preening that Fernande liked to carry out on a regular basis. The work suggests that Picasso alone, with brush and paint, could enhance her beauty.

Below right
Three Dutch Girls, *1905*
Oil on board, 77 x 67 cm (30.5 x 26.5 in). Musée National d'Art Moderne, Centre Georges Pompidou, Paris

Picasso visited Schrool in Holland in the summer 1905, and stayed with the writer Tom Schilperpoort at a village near Alkmaar. *Three Dutch Girls* is taken from the image of the *Three Graces*. The solidity of the figures hints at the classical forms that the artist encountered during his early academic training.

Above

***Bonheur de Vivre**, 1905–06, Henri Matisse*

Oil on canvas, 175 x 241 cm (69 x 95 in). Barnes Foundation, Merion, Pennsylvania

Picasso's painting of *Les Demoiselles* was clearly an attempt to distance himself from the hedonistic primitivism of Henri Matisse's *Bonheur de Vivre*. This work is a kind of paradise lost: a joyous sensual painting in brilliant colours and filled with dancing groups and noble individuals, in writhing ecstasy or in states of supposed primitive abandon.

Gallery 1

Special documents, photographs and illustrations

Above
Picasso, Bullfight with Pigeons, *1892*
Graphite pencil on paper, 13.5 x 20.2 cm (5.3 x 7.9 in). Museu Picasso, Barcelona

Picasso's childhood bullfighting scene looks ahead to Picasso's later images of the bullfight, and a subject most famously reiterated in the 1937 painting *Guernica*. The birds are perhaps copied from one his father's pigeon paintings.

Left
Picasso and Lola, *1888*
Photograph. Musée Picasso, Paris

Picasso was the little pasha of the family, which led him to enjoy the company of a household of females. Here he is pictured with his sister Lola, from whom he may have observed (alongside other female family members) the art of dress-making, which possibly inspired his papiers collés.

Above
Picasso. La Coruña, *1894*
Double-page manuscript from 16 September 1894, brown ink on paper, 21 x 26 cm (8.3 x 10.2 in). Musée Picasso, Paris

This page of sketches derives from one of Picasso's early attempts at creating a "journal". The work shows cartoons, caricatures and chronicles of daily life in La Coruña, where the artist moved with his family in 1891.

Above

Picasso, Els Quatre Gats, Barcelona, *1900*

Menu card, 21.8 x 16.4 cm (8.5 x 6.5 in). Museu Picasso, Barcelona

This menu card advertises Pere Romeu's café-cabaret Els Quatre Gats in Barcelona. The modernista house style imitates decorative posters by fellow Spaniards Ramon Casa and Miguel Utrillo, and illustrations by French artist Henri de Toulouse-Lautrec.

Right

Etude de chiromancie: le main de Picasso, *1902*

Graphite pencil (drawing) and sepia ink pen on paper, 29 x 18.9 cm (11.4 x 7.4 in). Museu Picasso, Barcelona

In Jacob's sketch, the poet gives a reading of his friend's left hand, in a bid to teach him the rudiments of palmistry. Jacob suggests that Picasso is a cultivated individual with a creative streak and an energetic personality.

MXJ.B FECIT

tempérament ardent, réussites

1 ligne de vie. Jusqu'à 68 ans
faiblesse et maladie (à la fin de la prem. jeunesse)

2 ligne de chance
brillant début dans la vie
au point de vue pratique. Études déceptions
et changement de fortune avant 30 ou 35 ans
mais réussite dans les arts — brillante. (carré sur la ligne de vie)
La vie sera apaisée vers la fin.
On peut espérer la fortune (bracelet 3)
No 4. La ligne hépatique est divisée, faible
signe d'une santé médiocre
5 le Mt de Mercure est développé. Intelligence
mais la 1ère phalange du petit doigt est courte
naïveté.

Remarque particulière. Toutes les lignes semblent
naître à la base de la ligne de chance de cette main,
c'est comme la première étincelle d'un feu d'artifice.
Cette sorte d'étoile vivante ne se rencontre que
rarement et chez les individus prédestinés. Une gerbe
serrée vers le mont de l'inspiration nous indiquerait un
tempérament poétique si la forme allongée de la main ne
nous avait déjà induit à le juger tel.

La base de la main est large, carrée, signe de
sensualité mais aussi de franchise et de [illegible] honnêteté.
La main en forme de flamme est aux natures charmantes,
sociables.
Le pouce est court, peu de volonté. La ligne de [illegible] [illegible]

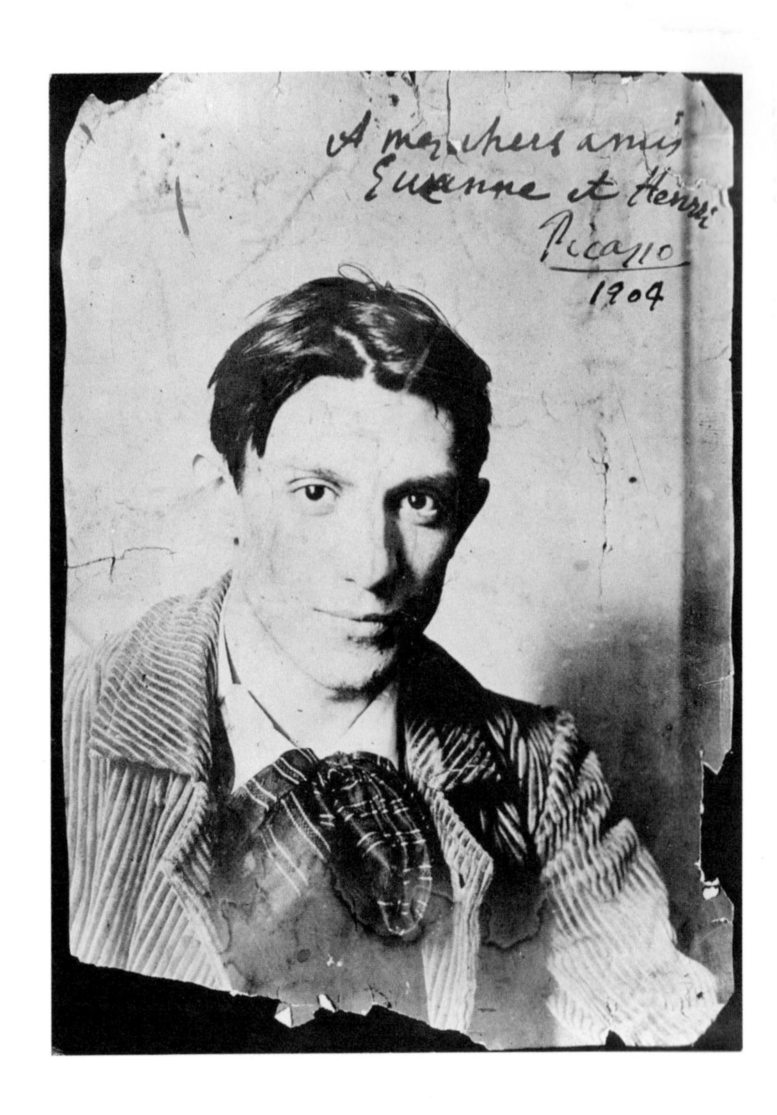

Left

Self-portrait, *1899–1900*

Charcoal and crayon on paper, 22.5 x 16.5 cm (8.9 x 6.5 in).
Museu Picasso, Barcelona

Picasso's charcoal drawing is a moody, self-conscious and soul-searching portrait that demonstrates both an interest in the expressionism of German artist Edvard Munch and the soulful art of Spanish master El Greco.

Above left

Apollinaire in Picasso's Studio, *1910.*

Photograph taken by Pablo Picasso. Private Collection

Apollinaire and Picasso were the very best of friends, and the two shared an eclectic taste in tribal artefacts (l'art nègre). Here the artist photophraphs the poet seated next to a wooden figure from the Marquesas Islands.

Above right

Picasso, with an inscription to his musician friends Suzanne and Henri Bloch, *1904.*

Photograph. Musée Picasso, Paris

Picasso met brother and sister musicians Henri and Suzanne Bloch through Max Jacob. Henri was a violinist, whereas Suzanne was a Wagnerian opera singer. Picasso would later paint Suzanne's portrait in a Blue Period style.

Above
Roofs of the Bateau-Lavoir, annotated by Picasso to show the windows of his studio, *1904*
Bibliothèque Nationale, Paris

The studio's close proximity to the Théâtre de Montmatre and Cirque Medrano, was crucial to the artist's development.

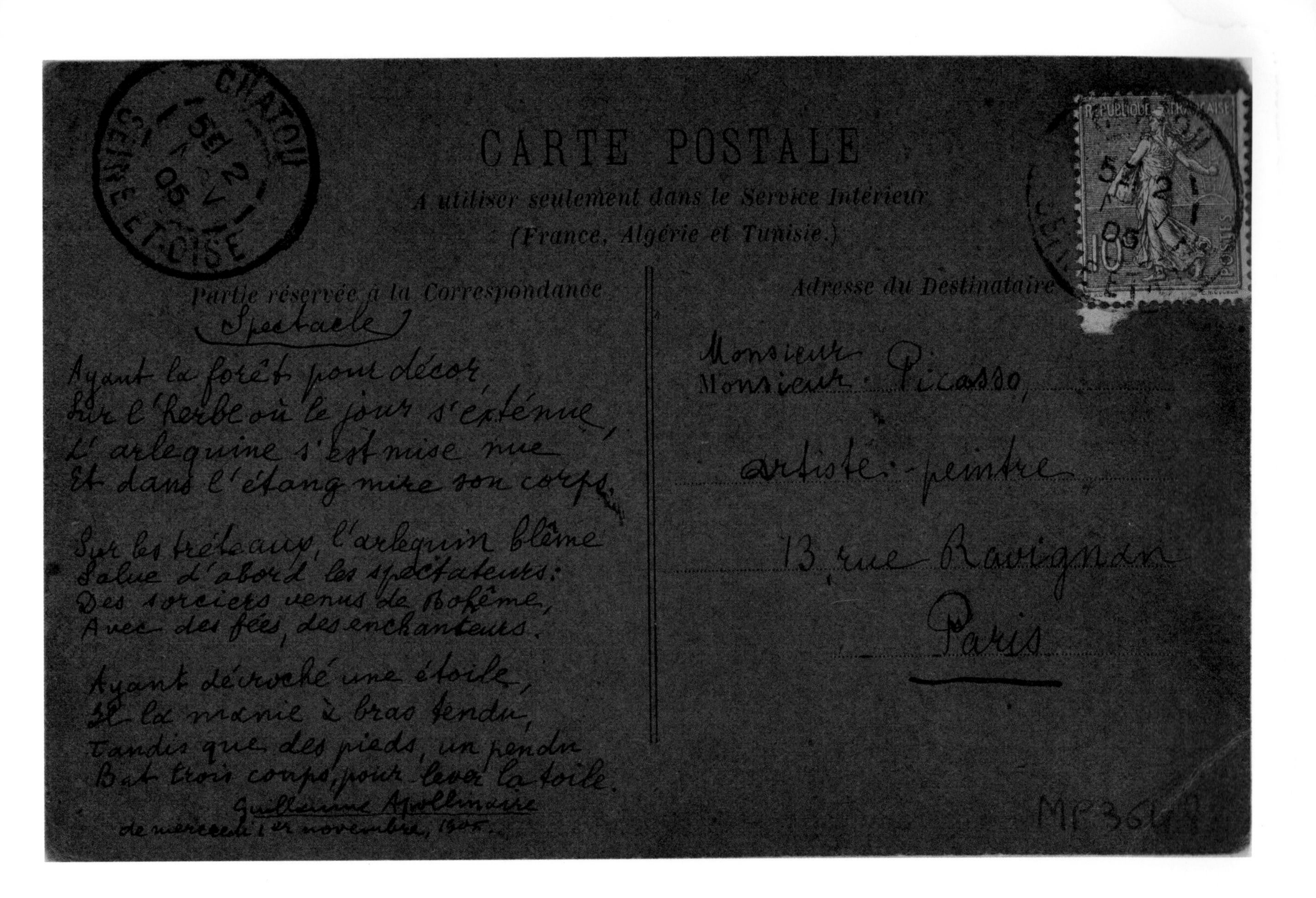
CHATOU SEINE-ET-OISE

CARTE POSTALE

A utiliser seulement dans le Service Intérieur

(France, Algérie et Tunisie.)

Partie réservée à la Correspondance

Spectacle

Ayant la forêt pour décor,
Sur l'herbe où le jour s'exténue,
L'arlequine s'est mise nue
Et dans l'étang mire son corps.

Sur les tréteaux, l'arlequin blême
Salue d'abord les spectateurs:
Des sorciers venus de Bohême,
Avec des fées, des enchanteurs.

Ayant décroché une étoile,
Il la manie à bras tendu,
Tandis que des pieds, un pendu
Bat trois coups, pour lever la toile.

Guillaume Apollinaire

de mercredi 1er novembre, 1905.

Adresse du Destinataire

Monsieur
Monsieur Picasso,
artiste-peintre,
13, rue Ravignan
Paris

Above

Postcard sent to Picasso by Apollinaire on 2 November, *1905*

Musée Picasso, Paris

The only message on this plain blue post card, addressed to "Monsieur Picasso, Artist, 13 rue Ravignan Paris", contained two poems, one on each side of the card, "Spectacle" and "Les Saltimbanques", two of the most popular works in modern French poetry.

Left
Picasso with New Caledonian sculpture in his studio at the Bateau-Lavoir, *c. 1908*
Photograph taken by Burgess Gelett Frank. Musée Picasso, Paris

Picasso with New Caledonian sculpture in his studio at the Bateau-Lavoir, in Montmartre, a floating laundry so-called because it was filthy, creaky and located on a hill. This photograph was most probably published in connection with Gelett Burgess's article the "Wild Men of Paris", "The Architectural Record", May 1910.

Above
Gertrude Stein, *(1874-1946)*
Photograph. Jewish Chronicle, London

American writer, poet and art collector Gertrude Stein was a keen supporter and a patron of Picasso. In the early part of the twentieth century, artists including Cézanne, Renoir, Matisse and Picasso dominated her studio.

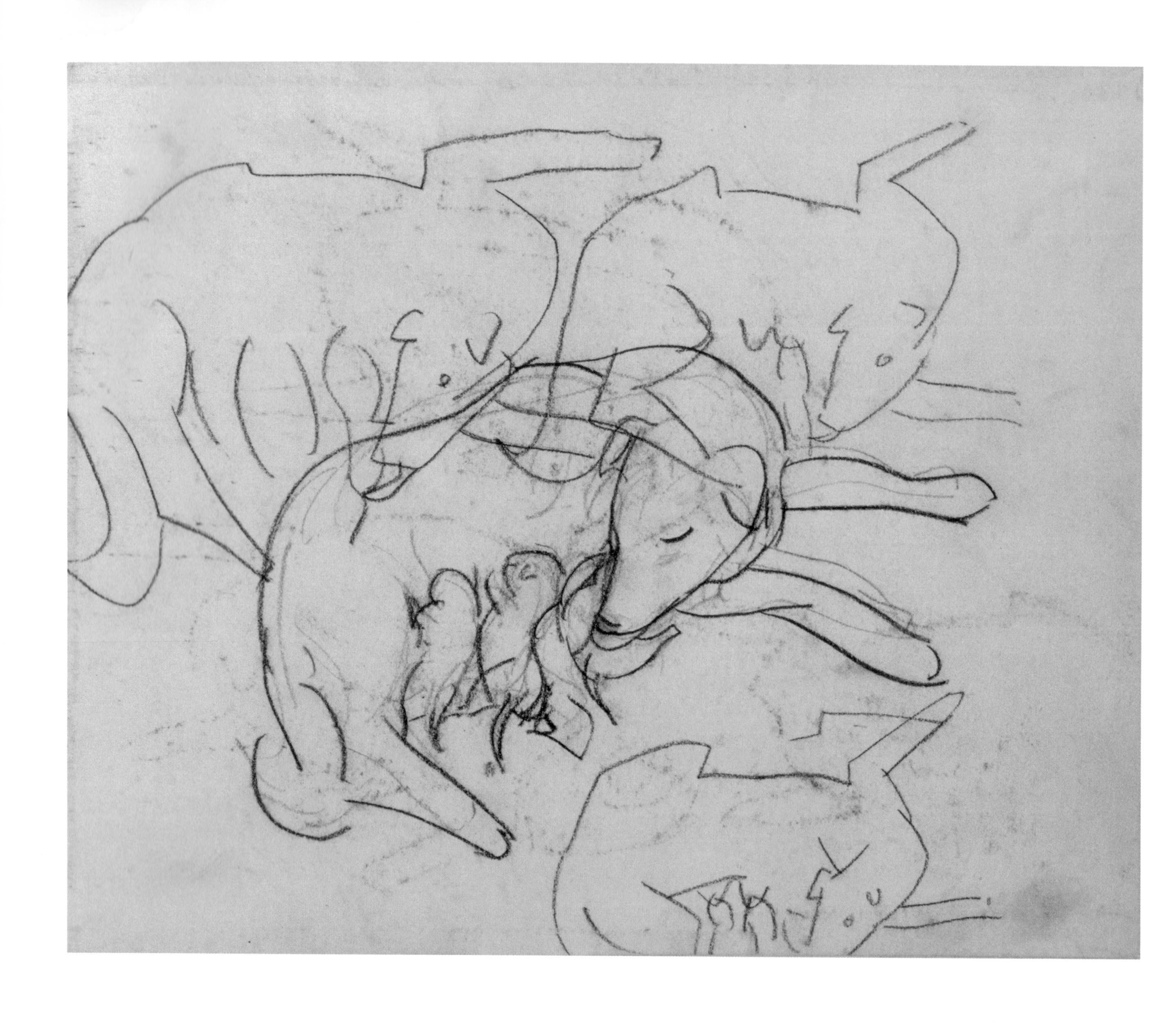

Above
Dog Suckling Her Young (Fricka), *1907*
Black crayon drawing, 19.3 x 24.2 cm (7.5 x 9.5 ins).
Musée Picasso, Paris

The drawing is part of a series of studies related to Picasso's 1907 *Demoiselles d' Avignon*, and perhaps a moralistic reference to fallen behaviour and wanton whorishness.

Right
Studies for illustrations of Le bestiaire ou cortège d'Orphee, *1907*
Pen and ink, 26 x 20.7 cm (10.2 x 8.2 in). Musée Picasso, Paris

Picasso produced these drawings for Guillaume Apollinaire's *Le Bestiaire or Cortege d'orphée* on the back of a letter from Fernande Olivier. The free-flowing sketches echo the poet's most lyrical and uninhibited writing.

Left
André Salmon infront of Picasso's *Three Women*, *1908*
Photograph taken by Pablo Picasso. Musée Picasso, Paris

The poet and critic André Salmon was among a small coterie that included Picasso, Apollinaire, Jacob and Braque. He was a proponent of Cubism, as seen in his eyewitness account of twentieth-century art, *La jeune peinture française*.

Above
Study for Demoiselles D'Avignon, *1906*
Black crayon drawing, 14.7 x 10.6 cm (5.7 x 4.2 ins).
Musée Picasso, Paris

This is a study for the central figure of *Les Demoiselles D'Avignon* that depicted five nude figures in a shallow space and paved the way for Cubism. The work marks a dramatic shift in the history of twentieth-century art.

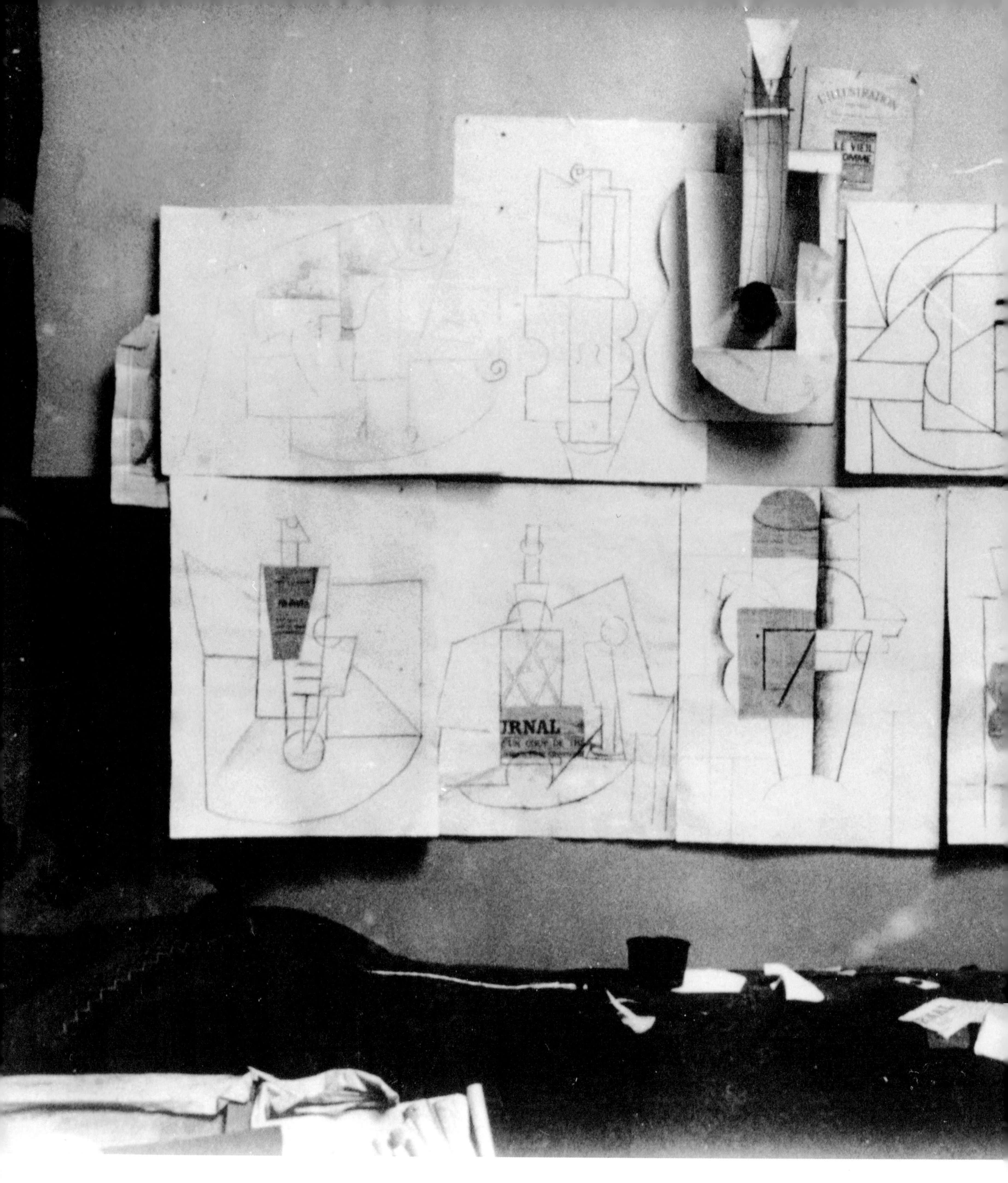
LE VIEIL
URNAL

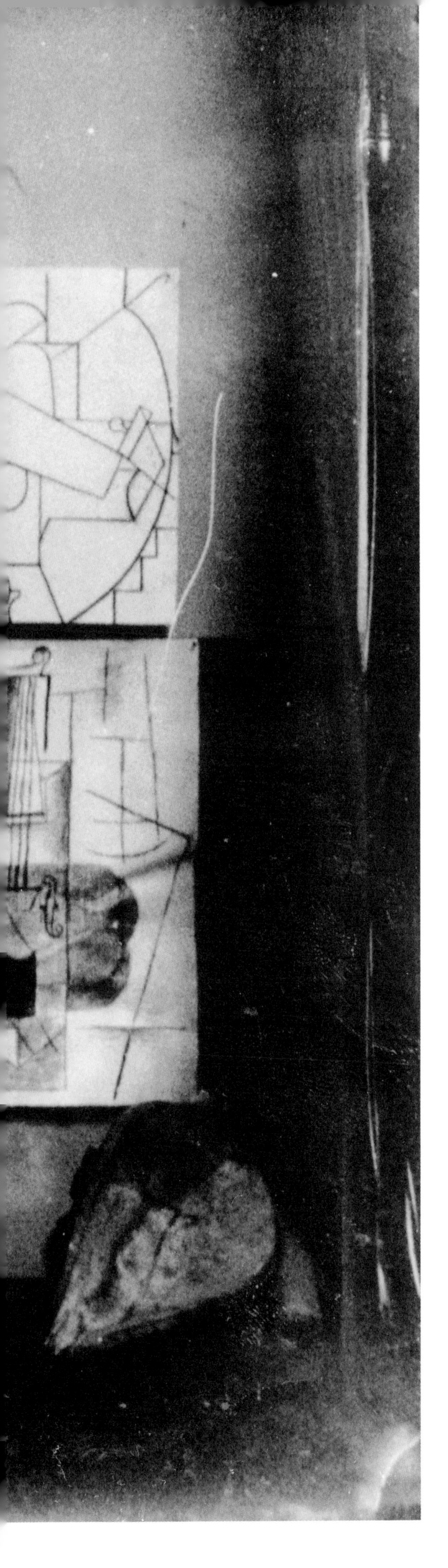

Left
Wall Arrangement of Papiers Collés and Guitar in the Boulevard Raspail, *1912*
Photograph taken by Pablo Picasso. Musée Picasso, Paris

A photograph of a wall arrangement of drawings in Picasso's Boulevard Raspail studio illustrates the connection between the artist's Synthetic Cubism, construction techniques and bricolage. The *Guitar* stands out against the collage of drawings.

Above
Frontispiece portrait for Apollinaire's book of poetry Alcools, *1912*
Pencil, ink, and wash on paper, 21 x 15 cm (8.3 x 5.9 in).
Musée Picasso, Paris

When Apollinaire's *Alcools* was published in 1913, it established his reputation. *Alcools* marked a unique collaboration between poet and painter: it contained the poem "Spectacle", celebrating the magical power of Harlequin Trismegistus.

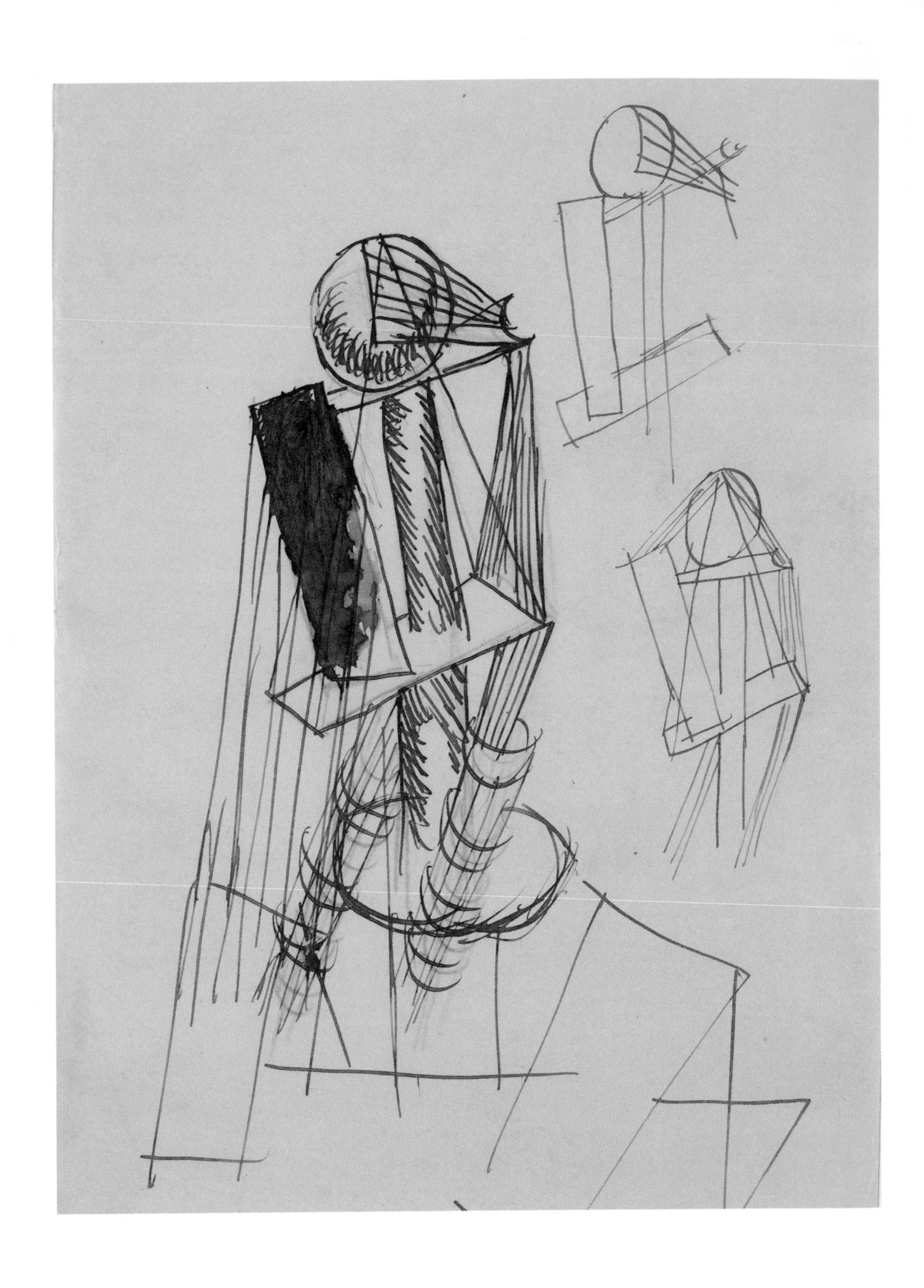

Left
Personnage, *1912–13*
Pen and black ink on black chalk outlines, 31.2 x 20 cm (12.3 x 7.8 in). Musée Picasso, Paris

Personnage alludes to the composite nature of Picasso's *Guitar* and captures his understanding of the relationship between painting and sculpture.

Above
Three Head Studies, *1912–13*
Pen and black ink on black chalk outlines, 31.2 x 20 cm (12.3 x 7.8 in). Musée Picasso, Paris

Picasso made numerous studies for sculptural projects around this time. The geometrical spatial analysis of human anatomy and integration of multiple viewpoints would prove key to the assemblage character of his Manager constructions in *Parade* in 1917.

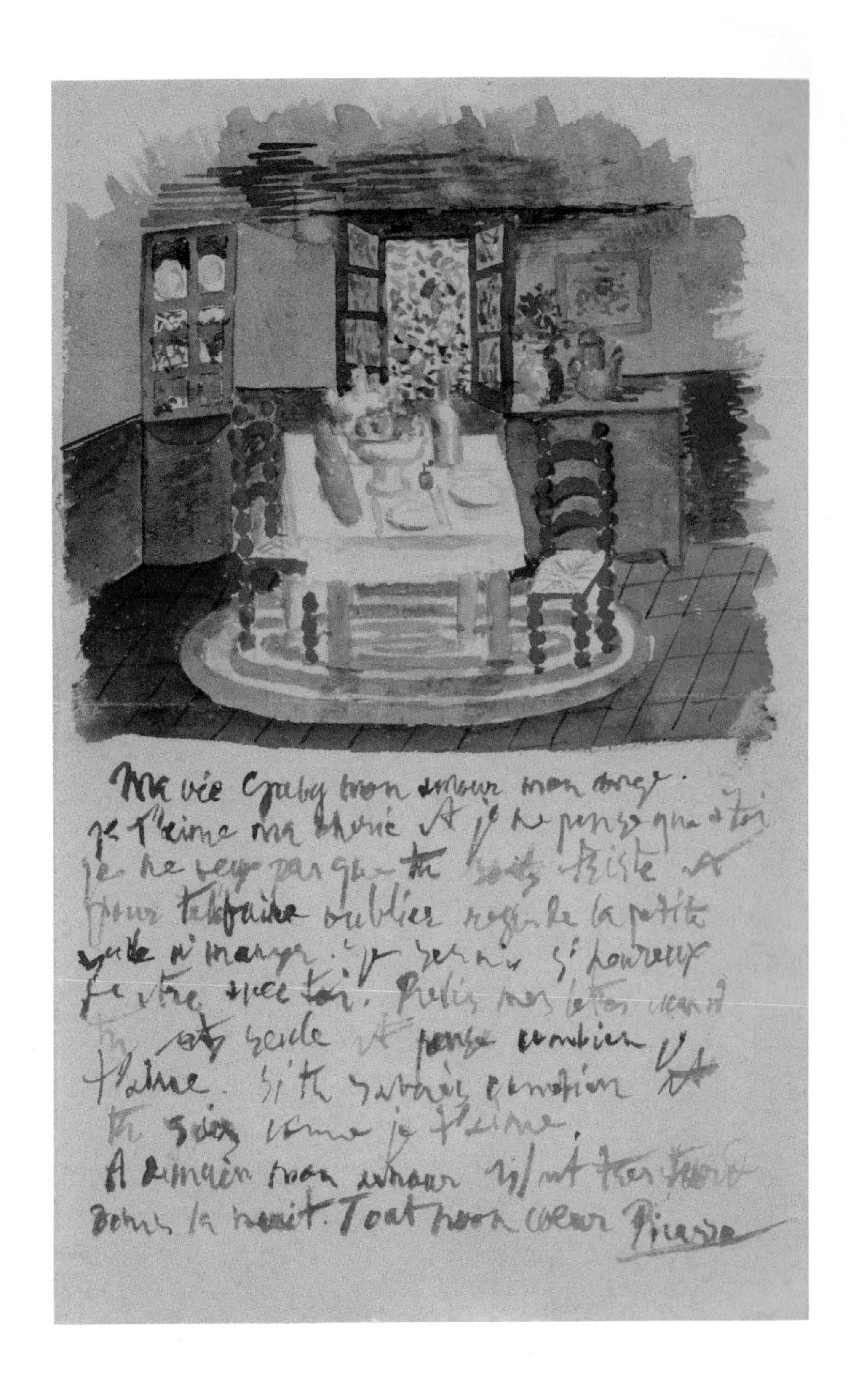

Left
Portrait of Apollinaire with a bandaged head, *1916*
Black pencil, 29.7 x 22.5cm (11.6 x 8.8 ins). Musée Picasso, Paris

This drawing depicts Guillaume Apollinaire with his head swathed in bandages, after he was wounded during the First World War. The Croix de Guerre is pinned over Apollinaire's heart. He was awarded this for courageous behaviour under fire. This drawing became the frontispiece for *Calligrammes* in April 1918 where he recorded his war experiences. It was published a few months before he died of influenza.

Above
Letter to Gaby Lespinasse, *1916*
Watercolour and ink drawing, 17.5 x 11 cm (6.8 x 4.3 ins). Musée Picasso, Paris

This is a love letter that Picasso wrote to Gaby Lespinasse. He wrote: "I would be so happy to live with you. Read my letters again when you are alone and think how much I love you."

Left
Serge Diaghilev, *1916*
Photograph. Bibliothèque de l'Opéra, Paris

Russian impresario Serge Diaghilev combined ballet, music and art into an immersive form of theatre with his company the Ballets Russes, which he ran from 1909 until 1929. Collaborators included Chanel, Picasso, Matisse, Nijinsky and Stravinsky.

Above

Picasso, Olga Koklova and Jean Cocteau in Rome, *1917*

Photograph. Collection: Réunion des musées nationaux/Madeleine Coursaget

This black-and-white photograph portrays a young Picasso with his with his soon-to-be first wife, the Russian ballet dancer Olga Koklova, in the company of the French poet, writer, artist and film-maker Jean Cocteau.

Above

Artist's studio at rue La Boétie, *1920*

Pencil, 24 x 34.1 cm (9.4 x 13.4 in). Musée Picasso, Paris

As this drawing of the upstairs floor of Picasso's studio reveals, the artist was in his natural element amongst clutter and chaos, which he liked to surround himself whenever he was working in the studio environment.

2

With the aid of Georges Braque, Picasso began to formulate Cubism around 1908, and the movement's various phases up until 1915 epitomizes Modernism as an idiom, and as a search for re-invention in art. Cubism created many new pictorial forms and triggered an unending quest for fresh materials and objects so as to help reach beyond traditional descriptions of visual reality in art. Cubism not only opened up new methods of painterly representation, but inspired Picasso's radical approaches in three-dimensional work and the creation of collage, *papier collé*, construction and assemblage techniques. Picasso explored sculpture throughout the Cubist epoch, and his work culminated during 1912–15, in a number of constructions and assemblages made from cardboard, wood, sheet metal, and cobbled together with "junk" and other "found" objects and materials.

Section 2: 1908–1916

Chapter 6

Picasso, Primitivism and Magic: The Beginnings of Cubism, 1907–08

Picasso's involvement with *art nègre* was a key factor in his carving an identity for himself as a modern conjurer of "primitive" works. *Art nègre* (Negro Art), and related derivations such as "primitive" or, even, "savage" art, are now universally seen as offensive and derogatory. Nevertheless, the terms were habitually used in France, Germany and other European countries to described non-western artefacts, primarily from Africa and Oceania, up until about 1940. The connection between Picasso's art and magic is well-documented. In *La Jeune Peinture Française* (1912), André Salmon makes a direct link between Picasso the magician and his painting of *Les Demoiselles d'Avignon* (now on display in The Museum of Modern Art, New York, 1907). Salmon claims: "The apprentice sorcerer was still seeking answers to his questions among the enchantments of Oceania and Africa".[1] As historians of Picasso's work have argued, his knowledge of *art nègre* clearly shaped the formal structure of his Cubist paintings. Tribal artefacts amassed from Oceania and Africa in the Trocadéro in Paris had a great impact on Picasso and his contemporaries, and he would go on to describe these revelatory discoveries to André Malraux in 1937. In summoning up imagined *nègre* spirits, hidden deep within the magic-making masks, carvings and fetishes, Picasso evoked sorcery and revealed his life-long superstitious nature. The artist recalled: "[The masks] were weapons to help people escape the power of the spirits and become free".[2]

Art and artists have long been associated with magic and magicians. In *Totem and Taboo* (1913), Sigmund Freud remarked that the only discipline in our civilization to have retained an element of magic was the field of art. Freud's interest in magic was restricted solely to a fascination with animism and the "omnipotence of thoughts", in what he called primitive or savage societies. Freud likened a so-called primitive mentality to the mental life of children and, more crucially, to the narcissistic, neurotic and paranoiac states in modern civilization.

Freud's ideas about the roots of the magical arts in supposed primitive cultures relied heavily on James Frazer's *The Golden Bough* (1890–1915), which by and large was regarded as a foundational book on religious customs by French sociologists. The suppositions of the psychiatrist and anthropologist did much to popularize and determine primitivizing stereotypes in relation to the principles of religion and magic among French and German avant-garde circles. Modernist groups of artists, such as the Fauvists, Cubists and Surrealists, appropriated *art nègre* in such a way as to establish what can only be described as "a cult of the primitive". At the dawn of the twentieth century, artists, writers, poets were fashioning interconnected ideas regarding exotic/erotic fantasies about the supposed savage peoples in order to critique their own society's values, philosophical viewpoints and traditional artistic canons of beauty and noble subject matter, established during the Renaissance.

The rupture between traditional forms of painting and sculpture, seen especially with the invention of Cubist and collage techniques, and conflated with the imagined fetishes, rituals and magic attributed to tribal or non-Western artefacts, was brought about through the alignment of various notions of magical thinking. Parallels can be observed in the references that Frazer and Picasso make to the virtues of sympathetic magic. In *The Golden Bough*, Frazer writes about the "private magical rites and incantations practiced for the benefit or injury of individuals"[3]. In his practice, Picasso appears to have been fascinated by the mysterious powers of tribal objects: "[Spirits] are tools. If we give spirits a form, we become independent".[4]

The precise nature of Picasso's interest in anthropological artefacts, including how he first saw tribal objects, and to what degree they aided his visual art, is a much-debated topic when considering the beginnings of Cubism. The connection between Picasso's art and tribal objects is traditionally dated to the spring of 1907, during which Picasso went alone to visit the dusty and overlooked rooms of the Musée d'Ethnographie at the Trocadéro (now the *Musée de l'Homme*) in Paris. Guillaume Apollinaire's typed quotations of "Sayings by Pablo Picasso" record his epiphany when standing among the unkempt and neglected tribal objects of the Trocadéro: "I experienced my greatest artistic emotions when the sublime beauty of the sculptures by unnamed artists of Africa suddenly appeared before me. These religious, passionate, and rigorously logical works of art are the most powerful and beautiful products of the human imagination".[5]

1 André Salmon, *La Jeune Peinture Française*, Paris, Société des Trente, Albert Messein, 1912 p. 44. Translated in Cowling, *Picasso: Style and Meaning*, p. 176.

2 André Malraux, *La Tête d'Obsidienne*, p. 17–19. Trans in Cowling, p. 176.

3 James George Frazer, *The Golden Bough: A Study in Magic and Religion*, Macmillan and Co. Limited, 12 vols., London, 1949 [first edition: 1890–1915], Chapter III, "Sympathetic Magic", p. 11–48 (p. 45).

4 André Malraux, ibid.

As Peter Read explains, however, the artist first encountered African sculpture while visiting Gertrude Stein in the autumn of 1906, when Henri Matisse showed him a Congolese mask bought from a junk shop. We also know that Matisse, André Derain and Maurice de Vlaminck were all collecting African objects in Paris by 1906. For example, Picasso greatly admired Paul Gauguin's retrospective exhibition of the same year at the Salon d'Automne, which included examples of Polynesian ceramics and sculpture. Picasso also began acquiring *art nègre* himself from curiosity shops and flea markets around the time of working on *Les Demoiselles d'Avignon*, as seen in a photograph of his studio at the Bateau-Lavoir (see pages 44). Perhaps as a distraction to creating this huge canvas, the artist embarked on a number of primitivizing works, imitating and combining examples of Polynesian and African sculpture. Picasso, for instance, executed several figures with heads inspired by masks, such as *Nude with Raised Arms* (see opposite) and *Head* (both 1907), which bear striking similarities to the Oudombo *Reliquary Figure* from the Gabon, which has belonged to the collection of the Trocadéro since 1897, and features glaring eyes, facial striations and a feather headdress. The reliquary, which used strips of skin and was designed to contain human bones, must have instantly appeared to the artist, and others who viewed the piece as some kind of magical guardian watching over the dead. According to William Rubin, Picasso acquired two Kota reliquary figures from the Gabon in 1907, and the diamond-shaped legs and arms of Picasso's *Nude with Raised Arms* have much in common with certain types of Kota sculptures, which have projections extending from both sides. More importantly, Kota figures held a magical role in Picasso's painting and his reconfiguration of the non-representational forms of the Kota and Oudombo figures were in all likelihood driven by an attraction to the imagined, invocatory character of these strange-looking museum exhibits. Picasso undoubtedly understood the basic meaning behind these reliquary figures and chose to romanticize and reinterpret their forms and styles according to his own superstitions, by bringing together elements drawn from different tribal sources. As Elizabeth Cowling argues, Picasso's appreciation of tribal art was clearly based upon popular literary ideas that associated tribal artefacts with rites for the dead and meant to provide protection from, or ward off, evil spirits. *Nude with Raised Arms* was perhaps a similar attempt to cultivate the terrifying experience Picasso encountered during his first visit to the Trocadéro Musée d'Ethnographie in Paris and, to conjure up, through association with *art nègre*, a painting of identical "savagery" and supposed magical power. In taking on the persona of "primitive" magician, Cowling suggests that Picasso created a primitive idol (note the figure's petrifying, Medusa-like, gaze) that fuses concept and form, and which is a direct equivalent to Christian icons and other religious imagery.

Nude with Drapery (1907) evolved out of studies for *Les Demoiselles d'Avignon*, and the work recalls the poses and gestures of the two women in the centre and to the left of Picasso's great masterpiece. Following the canonical style of Michelangelo's *Dying Slave* (c.1515–16) and Ingres's *La Source* (see page 65), the woman stands on some kind of podium with her right arm behind her head, gazing downwards in supplication and emulating the *contrapposto* pose of classical proportions. Here, Picasso parodies morally pure images or archetypal expressions of beauty by supplementing the idealized display of divine loveliness for a body that is almost skeletal, jagged, misshapen, distorted and covered in striations that suggest the markings (tattoos, dog tooth and basket weave patterns) on tribal carvings. The figure also begins to fracture and meld with the surrounding drapery, its faceted forms stabbing and beginning to envelop the model in a way that anticipates the Cézannesque, Analytical Cubism developed by Braque and Picasso in the summer of 1909 (see Chapter 7).

John Richardson and Elizabeth Cowling have suggested that *Nude with Drapery* and other works, such as Picasso's magnificent painting *The Dryad* of 1908 (see page 66), were influenced by *ecorché* (flayed) figures in Vesalius's sixteenth-century *De Humani Corporis Fabrica* of 1543 (see page 66), or by comparative anatomy models displayed in the Museum of National History, Paris. Whatever their origins, Picasso referenced the human *ecorché* through his gruesome anatomical details of bone and flesh, so as to usurp the figuration underpinned by a classical tradition. Yet Picasso's stylizations of *art nègre* also served as a critique of contemporary paintings such as Matisse's *Blue Nude: Memory of Biskra*, whose fauvist pastoralism, bright colour scheme and distortion of the beautiful and grotesque shocked visitors to the Salon des Indépendants in 1907. Picasso bitterly complained to Walter Pach, a friend of the Steins, that Matisse's casual approach to the sensual and decorative genre of portraying the female nude was a failure.

Picasso followed up his experiments in *art nègre* and his early Cubist works with a small idol-like *Figure* (1908, see page 67), loosely carved in blocky oak forms, striking a hefty pose and holding its weight on one leg, in a fashion similar to the wooden Fon Figures from Dahomey, installed in the African art gallery of the Trocadéro in 1895. These were essays in his new primitivist style, derived from caryatid figures and recalling his acquisition of a freestanding Marquesan wood *tiki* figure in 1907 – which reveals the influence of his association with André Derain, himself an avid and knowledgeable collector of primitive artefacts. These carved figures have the same block-relief, hard and wood-grain appearance as Picasso's *Three Women*, whose rough-hewn finish and composition mirrors Derain's *Bather* composition of 1907, which was close in style to the monumental figures of Cézanne. Derain played a crucial role in redirecting Picasso's response to tribal art, away from the influences of magic-making masks and expositions in sorcery, and towards more realistic sources. As Salmon reported in *La jeune peinture française* of 1912: "The imagery of Polynesia and Dahomey struck [Picasso] as *raisonnable* (sensible or rational)".[6]

In relation to other non-Western art when painting the faces of his *Three Women*, Picasso may still have been influenced by fifth-century Iberian statues from Cerro de los Santos and Osuna (about 80 kilometres or 50 miles from Picasso's birthplace in Málaga). Both pieces were stolen from the Louvre by Apollinaire's "secretary", Gérey Pieret, and sold or given to Picasso, probably sometime in March 1907. The facial stylization of these busts looks remarkably similar to the primitivized expression of faces in Picasso's painting. These limestone carvings also appear to have influenced Picasso's 1906 terracotta sculpture of *Woman Combing her Hair*, and the connection might be more significant than at first appears, because the sculpture can be seen in the photograph of Picasso in his studio of the summer of 1908, positioned to the right on a chest of drawers, just behind the unfinished *Three Women*. Apollinaire later informed Madeline Pagès that he had desperately tried to persuade Picasso to return both Iberian pieces but "Picasso wanted to keep his statues".[7]

5 Picasso and Apollinaire, *Correspondence*, ed. Pierre Caizergues and Hélèn Seckel, Paris Gallimard, 1992, p. 201–204.

6 André Salmon, *La Jeune Peinture française*, 1912, p. 43.

7 Guillaume Apollinaire, *Letters à Madeleine: Tendre comme le souvenir*, ed. Laurence Campa, Paris, Gallimard, 2005, p. 96–97. Cited in Peter Read, *Picasso and Apollinaire*, p. 62.

Right

Nude with Raised Arms, *1907*

Oil on canvas, 150 x 100 cm (59 x 39.5 in). Private Collection

The pose of this strange and haunting figure is similar stylistically to a number of African Kota reliquary figures, which were associated, in Picasso's mind, with sacred rites for the dead, and seen as protective guardians to ward off evil spirits. The artist was very superstitious and throughout his life viewed himself and his work as a receptacle for magical forces.

Three Women, *1908*

Oil on canvas, 200 x 178 cm (78.5 x 70 cm). State Hermitage Museum, St Petersburg

The single, most ambitious *art nègre* painting that Picasso produced after *Nude with Drapery* (1907) was his great work *Three Women* (1908, see left). The canvas went through a series of protracted re-workings, and a large number of highly coloured preparatory studies and photographs suggest that the picture was originally very primitivized in feel and appearance. Pierre Daix is convinced that the painting, which was begun in the autumn of 1907, was far more barbarous in its first African-looking state. Indeed, photographs demonstrate that *Three Women* depicted rather androgynous-looking figures, with masks for faces, amid a darker, primordial forest setting. It was perhaps for these reasons that Gertrude Stein claimed that the work was initially puzzling and "rather frightening".[8] The submissive countenances and dream-like gazes of Picasso's women are reminiscent of the large compositions with trios of nudes by André Derain and Georges Braque, which were exhibited at the Salon des Indépendants in the autumn of 1908. The facial stylization of Picasso's women is remarkably similar to the expression of fifth-century Iberian statues from Cerro de los Santos and Osuna, which the artist temporarily acquired in the spring of 1907. In the autumn of 1908, then, Picasso returned to his own large canvas, re-painting the faces, background and other anatomical details, giving his figures and their drapery a more sculptural appearance by faceting the forms to suggest gravitas, weight and solidity, as if they had been carved in stone. In comparison to *Les Demoiselles d'Avignon*, the *Three Women* is more meditative and lacks the explosive punch, sexuality and exorcist mode of Picasso's 1907 work, as well as being discernibly closer in formal logic to Paul Cézanne's bather paintings, from which Braque and Derain had both drawn their inspiration. In pitting himself against Cézanne's *Grandes Baigneuses* (1906, see pages 68–69), Picasso laid the foundations of a movement that would become one of the most important and debated idioms of twentieth-century art history: Cubism.

8 Gertrude Stein, *The Autobiography of Alice B. Toklas*, Harcourt, Brace, New York, 1933, p. 22.

Above

La Source, *1856, Jean-Auguste-Dominique Ingres*

Oil on canvas, 165 x 80 cm (65 x 31.5 in). Musée d'Orsay, Paris

This was an icon of French painting, expressing the innocence, freshness and vitality of the female body in nineteenth-century academic classicism. Picasso's primitivising images of female figures of the period were surely an attempt to undermine academic canons, with regard to femininity and beauty.

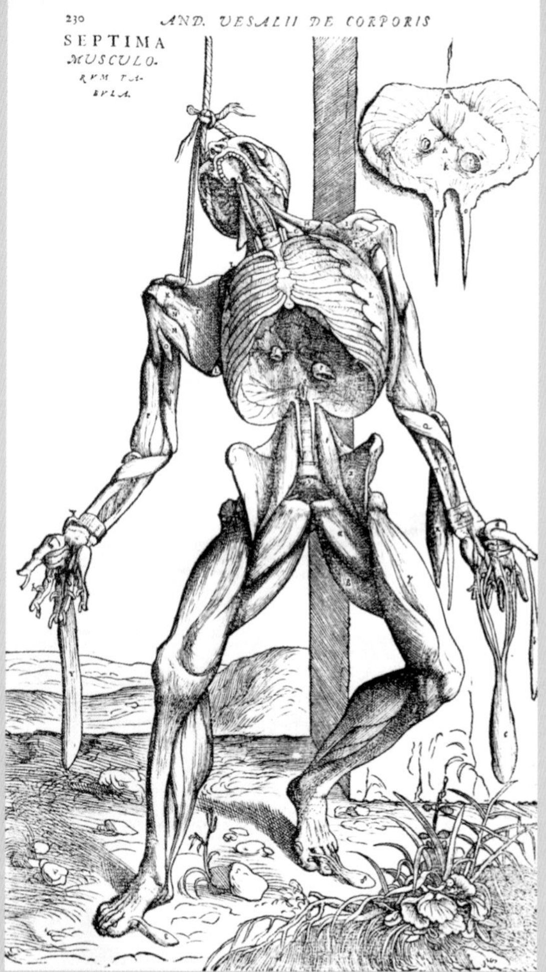

Left
The Dryad, *1908*
Oil on canvas, 185 x 108 cm (73 x 42.5 in). State Hermitage Museum, St Petersburg

Picasso's *Dryad* is another great painting from the summer of 1908. The half-standing/sitting figure, emerging out of a dark woody glade, blurs the distinctions between horizontal and vertical, so as to heighten ambivalence in the picture. This visual trope was used in subsequent Cubist paintings.

Above
Seventh plate of the muscles from the second volume of *De Humani Corporis Fabrica*, *1543, Vesalius*

Picasso's *Dryad* painting is distinctly reminiscent of this sixteenth-century engraving. It is likely that the artist gleaned his knowledge of Vesalius' engravings in *De Humani Corporis Fabrica* from the bibliophile Apollinaire, who had an eclectic collection of antiquarian medical texts.

Right
Figure, *1908*
Carved oak, 80.5 cm (31.5 in) high. Musée Picasso, Paris

This rare wooden carving by Picasso suggests a woman carrying a bowl above her head and was probably inspired by a firm knowledge of African and Oceanic sculpture. Picasso was on close terms with André Derain, who made his own primitivized carvings, and was a highly knowledgeable and enthusiastic collector of tribal objects.

Left
Grand Baigneuses, *1906, Paul Cézanne*
Oil on canvas, 209 x 252 cm (82.5 x 99 in).
Philadelphia Museum of Art

Picasso was deeply affected by Paul Cézanne's large bather compositions, particularly the monumentality and structural arrangements of his female figures, which were often associated with the avant-garde's "discovery" of *art nègre* around 1906. Picasso's nude paintings of *Three Women* and *Nude with Raised Arms*, as well as many other primitivizing works of the period, would be unimaginable without the influence of the French master's late great figure compositions and the upsurge in the interest of tribal artefacts.

Chapter 7

"Cézanne's Lesson": Picasso, Braque and Towards Cubism, 1908–10

Primitivism had been an especially fertile field for Picasso: the rigorous forms and totemic aspects of Iberian, Egyptian, Oceanic and African artefacts lent themselves to some extremely unconventional paintings and sculptures by the artist. But now Picasso was searching out a new spiritual guide and beginning to adopt the tactic of reductionism, extracted from the statuesque images of Cézanne's *Grandes Baigneuses* (see Chapter 6). *Three Women* and *Friendship* (1908) could not possibly have been conceived without the reduction of simple constituents to create androgynous-looking figures with hefty bodies, which have a sculptural sense of mass, weight and presence. Picasso had previously been exploring in a series of watercolours the idea of a large figure composition, entitled *Five Women (Bathers in a Forest)*, which would have been a wonderful companion to *Les Demoiselles d'Avignon*, and a work that had all the hallmarks of the theatrical, spatial construction of Cézanne's pictures. Historians have long touted the idea that Cézanne's work was fundamental to the development of Cubism. However, as Pepe Karmel, an authority on Picasso's Cubism, points out, the artist rarely mirrored the patterning or grid-like brushwork seen in Cézanne's paintings. Instead, he imitated the proscenium space of his still lifes or the tilted-up picture planes of his landscapes. Cézanne's still-life subjects, according to Karmel, replicate the visual tropes of many Renaissance masterworks such as Giovanni Bellini's Madonnas, where curtains function to create shallow spaces or shelves project forward so as to better reveal the space and objects within the painting. Karmel cites Cézanne's famous *Grandes Baigneuses* (1906), currently in the Philadelphia Museum of Art, as an example of the artist adopting this age-old theatrical practice of the High Renaissance, where the figures appear are on a stage-like proscenium set before a "curtain" of trees, which open to reveal the distant landscape, and a traditional device intrinsic to Cézanne's late painting.

Picasso had been aware of Cézanne since 1901, and developed his interest in the French master on seeing his works in Ambroise Vollard's gallery, a display of ten paintings at the Salon d'Automne in 1906 and a show of 79 watercolours at the Bernheim-Jeune in June 1907. In the wake of the French master's death on 22 October 1906, Picasso visited a memorial exhibition held the following year. The watercolour show, in particular, was a revelation for Picasso, who seems to have been struck by the fluidity of Cézanne's brushwork and the sense of completeness associated with his watercolour technique. Picasso commented: "As soon as he begins to make the first stroke the picture is already there".[1] Cézanne's exploitation of the white ground in his watercolours and canvases became an intrinsic part of his descriptions of light falling upon objects, and allowed him to render space more palpable to the eye. For example, in Cézanne's *Trees by the Water*, the variations in viewpoint and the gaps in the work allow the observer to imaginatively sketch in certain possibilities offered by perception. As the art critic John Berger suggests, these blank spaces provide "the silence demanded [by] echoes".[2] Cézanne's watercolour records a shifting, mobile perspective, in which engagement with the subject is constantly changing, and the elision of planes encourages the viewer to become almost part of the view. This was Cézanne's real lesson, and as the Salon Cubist Robert Delaunay would later write in a sketchbook, "the watercolours of Cézanne announce Cubism".[3]

George Braque's passion for Cézanne can also be traced back to the commemorative exhibition of 1907, and a sojourn to paint a number of canvases of L'Estaque in the South of France, where Cézanne had once worked, in the summer of 1908.

Braque probably met Picasso in the spring of 1907 during the course of Salon des Indépendants exhibition (20 March-30 April) and, in November or December, was accompanied by Apollinaire to Picasso's studio at the Bateau-Lavoir, and marking the beginning of their Cubist adventure. Braque was slightly younger than Picasso (seven months to be exact), but both were entirely different in character: Braque being clear, measured and bourgeois, Picasso fiery, temperamental and bohemian in nature, he was the Apollo to Picasso's Dionysus. Braque hailed from a family of housepainters and colour merchants, and his skill as a decorator and knowledge of the techniques of lettering, marbling and wood-graining effects would become crucial to the matière of Synthetic Collage Cubism. Late in life, Braque described to Dora Vallier the pioneering Cubist adventure in terms of mountaineering expedition, where both artists – who met on an almost daily basis during an intense, six-year period of closeness.

1 Hélène Parmelin, *Picasso dit…*Paris, Gonthier, 1966, p. 72.
2 John Berger, *The Success and Failure of Picasso*, Readers and Writers Publishing Cooperative, London, 1965 [1980], p. 55.
3 Meyer Shapiro, *Cézanne's Watercolours*, Knoedler's, New York, 1963, p. 15.
4 Louis Vauxcelles, *Gil Blas*, 14 November, 1908. "Braque, la peinture et nous", *Cahiers d'art 29*, no.1, October 1954, p. 14.
5 Alfred J. Barr, *Cubism and Abstract Art*, The Museum of Modern Art, New York, 1936, p. 672–673.
6 Dora Vallier, Georges Braque, "Braque, la peinture et nous", *Cahiers d'art 29*, no.1, October 1954, p. 13–24.
7 Roland Penrose, *Picasso Sculpture, Ceramics, Graphic Art*, Tate Gallery, London, 1967, p. 10.

Braque returned with the hope of showing his L'Estaque landscapes at the 1908 Salon d'Automne, but when the jury rejected his works, he exhibited them at Daniel-Henry Kahnweiler's gallery in November of the same year. It was at this show that the artist's landscapes inspired Louis Vauxcelles to come up with the maxim that Braque "reduces everything, sites and figures and houses to geometric schemas, to cubes".[4] Although Braque's *Landscape at L'Estaque* (see page 73) and Picasso's *Cottage and Trees* (1908–09, see page 73) betray differences, in terms of Braque's elimination of sky and Picasso's use of a standard backdrop, both flout traditional conventions of perspective and modelling by transforming their landscapes into blocks of colour that seem to pile up or push outward, so that where the pictorial space becomes open-ended, planes and objects bleed into one another. Braque's landscape painting reinterprets Cézanne's elision of planes and his device known as *passage*, defined by Alfred Barr as "the merging of planes with space by leaving one edge unpainted or light in tone".[5]

His and Picasso's awareness of Cézanne's pictorial inventions was a crucial first step in the development of Cubism, which allowed both artists to create new kinds of pictorial space and artifice that would influence the course of modern art. This marked the beginning of a relationship that would establish Cubism as the style and rhetoric of the twentieth-century. Braque likened their project and daily exchanges to those of a pair of "two mountaineers roped together"[6]. Picasso described that his discussions with Braque happened on an almost daily basis, with Picasso and Braque going to each other's studios. Both were eager to see what exactly each had made during the day, comparing, discussing and testing various ideas with regard to their respective works. Furthermore, Braque detailed the artists' quest for anonymity in their practice as an attempt to efface their own personalities in order to seek out originality. Although amateurs often mistook both painters' works – Picasso's for Braque and visa versa – this was of little importance since both were fundamentally interested in each other's art and the resulting problems that it presented on a daily basis.

The problem that Braque described most probably surfaced with Picasso's discovery of broken geometrical facets in drawings and paintings of the village and mountains at Horta de Ebro in Spain during the summer of 1909. Works such as *Houses on the Hill, Horta de Ebro*, fluctuate between the use of Cézannesque passage, in the landscape, buildings, trees and sky viewed from all sides, as if Picasso had travelled all over the hilly terrain; and the empty pathways and solid cube-like formations that delineate the elaborate facets. The cubic forms showing houses neatly packed together on the hillside also imply a sculptural relief. Most notably, the blocks and flat, contradictory spaces on the hill are strikingly similar to the forms of a life-size sculpted *Head of a Woman* (*Fernande*, see page 73), which Picasso modelled in clay on his return to Paris from Spain in 1909. Here the deeply-cut, illuminated facets of Fernande's hair-bun and head appear to climb upward like the buildings of the Horta landscape. Clearly, then, Picasso sought to bring together and elaborate upon all the discoveries that he made at Horta within this single sculpture: angles, tonal subtleties and multiple viewpoints create an analogy between the architectural volumes on the hill in his Horta paintings and the tendency to build up the forms in *Head of a Woman*. This important work is not simply an academic or superfluous exercise (as scholars have often suggested), but depends fundamentally upon our understanding of the Cubist idiom. *Head of a Woman* is, despite all claims to the contrary, the first Cubist sculpture appealing to an imaginative integration of the spatial and the visual, and therefore an invaluable piece in the development of Picasso's later Cubist painting and constructed sculpture.

The term Analytical Cubism is a fitting description for *Head of a Woman*, because it is the result of a pseudo-scientific process of experimentation. As Picasso famously told Roland Penrose "it was pointless to go on with this kind of sculpture" and he had initially thought of using wire to define some of the planes of the head, but relinquished this concept because it was "too like painting".[7] As a result, we may conclude that the sculptural effects of *Head of a Woman* did not achieve the fullness of his drawing and painting at this time, or the "open form" construction that would first appear in the autumn of 1912 (see Chapter 8). However, the solidity of *Head of a Woman* and the Horta landscape paintings as a whole, would point the way forward as Braque and Picasso pressed on with their experiments, testing the limits of Analytical Cubism over the course of 1910. Picasso's *The Guitar Player* (see page 74) and Braque's *Still Life with Candlestick and Playing Cards* are examples of their increasingly abstracted works, which describe the human frame and objects in schematic terms. These vaguely decipherable elements, made out of numerous geometric planes and facets, are intimately bound up with the grid-like space merging with figurative or still life elements. They induced the Surrealist leader André Breton to interpret these paintings as "great grey beige scaffoldings" in *Surrealism and Painting* (1928).[8]

Drawings such as *Standing Nude* (better known as *The Fire Escape*, see page 75), like many other works from this period, suggest the anatomization of the human body. In particular, they also recall the ecorché figures in Vesalius's *De Humani Corporis Fabrica*, as well as confirming Kahnweiler's idea that Picasso had "shattered the closed form" with these works.[9] Apollinaire reflects on such formal concerns about painting in *The Cubist Painters* (1913), in which he points out that "the artist had to assassinate himself as scientifically and methodically as a great surgeon".[10]

The rising use of X-rays in medicine was perhaps a key factor behind the artist's fascination with the internality of the human anatomy. His awareness of the possibility to view the interior structure of the body, which was opened up by new experiments in radiography, would have been stimulated by the Futurists' writings on the power of X-rays in their *Manifesto of Futurist Painting* (1910), and through seeing Fernande Olivier's X-ray while she was ill in hospital in January of the same year.

Besides X-rays, Picasso also drew upon an imaginative and magical source when making the fragile, constructed works of Cadaqués in 1910: Cervantes's concept of a glass body in his book *El Licenciado Vidriera* (*The Scholar Made of Glass*). This tells the tale of a bewitched scholar who is given a magical love potion that relieves the young man of his incurable shyness, but leaves him convinced that he is made of glass – which Apollinaire had asked Picasso to translate during the summer of 1910. Whatever the precise source, it is clear that the artist exhibited a fascination for the anatomical aspects of portraits and still lifes, and this was stimulated by his experiments with Analytical Cubism at Horta. The techniques that he developed at Horta, in works relating to *Head of a Woman*, enabled him to invent a language of "open form" sculpture, which would propel the development of construction techniques in years to come.

---

8 André Breton, *Le Surrealisme et la Peinture*, 1928. Translated by Simon Watson Taylor, *Surrealism and Painting*, MacDonald, London, 1972, p. 67.

9 Daniel-Henry Kahnweiler, *Der Weg Zum Kubismus*, Delphin Verlag, Munich 1920 (republished Stuttgart, 1958), Chapter V, p. 38 and p. 49. Translation by Henry Aronson, *The Rise of Cubism*, The Documents of Modern Art, Wittenborn Schultz, New York, 1949, p. 10.

10 Guillaume Apollinaire, *Les Peintres Cubistes*, Eugène Figuière, Paris, 1913, p. 38. Peter Read, translated as *Guillaume Apollinaire: The Cubist Painters*, The Documents of Twentieth Century Art, University of California Press, Berkeley and Los Angeles, 2004, "New Painters: Picasso", p. 38.

Women with a Fan, *1908*

Oil on canvas, 152 x 101 cm (60 x 40 in). State Hermitage Museum, St Petersburg

Woman with a Fan, 1908, is loosely based on the likeness of Fernande Olivier. Picasso used his pencil drawing *Portrait of Fernande* as a basis for the painting, employing the same facial characteristics, but with eyes cast down and a slight change in hairstyle to align the head with the oval shape of the face. An X-ray of the painting demonstrates that Picasso's original intention was to create a full-face portrait recalling the generic frontal aspects of ancient Egyptian or Greek statuary. However, the artist opted for a highly geometrical facial style that recalls the appropriation of African tribal masks. By tilting the face downwards, closing the eyes and negating the features of the mouth, Picasso gave the figure a primitivized appearance in his painting. Seemingly less influenced by the rugged atavism of *Nude with Raised Arms* and *Nude with Drapery*, the portrait nevertheless bears a remarkable resemblance to an African Fang mask bought by André Derain in 1906 (see below). Picasso's adaptation of the features of the mask, inverting the shape of the eyes and blending the mouth with the nose, suggests that he was aiming to assimilate the plastic values of African statuary and masks for his hieratic twentieth-century modern woman. This mask-like face reappears in a number of contemporaneous figure works, such as *Portrait of Max Jacob* (1907), *Bust of a Peasant Woman (Madame Putman)* and Picasso's charcoal drawing of the head of Guillaume Apollinaire. John Richardson suggests that the facial style of these works is borrowed from *art populaire* and Picasso's love for the naïf imagery of Douanier Rousseau. Picasso was nevertheless still absorbing the lessons of *art nègre*, and his African borrowings in *Woman with a Fan* coincided with an upsurge of interest in the Post-Impressionist painter Paul Cézanne, whose monumentally "primitive" and hieratic portraits, or bather compositions, with their abstracted geometry and somewhat arbitrary anatomical figure style, aided the understanding, reception and assimilation of avant-garde investigations into *art nègre*. Hence the African forms of Picasso's *Woman with a Fan* are moulded with an awareness of the structure and gravitas of Cézanne's figure compositions. For instance, the mask-like majesty, countenance and tilted balance of the French master's stately late portraits, such as *Madame Cézanne in a Yellow Armchair* (c. 1893-5), give Picasso's female, by association, the presence of a priestess and a timeless attitude. As Picasso later told Brassaï, "[Cézanne] was my one and only master".[11]

Left

Fang Mask, *1900, Anonymous*

Gabon, wood, 48 cm (19 in) high, formerly owned by Maurice de Vlamink and André Derain. Musée National d'Art Moderne, Centre Georges Pompidou, Paris

Fang masks were not only collected by Picasso, but also Braque, Derain, Vlaminck and many other modern artists, collectors and dealers in Picasso's circle. The physiognomies of these masks, with elongated faces and long tapering noses, are unquestionably related to a number of Picasso's paintings during the period of 1908.

11 Brassaï, *Picasso and Company*, translated, Francis Price, Doubleday, New York,1966, p. 79.

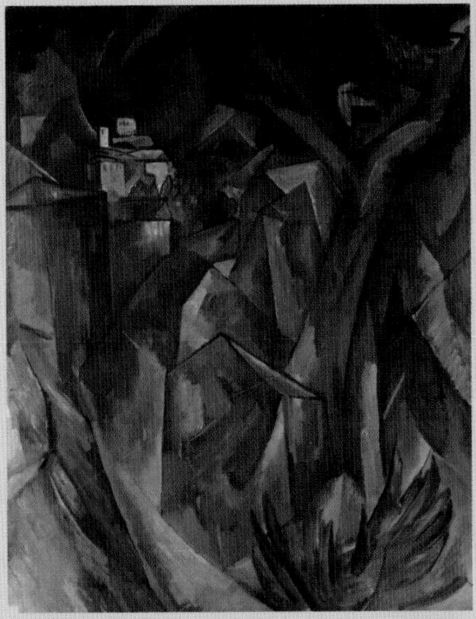

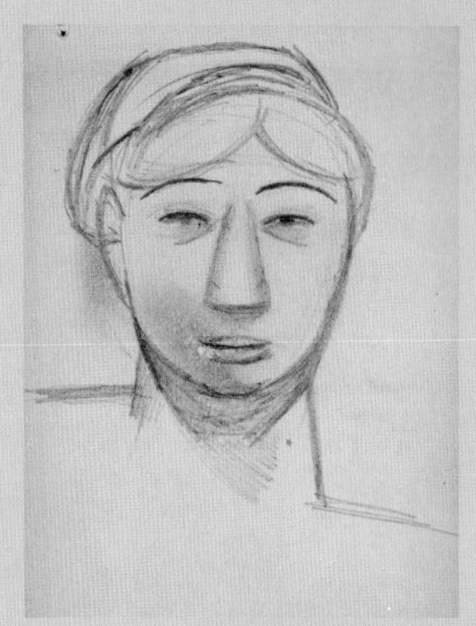

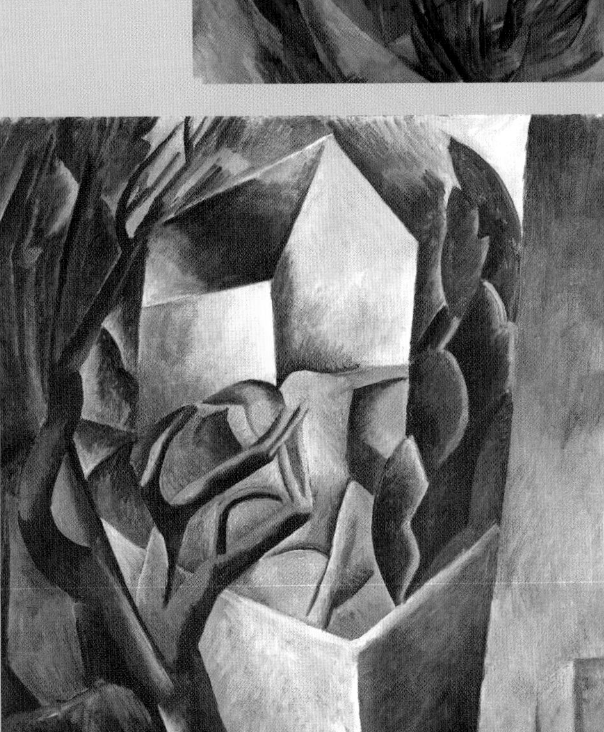

Top centre
Head of a Woman (Fernande), *1909*
Bronze, 41.3 x 24.7 x 26.6 cm (16.5 x 9.5 x 10.5 in).
Art Gallery of Ontario, Toronto

Picasso famous Cubist sculpture builds on the discoveries made at Horta de Ebro in Spain, and its mass of ridges and light-catching facets recall the hills and mountains around the Spanish landscape. Picasso's sculpture also bears a clear resemblance to tribal art, particularly African Fang masks of the type that he himself owned.

Above
Cottage and Trees, *1908–09*
Oil on canvas, 92 x 73 cm (36 x 28.5 in).
Pushkin Museum of Fine Arts

There is evidence to suggest that *Cottage and Trees* was not actually painted in La Rue-des-Bois in the country, but back in Paris during the winter of 1908–09. If this is correct, we can assume that Picasso was attempting to identify more closely with Braque's Cubist project by means of imitation, rather than actually painting similar, *plein air*, landscapes.

Top left
Landscape at L'Estaque, *1908, George Braque*
Oil on canvas, 81 x 65 cm (32 x 25.5 in). Kunstmuseum, Basel

Braque spent the summer at L'Estaque, a small port in Marseille. Where Cézanne had once worked, he painted in a Cubist style, which lends proximity to the landscapes. Along with Picasso's paintings created at La Rue-des-Bois at Criel, Verneuil, Oise, in 1908, these Cubist paintings would change the direction of twentieth-century modern art.

Top right
Portrait of Fernande, *1908*
Pencil on paper, 20 x 13.5 cm (8 x 5.5 in). Musée Picasso, Paris

This drawing clearly relates to *Woman with a Fan* (1908), and whose countenance must surely have been triggered by the stylizations of African Fang masks.

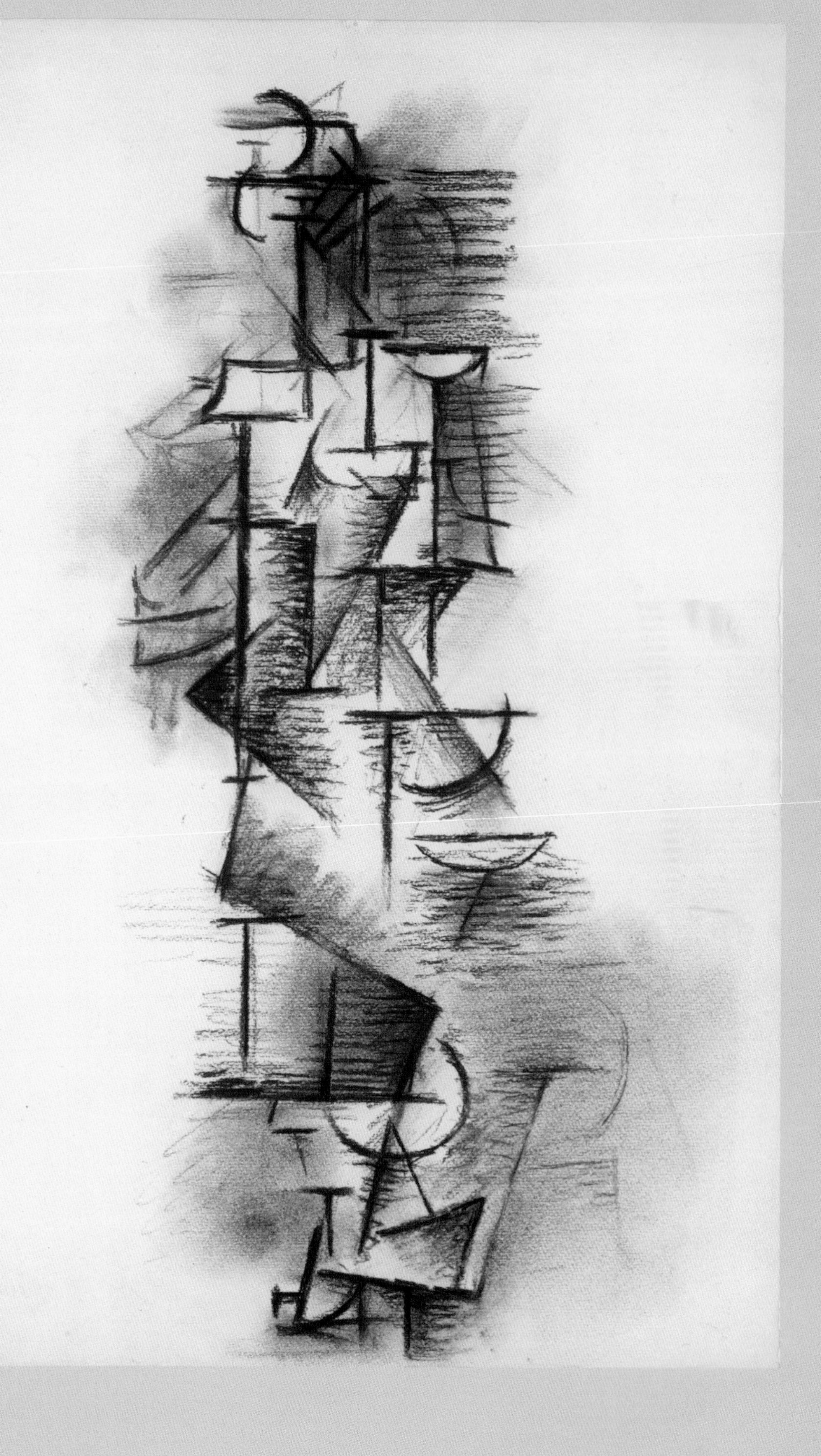

Opposite
The Guitar Player, *1910*
Oil on canvas, 100 x 73 cm (39.5 x 28.5 in). Musée National d'Art Moderne, Centre Georges Pompidou, Paris

Painted in the summer of 1910, Picasso's guitarist becomes a mass of horizontal/diagonal lines, that suggest abstracted planes, features and forms, which splinter the figure into a multiplicity of parts. By using shading and chiaroscuro techniques, the artist emphasizes the hazy atmosphere of light and dark deep within the painting's interior.

Right
Standing Nude (The Fire Escape), *1910*
Charcoal, 48.5 x 31.5 cm (19 x 12.5 in). Metropolitan Museum Art, New York

The standing female figure, created out of a series of flat, intersecting and almost transparent planes, confirms Picasso's attempt to break up solid masses into a series of Cubist facets and shifting, abstract components that prefigure many of his open form constructions in 1912.

Chapter 8

Pasting Papers: Invention of Collage, *Papier collé* and Construction, 1910–12

In 1910–11, the ever-increasing abstraction of Braque and Picasso's paintings expanded to include not only the mundane character of everyday life – candles, cups, glasses, pipes, watches, musical instruments, cupboards and drawers – but also incorporated phenomenological details of letters, numbers, words, phrases, musical notation, excerpts from adverts, newspapers or popular songs. Portraits also include the suggestion of eyes, eyebrows, tousled locks or waves of hair, an ear lobe, a sleeve, clasped hands and other descriptive details in this Cubist lexicon. This game playing was part and parcel of the alliance between the two artists, and they took great pleasure in trumping each other's latest discoveries. Braque's *Violin and Palette* (1909) shows the descriptive detail of a nail holding the artist's palette to the wall, and casting what appears to be a naturalistic shadow. This was all part of a game of illusion perpetrated by the two friendly rivals, so as to lend a teasing accessibility to what were often highly complex pictorial images.

In comparing Picasso's *Accordion Player* (1911) with Braque's *Man with Guitar*, also painted in the summer of that year, we can observe how greatly Braque's and Picasso's styles of Cubism had converged. For instance, Picasso's *Mandolin Player* (1911) uses a pyramidal structure to display the fragments of reality – the mandolin, the player's fingers, the fret box and the upholstery fringe, braided curtain cords and tassels – against a head, body and limbs that are almost indecipherable amid the shimmering, silvery, planes of light, and the dark, abstracted spaces.

The assemblage of piecemeal, symbolic elements is characteristic of the constructive syntax used in many of Picasso's 1912 Cubist paintings, collages and sculptures, such as his *Guitar* (1912), and evokes Stéphane Mallarmé's aesthetic of visual poetry. Indeed, the painter and critic André Lhôte was so struck by the connection between Mallarmé's theory regarding "la substance du néant" ("the substance of nothingness") and the "light tones of sepia and Chinese ink" in Picasso's paintings that he described them as "constructions mallarméenes".[1] The poetic style of many of Picasso's paintings and sculptures was possibly partly influenced by hermetic texts, beloved by Apollinaire and the painter alike (see Chapter 15). Greek Hermetic treatises may even have provided a basic model for the language, spatial relationships and constructive play of Picasso and Braque's most radical Cubist paintings, *papiers collés* and sculpture created during 1912–14. The idea that the solid, yet highly fragmented elements of Braque's and Picasso's Cubist works were actually integers capturing the fullness of space is also analogous to Mallarmé's poetic sensibility in the posthumous *Igitur*, which describes a glass flask in terms of "purity… [enclosing] the substance of nothingness".[2]

Thus in "*Ma Jolie*" (*Woman with a Zither* or *Guitar*, see page 81) of 1911–12, the bold, stencilled letters, taken from a popular song "Dernière Chanson" ("Last Song"), invite the viewer to compose their own picture and draw their own meaning out of the spaces of apparent "nothingness". Even the gender of the figure is difficult to determine, given that the face is described by just a few, highly schematic lines on the canvas. The lettering perhaps infers that the piece is a covert love token to Picasso's new mistress Eva Gouel (real name Marcel Humbert), whom Picasso liked to call "Ma Jolie", or it may borrow its name from the popular music-hall song "Ma Jolie", which was highly fashionable at the time. The use of "Ma Jolie", meaning pretty or lovely in French, is ironic in this context, since the hard edges of the geometry and shadowy, chiaroscuro effects make it almost impossible to find a Venus amid the hermetic text of Picasso's canvas. The paradoxical pursuit of Picasso's "Ma Jolie" simultaneously elucidates (through descriptive clues or readings of objects) and obfuscates (with its fluctuating interpretations of words) traditional ideas of *belle peinture* with regard to both feminine and representational beauty – the painted canvas itself.

Interestingly, Braque and Picasso would soon include sand, sawdust, domestic commercial paint (particularly Ripolin) and synthetic papers in their canvases, thus rejecting conventional ideas of beauty in painting. Picasso expresses these concerns in a letter to Kahnweiler on 17 June 1912, at a time when materials, structure and facture were key to the development of his Synthetic Cubism: "Maybe we shall succeed in disgusting everyone, and we have not said everything yet."[3] Picasso was out to defend the brilliant Ripolin colours used in two oval canvases entitled *Souvenir of Le Havre* (1912) and *The Scallop Shell: "Notre Avenir est dans l'Air"* ("*Our Adventure is*

---

1 André Lhôte, "Chronique des Arts: Exposition Picasso; Exposition Manet", *Nouvelle Revue Française*, 1 August 1932, p. 286.

2 Stéphane Mallarmé, *Igitur* (1897). Cited and translated by Mary Ann Caws in *Stéphane Mallarme, Selected Poetry and Prose*, New Directions, New York, 1982, p. 91–101 (especially p. 97).

3 Isabelle Monod-Fontaine, "Braque: The Slowness of Painting", in *Braque: The Papiers Collés*, p. 40.

4 Patricia D. Leighten, "Picasso's Collages and the Threat of the War", 1912–13, *The Art Bulletin* 67, no. 4, December 1985, p. 653–672.

5 Pierre Daix, *Dictionnaire Picasso*, Paris, Robert Laffront, 1995, p. 130.

in the Air"), which he showed to Braque as part of their friendly rivalry. Indeed, the pioneering spirit of Cubism lay in both artists' attempts to trump – by means of modern or mass-produced techniques and materials, words and "signs" – each new discovery, and something that happened regularly during the Cubist epoch. This competitiveness between the duellists may have inspired a political dimension in their works. Patricia Leighten and other scholars have insisted that French nationalism was an important element of Picasso's French flag and informed the belief that the war with Germany would be fought "in the air".[4] However, it is very unlikely that Picasso would have made such a glib comment in relation to militarism or nationalism, and his reference to "Our Adventure is in the Air" most probably refers to the aesthetic challenges he encountered with his adversary Braque, with whom he was engaged in a pioneering flight. This lively dialogue was one of the quick-fire exchanges between Braque and Picasso. The fact that the use of bright Ripolin paints was perceived as shocking, revolutionary and ugly can be observed in Braque's acidic remark that "the weapons have changed" on encountering Picasso's *Souvenir of Le Havre*.[5] This belief in provoking each other to experiment with the *matière* (substance) of their painting encouraged the artists to explore the possibilities for incorporating various media, such as sand, dust and metal fillings, into their pictures and sculptures. In January 1912, Braque returned from Céret with a new painting entitled *Homage to J S Bach* (see page 81), which he immediately showed to Picasso. Braque had been an apprentice painter-decorator and soon employed the lowly decorator's technique of *faux-bois* (imitation wood grain) to render the wavy pattern in the lower left-hand section of his canvas. Picasso must have been impressed by his colleague's pictorial stunt (affecting workmen's habits and wearing their clothing was something of an in-joke between the artists at the time), and this was brilliant mix of high and low culture that used stencils for the lettering. More importantly, the work shows that Braque identified with the artisan rather than the artist. As Kahnweiler recalled, Braque and Picasso took the greatest pleasure in projecting the persona of workmen when coming to his gallery at the end of each month to get paid. They arrived at Kahnweiler's gallery, imitating and dressed as labourers, with their caps in hand: "Boss we've come for our pay!" [6]

Despite using the decorator's comb to fake wavy hair and moustaches in humorous paintings such as *The "The Aficionado"* (1912, Kunstmuseum Basel), Picasso did not immediately react to Braque's punning *trompe l'oeil* techniques. Nevertheless, *Homage to J S Bach* played a crucial role in the lead-up to Picasso's next artistic invention: collage. It is generally accepted that the first collage was *Still Life with Chair Caning* of May 1912 (see page 81), which incorporated a cut-out and glued-on sheet of commercial oilcloth, representing a caning pattern usually reserved for covering tables and chairs in restaurants. Picasso's introduction of a foreign material into the traditional domain of illusionism signalled a crisis in painting that shattered all previous notions of stylistic unity in twentieth-century art. The appropriation of this everyday, material object alongside a real twisted rope (simulating popular carved wooden frames), was a stunning and iconoclastic coup for the Cubists: a disruptive invention that parodied the traditional *trompe l'oeil* techniques of still-life painting (by short-circuiting the illusion of the painted surface) and rendered heterogeneity a compositional standard for all subsequent Cubist works.

While Picasso was away from Paris, Braque hit upon another stunning invention. While wandering around the streets of Avignon, the artist happened upon a shop selling rolls of wood-grain patterned wallpaper, which produced a very similar effect to the *faux-bois* technique he had used in *Homage to J S Bach*. This printed type of *faux-bois* became the main focus of the first *papier collé*, *Fruit Dish and Glass* and was used to signify the wood panelling in the background and the table on which the still life rests. Braque also drew in standard Cubist motifs, including a bunch of grapes, a fruit dish and a fluted glass and, at the top and bottom of the composition, references to both a poster for Burton's Ale and the Austin Fox Bar near the Gare Saint-Lazare in Paris. The floating strips of faux-bois mirror the in-and-out-of-focus character of Picasso and Braque's earlier Cubist figure paintings, and open up his *papiers collés* to multiple interpretations and momentary impressions. The stuck-on *faux-bois*, representing foreground and background elements, undermines the sense of depth and space within the work, and brings a touch of artificial illumination. Even though it seems that Braque was simply extending Picasso's ideas in *Still Life with Chair Caning*, Braque's use of wood-grain wallpaper achieved much more by asking new questions about alien objects, introduced into the field of painting and art in general. As Braque explained, subsequent to the creation of *Fruit Dish and Glass* he "felt a great shock", and he stated that the *papier collé* was a much "greater shock for Picasso when I showed it to him".[7] Imitating popular imagery, standard rules of representation and employing materials and objects from modern life thus helped Braque and Picasso to innovate a thoroughly modern approach to creating works of art. In addition to the tribal arts of Oceania and Africa, caricature, theatre, plays and performances, literature, pulp fiction, news pieces (often referring to political incidents), photography and the cinema were vital to Picasso's early Cubist work and its development. By October 1912, the works using the techniques of collage and *papier collé* had instigated a new type of sculpture: Cubist construction.

However, Picasso's *Guitar* continues to pose challenges for the viewer. Although there is no mention in the artist's September correspondence of any shock at Braque's *papier collé* technique, Picasso must have felt its impact and been determined to outdo his fellow collaborator by using a new kind of *matière* in his Cubist painting. We know that by early October, Picasso was experimenting with Braque's "papery procedures" and "in the process of conceiving a guitar".[8] Even though we shall never know whether this was a two- or three-dimensional work, it is unlikely that Picasso would have made any real distinction between *papier collé* and constructed sculpture, given the artist's comments in letters to Braque, and, in any case, this appears to be the whole point of his cardboard *Guitar*. An important crayon drawing from 1912, entitled *Personnage*, alludes to the composite nature of *Guitar* and Picasso's own understanding of the relationship between painting and sculpture at the time. The inscription by Picasso on the verso reads: "Perfil [profil] et objets | en d'espace | silhuete [silhoutte] et | aspects du objets." ("Profile of objects | in space | silhouette and | aspects of objects.") The reference to "Perfil" obviously refers to the constructed figure drawing on the *recto*, whereas the use of the word "Siluette" (again in its Spanish form) implies the shadows cast by objects in painting and sculpture. Conversely, the use of the word "aspects" is presumably a reference to the different viewpoints operating within the Cubist idiom. Similarly, Picasso's *Guitar* oscillates somewhere between being a picture and an object, and should rightly be called a *tableaux objet*. Thus the combination of pictorial and constructional processes anchors *Guitar*. The dual approach was also essential to Picasso's other Synthetic Cubist collages, whose visual language is clearly different to the impressive Grebo mask that he purchased in a flea market in the busy port of Marseille in August 1912. Picasso's overall commitment to relief sculpture as opposed to more fully three-dimensional sculpture can be observed in *La jeune sculpture française*, where André Salmon describes a visitor's reaction to a construction in Picasso's studio. At the spectator's insistence on finding an orderly coherence to this object, he gave the curt response: "It's nothing. It's a guitar! And that's it. The airtight partitions are demolished. We are delivered from painting and sculpture".[9] As we shall now see, Picasso remained committed to both painting and relief sculpture before and after the First World War, and this is of vital importance if we are to understand how his sculpture and painting evolved over the subsequent years.

---

6 Kahnweiler, David-Henry *Mes Galeries et mes peintres: Entretiens avec Francis Crémieux*, Paris, Éditions Gallimard, 1961, p. 122.

7 André Verdet, "Avec Georges Braque", *XXe Siècle*, Paris 24, no. 18, February 1962, supplement, not paginated. Cited in Rubin, *Picasso and Braque: Pioneering Cubism*, p. 40.

8 Isabelle Monod-Fontaine, Braque: The Papiers Collés, p. 40.

9 André Salmon, *La jeune sculpture française*, Société des Trente, Albert Messein, Paris, 1912, p. 103–4.

Guitar, *1912*

Cardboard, string and wire maquette, 61.5 x 33 x 19 cm (24 x 13 x 7.5 in). The Museum of Modern Art, New York

It is with hindsight that we can now reflect on perhaps the single most important innovation affecting Picasso's sculpture: his invention of a constructed cardboard *Guitar* in 1912 (see right). Developed as an open construction of planes, which project into space rather than being a solid block, *Guitar* usurps all the traditional concepts of monolithic sculpture. The work's piecemeal assembly was undoubtedly a vital technical weapon against tradition. Picasso's statements at this time give primacy to the material aspects of his work; in a letter to Georges Braque on 9 October 1912, he mentions his use of the "latest paperistic and powdery procedures". Picasso writes: "I am in the process of imagining a guitar and I use a little dust against our horrible canvas".[10] Yet it is clear that *Guitar* is also a built image: a construction with definite pictorial and iconographical characteristics, its simple, cut-out shapes imitating a real guitar. The debris of the construction, perhaps found in and around the studio, includes the odds and ends of cardboard, strings and pieces of wire, and is assembled to form new signs, giving meaning to the material in its most physical sense, and to the flat shapes arranged in simple, semantic relationships. This juxtaposition between the constructed and pictorial elements anchors Picasso's *Guitar*, and underpins the method used in many of his other Synthetic Cubist collages of this period.

The impact of African masks upon Picasso's *Guitar* has been well recorded in the twentieth-century annals of art history. In a letter to Daniel-Henry Kahnweiler, dated 11 August 1912, Picasso tells the dealer that he has "bought a very good masque"[11] and, historically, this Grebo mask appears to have provided the inspiration for *Guitar*. Yve-Alain Bois and Rosalind Krauss single out this mask as a catalyst in the creation of Picasso's *Guitar*, arguing that this tribal object would mark a shift away from the mimetic processes used in the artist's Analytical Cubist works, toward the more logical, semiotic language of Cubism. That is to say, the concept of *Guitar* appears to be derived from signs, such as the projecting sound hole taken from the protruding eyes, indicated by the Grebo mask. Apart from this analogy, however, there is little resemblance between what is a construction and a wood carving relief. The drawings related to *Guitar* tend to represent the instrument as a relief. Such a supposition casts serious doubt on the established historical notion that the structural syntax of *Guitar* was inspired by an African mask. As Elizabeth Cowling observes, the carved African masks Picasso acquired or saw do not have the same transparency, openness or hollowness of *Guitar*, let alone the weightless, force-defying characteristics of the artist's sculptural work created during 1912-14. Thus, if Picasso had sought to imitate African tribal objects, it is highly unlikely that he would have chosen cardboard as the material for his new radical construction sculpture. Picasso's *Guitar* oscillates between picture and object (painting and sculpture), in the same way as his *papiers collés* (pasted paper collages), constructions and assemblages shift between two-dimensional and three-dimensional mediums, and this is precisely what allowed the artist to perceive *all* his Cubist works as sculptural in essence. Such constructed works were true sculptures, as Picasso understood the term, which undoubtedly liberated him from "the tyranny of genres".[12]

10 Isabelle Monad-Fontaine, *Braque: The Papiers Collés*, National Gallery of Art, Washington, D.C., 1982, p. 40.
11 Isabelle Monad-Fontaine, *Donation Louise et Michel Leiris: Collection Kahnweiler-Leiris*, Paris, Musée National d'Art Moderne, Centre Georges Pompidou, 1984, p. 169.
12 André Salmon, *La jeune sculpture française*, Société des Trente, Albert Messein, Paris, 1912, p. 103–4.

Right

Man with a Hat, *1909–10*

Oil on canvas, 61 x 50 cm (24 x 19.6 ins).
Collection Heinz Berggruen, Geneva.

Many of Picasso's Cubist paintings of this time can, like Braque's, totally be misread. This work, for example, was also known as a *Portrait of Braque*, presumably because the figure in the painting is wearing a bowler hat of the sort Braque occasionally wore. However, Picasso told Pierre Daix that the man was not Braque, and that the work had been painted without recourse to a model, but that both artists later pretended that is was the Frenchman's portrait.

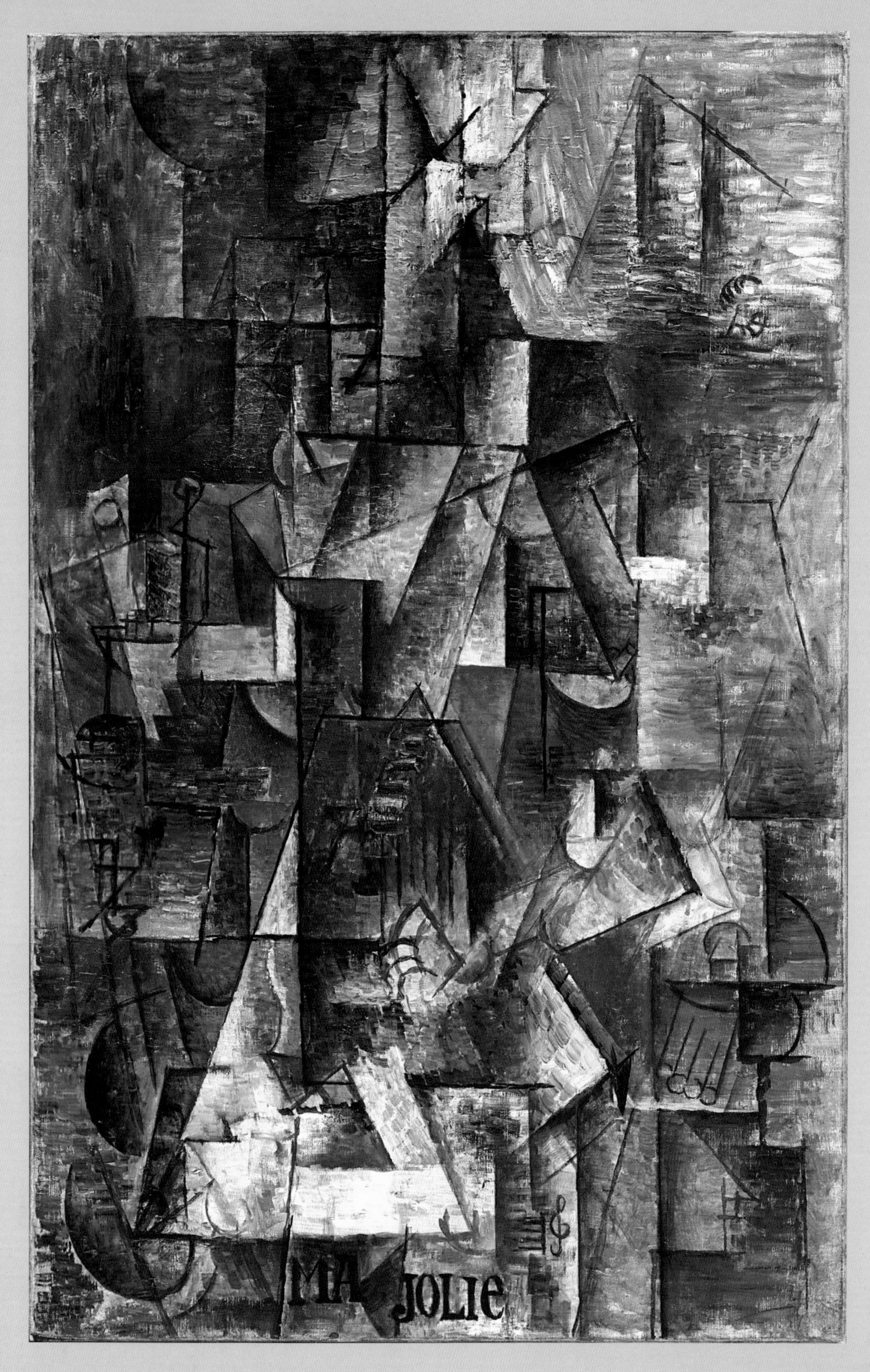
MA JOLIE

Opposite
"Ma Jolie" (Woman with a Zither or Guitar), *1911–12*
Oil on canvas, 100 x 65.5 cm (39.5 x 26 in). The Museum of Modern Art, New York

Picasso's hermetic Cubist masterpiece of 1911–12, with the stencilled capital letters "MA JOLIE" derived from a popular French love song ("O Manon, ma jolie, Mon coeur te dit bonjour!") is also an allusion to his secret love affair with Eva Gouel.

Above right
Homage to J S Bach, *1911, George Braque*
Oil on canvas, 54 x 73 cm (21.5 x 28.5 cm). Private Collection

Braque's painting cleverly makes use of *faux bois* and stencilling techniques to imply wood-grain and commercial lettering. Such technical innovations parody tradesmen's tools and materials. The decorator's steel comb was also used by Picasso to create curly hair in humorous Cubist portraits.

Right
Still Life with Chair Caning, *1912*
Oil and collage on canvas, 27 x 35 cm (10.5 x 14 in). Musée Picasso, Paris

Apart from Picasso's introduction of a postage stamp in an earlier work, this is his first Cubist collage, and the decision to allow alien objects drawn from other contexts into the sphere of traditional painting art, signalled a watershed in twentieth-century Modernism. Now there was no going back, and the use of objects would become intrinsic in the creation of Picasso's synthetic collages and constructions.

Chapter 9

"The Savage Mind": The *Bricolage* of Picasso's Cubist Sculpture, 1913–14

During 1913–14, Picasso continued to develop his *papier collé* (paper pasted collage), construction and assemblage techniques. The influence of these methods on his contemporary painting can be seen in the flat shapes and bold colours of *Woman in an Armchair* (1913), which recall the pasted newsprints and vibrant paper sheets of *papiers collés*, such as the Scottish National Art Gallery *Head* (see page 86), and the cardboard elements of the famous *Guitar* constructions. Meanwhile, construction and assemblage works replaced the highly abstract geometry and shadowy, esoteric aspects of the artist's earlier Cubism of 1910–12. Yet we should not be deceived, for this does not mean that the changes in structure made Picasso's two-dimensional and three-dimensional work any less mysterious. In fact, some of the artist's paintings and sculptures became extremely abstract, full of complex rhyming puns or strange contrivances related to the human body, as seen in *Woman in an Armchair*. What makes this painting so familiar yet different from previous works is its delicate balance of abstraction and naturalism. With witty visual puns and covert descriptions of female genitalia, Picasso portrays the figure with a "savage mind" that seeks to aggressively render her person and sexuality as objects (a chair for her body, pears or wooden knobs for her breasts, a slit for her face/vagina), but without sacrificing an underlay of sensitivity and compassion. This approach can also be seen in the references to "Jolie Eva": a secret Cubist sign of his new love Eva Gouel, better known as Marcelle Humbert, and confidante of Fernande Olivier. It is hard to say for certain when Picasso first met Eva because he was very secretive about her, but the affair probably began in early 1912. This happened around the time Picasso secretly and amorously began inscribing his painting with the words "Ma Jolie", so as not to alert Fernande to his clandestine lover. This approach can also be seen in the references to "Jolie Eva": despite the bright pink and mauve coloration of Picasso's painting, the work masks a state of anxiety and hints at a great sadness, loss or even a prediction of death. The plump breasts, delicately painted fabrics and the soft, round shapes of the chair/body intimate that this voluptuous nude may be a portrait of his sick and dying lover Eva Gouel. As John Richardson explains, "Jolie Eva" was suffering from cancer in 1913. Indeed, the amputated breasts that double as bloated lungs, the womb-like chemise, the inflamed and tumour-like pattern on the chair arms, and the stitched-up looking face of Picasso's female suggest a mastectomy, lung disease or a medical operation.

The anthropomorphism and wit of *Woman in an Armchair*, with its seemingly uncomplicated, flat shapes and clear lines, not only tally with a large number of Picasso's simple *papiers collés*, which are strangely torn and asymmetrically pieced together, but also the *ad hoc* arrangements of construction sculptures such as *Mandolin and Clarinet* (see page 85). Here the dislocated planes of the mandolin and the figuration of the clarinet reveal clear associations with other still-life constructions, such as *Violin and Bottle on a Table* (1915): their forms are composed of roughly sawn sections of wood, sometimes painted or pasted with paper, scored or drawn upon, and assembled with nails and string. There is almost nothing to distinguish this sculpture from the preceding *Les Soirées de Paris* sculptures: the work is a wall relief and, like the artist's other assemblages of this period, is intended to be viewed frontally. *Mandolin and Clarinet* features a number of contradictory effects of mass and space that are also relevant to an analysis of Picasso's techniques of this period. The body of the mandolin appears empty, whereas the tube of the clarinet is represented by a solid round section of wood. The result is a structure that is bent on the pursuit of the paradoxical and three-dimensional. The method by which Picasso flattens his quasi-architectural relief, fanning out the planes of the sculpture into an arc of 180 degrees, so as to give a buoyant impression of defying gravity, contrasts with the hefty materiality and hasty arrangement of planks and odd sections of wood. The hobbyist tomfoolery re-emerges in the shoddy-looking techniques of *Mandolin and Clarinet* and the hurried, playful appearance of the *papier collé Guitar, Glass, Bottle of Vieux Marc* (see page 87). The witty, contradictory spaces and hand-made constructive language of these works are reminiscent of the artisan play that provided the creative force behind Picasso's Synthetic Cubism of 1912–14. *Mandolin and Clarinet*, like many sculptures of this period, stresses the *matière* (substance) of its construction and appears to make use of objects from the artist's immediate environment. Paradoxically, the sculpture shams juvenile play in its use of found debris (old stretchers and wooden boxes lying in the artist's studio) and emphasis emphasizes crude carpentry techniques, so as to undermine the superior skills of the craftsman. In the process, Picasso revolutionizes the technique of making sculpture and re-invents the concept of *bricolage* as a sign of the traditional artisan at play. Picasso's crudity of fabrication – his is a travesty of fine workmanship – recalls Claude Lévi-Strauss's definition of the *bricoleur* in *La Pensée Sauvage* (*The Savage Mind*, 1962) as someone who has to make do with whatever materials are at hand. The *bricoleur*, Lévi-Strauss argues, does not limit himself solely to accomplishment with regard to technical expertise, but through expresses himself through "the medium of things", and by a series choices gathered from "limited possibilities".[1] More importantly, Lévi-Strauss defines *bricolage* as "a dialogue [between] materials and [the] means of execution", and equates the techniques of collage with old-fashioned craftsmanship, and with "the transposition of *bricolage* into the realms of contemplation".[2]

A photograph of a wall arrangement in Picasso's Boulevard Raspail studio reinforces the connection between the artist's Synthetic Cubism, construction techniques and *bricolage*. Here two cardboard guitars of 1912, propped against the wall and leaning on rolls of papers or canvas, lie among the clutter of Picasso's studio floor. The small *Guitar*, possibly created from a battered cardboard box, is so untidy that glue and thumb-prints can be seen all over the concertina fret board. Jagged scissor-marks, badly folded edges, tearing and patching indicate that this hand-made object has been produced from the cheapest of scrap materials, thus intentionally eschewing superior craftsmanship. Affixed to the wall in Picasso's photograph is the famous cardboard *Guitar*, overshadowing a series of half-finished *papiers collés*, as if to illustrate the interdependence and fragility of their construction and collage procedures. Braque outlined the *bricolage* nature of the artist's Synthetic Cubism in a letter to Kahnweiler on 17 October 1912: "I will have to buy a large portfolio to carry them in, they are so fragile".[3] Nor was Apollinaire, the defender of the new object-based Cubism, afraid to alert viewers to the down-market aspects of the materials used in Picasso's collages, *papiers collés* and assemblages, when he argued in the journal *Montjoie*, in March 1913, that the cheapest materials or objects could only liberate the imagination if the artist introduced "a two-penny song, a real postage stamp, a piece of newspaper, a piece of oil cloth".[4]

Indeed, Picasso's sheet-metal version of the *Guitar*, created in the spring of 1914 (see page 86) is almost proof of the "savage" nature of Picasso's technical procedures and the emphasis he placed on the aggressive structure of real, manufactured objects, especially musical instruments. As Elizabeth Cowling demonstrates, Picasso could easily have seen guitars being made in shops in Paris, near his old studio on the Boulevard de Clichy. Furthermore, as Cowling argues, Picasso would have found the key to the construction of his own *Guitar* by studying templates of musical instruments in manuals, books and illustrated encyclopedias, and because musical instruments are assembled from basic components parts and in a similar piecemeal fashion that discloses both the inner space and "the containing walls".[5]

Picasso's *Guitar* and other constructions from this period, including his *Les Soirées de Paris* works and *Guitar Player at a Café Table* (1913), may therefore be humorous references to the guitar or violin as a kit. This constructed sculpture could just as easily be taken apart or packed flat, and put away into a box – and, as such, perhaps makes a jibe at the mass production of Salon art.

---

1 Claude Lévi-Strauss, *La Pensée Sauvage*, Plon, Paris, 1962, Translated as *The Savage Mind*, Weidenfeld and Nicholson, London, 1966. Quotations are taken from page 17 and 21.

2 Claude Lévi-Strauss, *The Savage Mind*, p. 29–30.

3 Braque to Daniel Henry-Kahnweiler, 17 October 1912. Cited in *Rubin, Picasso and Braque*, 1989, "Documentary Chronology" (by Judith Cousins), p. 408–9.

4 Guillaume Apollinaire, *Montjoie!*, March 1914.

5 Elizabeth Cowling, *Picasso: Style and Meaning*, p. 258.

Guitar Player at a Café Table, *1913*

Assemblage with a painted figure, pasted newspaper arms, guitar suspended with strings, table, bottle, cup and pipe, no longer extant (painting probably preserved as Tête d'homme, Céret, 1913, Richard S. Zeisler Collection, New York), dimensions unknown, gelatin silver print, 12 x 8.5 cm (4.5 x 3.5 in). Photograph taken by Pablo Picasso. Private Collection.

The famous Boulevard Raspail *Guitar Player at a Café Table* of early 1913 was not a proper assemblage, nor a freestanding construction, but a comic elaboration on Picasso's probing figure/ground relationships in his Synthetic Cubist collages and constructed works, such as the cardboard *Guitar* (1912). Once more, *Guitar Player at a Café Table*'s emphasis falls on flat, simplified shapes and opaque forms, arranged on a two-dimensional surface. The assemblage ran the gamut from a Cubist painting on a flat paper surface, showing a harlequin with pasted paper arms, to a real guitar suspended from strings, to a still life on a table. The loose architectonic scaffolding implied by Picasso's sculpture envisions a rudimentary, puppet-like structure playing a guitar, and displays similarities to a large number of sketches depicting a *Guitarist*. In a way, the assemblage pre-empts the suggested movement of the Manager costume-constructions for *Parade* (1917) and the movable set decor for *Mercure* (see Chapter 15).

As with many of Picasso's designs and realized projects from this period, the assemblage projects from a flat back plane. Like the sketches, Picasso's assemblage has suspended or cantilevered elements (a guitar held in place with strings and glued-on *papier collé* arms and hands), a body created out of a vertical plane (a flat paper ground) and a table or easel-like support for legs. *Guitar Player at a Café Table* was a short-lived, three-dimensional work; it was quickly dismantled. There is strong evidence to suggest that the half-painted figure on sized paper was cut down and recycled to become the more elaborate composition of *Head of a Man* (Céret, 1913, Richard S. Zeisler Collection, New York). The facture of *Guitar Player at a Café Table* also recalls the tiny paper *Guitarist with Music Sheet* that Gertrude Stein rescued and placed in a wooden box to protect its brittle construction. The piece's delicate nature might well explain the fragility of Picasso's *Guitar Player at a Café Table*: the *bricolage* figure is composed of junk that littered the artist's studio. The flimsiness and comedy of its assemblage strongly recalls Cervantes's *The Scholar Made of Glass* and the transparency of the Cadaqués work produced in 1910. Of course, *Guitar Player at a Café Table* should be viewed in the context of Picasso's other constructions of this period, some of which were published in the November issue of Guillaume Apollinaire's *Les Soirées de Paris* in 1913, including a photograph of a relief construction that incorporated the famous cardboard *Guitar*. An immediate outcry among the magazine's readers caused a small number of them to cancel their subscriptions, and the photographs displaying the iconoclastic yet revolutionary execution of these works brought Picasso's fame to a number of avant-garde artists, including the Russian Constructivist Vladimir Tatlin. What some historians of Picasso's art do not mention is that some of the photographs featured in *Les Soirées de Paris* were actually shown in London, along with other works by the English Grafton Group, which produced a flurry of philistine comments and jokes. The painting of *Tête d'Homme*, depicting the Harlequin figure from *Guitar Player at a Café Table* was hardly seen as figurative at all. Notably, in the article "The Grafton Group Academy" in *The Saturday Review* of 31 January 1914, G.H. Barker comments on the "speckled bands and angles"[6] of Picasso's *Tête d'Homme* (no. 43), making a likely reference to the Richard S. Zeisler *Head of a Man*, which Roger Fry had originally acquired from Picasso's dealer Daniel-Henry Kahnweiler. The anonymous review of "The Grafton Group at the Alpine Club Gallery", published in the *Athenaeum* on 10 January 1914, like the articles on the photographs in *Les Soirées de Paris*, heavily criticizes the artist's use of debris and "deficiency in technique".[7] Both statements lay stress on the materiality of these works and indicate an awareness of the levels of shock that greeted the construction of *Guitar Player at a Café Table*, and many other sculptures by Picasso within academic and artistic circles at this time.

6 G. H. Barker in *The Saturday Review*, 31 January 1914.

7 Anonymous review in *Athenaeum* [Newspaper citation].

Above
Mandolin and Clarinet, *1913–14*
Construction in wood, with oil and crayon, 58 x 36 x 23 cm (23 x 14 x 9 in). Musée Picasso, Paris

Mandolin and Clarinet recalls the shoddy and crude carpentry of an amateur handyman, with its odds and ends of wooden planks hurriedly knocked together with nails. Scraps of found and recycled material, derived from the studio environment, were crucial to Picasso's "savage mind" and his persona as an inventor of heterogeneous objects.

Above left

Head, *1913*

Pasted paper, gouache, charcoal and pencil on cardboard, 43.5 x 33 cm (17 x 13 in). Scottish National Gallery of Art

One of a number of *papiers collés* that make use of abstract patterns to create severe-looking figures that are partly guitars. This work recalls the triangular form of *Woman in an Armchair* of 1913 that records Picasso's anxiety over the fate of his ill lover Eva. Alternatively, the fact that Picasso's *papier collé* is so brutally cut and pasted together suggests a latent sadness and, perhaps, even, despair: for Picasso's father died on 3 May, 1913.

Above right

Guitar, *1914*

Sheet metal, string and wire, 77.5 x 35 x 19.3 cm (30.5 x 14 x 7.5 in). The Museum of Modern Art, New York.

Picasso's sheet metal *Guitar* has a sturdier presence than its cardboard predecessor. A metamorphosis of gender occurs in the work's shadowy areas. The guitar's body suggests the female form while its projecting sound-hole evokes a masculine presence.

Above

Guitar, Glass, Bottle of Vieux Marc, *1913*

Pasted paper and pins with charcoal and chalk on paper, 47 x 62 cm (28.5 x 24.5 in). Musée Picasso, Paris.

Picasso used pins and wallpaper in his *papier collé*, and glued cut-outs together, to suggest the activity of tailoring. The bottle on the right appears to be a masculine symbol, whereas the flowery paper evokes the feminine art of dressmaking that Picasso would have seen occupy the women in his family.

Chapter 10

Modernity and Tradition: Cubism and the War, 1915–16

Picasso's new constructions engaged the artist in a witty dialogue with standard forms of representation and traditional techniques. His conversations with representational art became ever more complex, serious and timely as the prospect of war loomed, and as he swung increasingly between Cubism and more naturalistic styles of art. Visitors to Picasso's studio would have been mystified to see naturalistic portraits of friends and dealers, such as Max Jacob, Guillaume Apollinaire, Ambroise Vollard and Léonce Rosenberg, displaying an air of stubbornness, a uniform dress sense and poses befitting war heroes, alongside iconoclastic Cubist *papiers collés*, constructions and mysterious paintings such as the great, grim *Harlequin* of 1915 (see page 91). Rosenberg had begun to buy Picasso's work in 1913 and, by the end of the First World War, owned 20 important works as well as others by Cubists like Braque and Juan Gris. Rosenberg joined the French flying Corps as a liaison officer, but his duties were nevertheless slim enough to allow the dealer time to continue running his art gallery during the War. Picasso would later execute a marvellous Ingres-style pencil drawing of Rosenberg in uniform, standing in front of the recently purchased *Harlequin* painting. Commercial problems may have played a role in courting and pampering dealers and friends to help rescue Cubism and artists (including Picasso) in need of urgent financial support during the economically stagnant war period. Such circumstances seem to have beset many from the beginning of the First World War. It was not until 1916 that the market for modern art began to recover and galleries, which had been forced to close, often by a lack of foreign buyers, reopened along a stretch of rue La Boétie in Paris. Yet despite the fact that Picasso and others needed financial assistance from Rosenberg (who continued to trade regardless of the War and his duties in the French Flying Corps), the artist created a number of very important Cubist canvases in 1915–16. As Elizabeth Cowling points out, Marius de Zayas, who had opened an exhibition of Picasso's latest Cubist work at the Modern Gallery, was very happy (and relieved) to report that, "The intelligent public here is pleased to see the rumour that you have not abandoned your art to return to totally objective painting is false".[1]

As three contemporary still-life paintings of the period demonstrate, this rumour that Picasso's aberrant modernist styles and Cubist tricks were on the wane, was entirely inaccurate. In *Still Life with Fruit Dish on a Table*, *Still Life in a Landscape* (see page 91) and *Still Life with Cards, Glasses and a Bottle of Rum: "Vive La France"*, Picasso stylishly blends semi-naturalistic elements, luminous passages, rococo colour and decoration with the Cubist idiom. In the landscape painting, mottled green trees mingle with red stippled planes, and a beautiful patch of natural-looking blue sky is offset by puffy white clouds, while a stylized bunch of grapes contrasts with a Cubist fruit bowl. It is interesting to note that although these Cubist paintings of 1914–15 made humorous references to traditional still life genres, such as peeled fruit skins, abundant food and drink, or *memento mori* themes, they were not observed as radically different to Picasso's earlier Cubism.

In a volatile political climate, clamouring for "civilizing, Latin values", Apollinaire was keen to defend Cubism and Modernism through any means possible, notably by using precisely the same conservative language as those critics who saw Cubism as little better than a foreign enemy. He remarked: "The daring innovations of French painters were above all efforts to rediscover the authentic tradition of art… the first principles of art, and the disciplines to which these principles give rise".[2] If Apollinaire sounds like an apologist for Cubism, it is because given the current circumstances of the War, and the blatant propaganda surrounding him in the press, he must have felt obliged, or thought it necessary, to save Cubism from apparent financial and aesthetic ruin. In an article entitled "The Wonderful Flowering of French Art", published in *Den Franske Utstilling*, Oslo, in November–December, 1916, Apollinaire demonstrates that he had no reservations when it came to safeguarding avant-garde principles and idioms: "[France] is intelligent and ever open to ideas".[3]

Thus the patriotic emblems that Picasso employs in *Still Life with Cards, Glasses and a Bottle of Rum*, such as flags to suggest the motto "Vive La France", and allusions to pleasure and opulence, with black passages intimating wartime sobriety, ominous warnings and mortality, might have been a message of support for his adopted country. However, as always with Picasso, nothing is that simple, for the painter juxtaposes national symbols with new Cubist spatial tricks. He emphasizes the spread of the work across the picture plane using an approach derived from earlier works such as *Still Life: The Snack* and *Bottle of Bass, Glass and Newspaper* (see page 92), as well as a number of other picture relief works created at the same time. Most notable is Picasso's

1 Marius de Zayas, *How, When and Why Modern Art Came to New York*, Cambridge Massachusetts, MIT Press, 1996, p. 226.
2 *Apollinaire on Art: Essays and Reviews*, 1902–1918, London, Thames and Hudson, 1972, p. 446–7.
3 *Apollinaire on Art: Essays and Reviews*, p. 446–7.

ironic use of the word "Jou" – a standard Cubist motif – which suggests that Picasso was playing a "game" with himself, his fellow Cubists and possibly with his dealer and the buying public alike.

Setting these political issues aside, Picasso continued to make important Cubist sculptures in wood, such as *Violin and Bottle on a Table* and *Bottle of Anis del Mono and Fruit Bowl with a Bunch of Grapes*, as well as the sheet-metal construction *Violin* of 1915. The three constructions feature elements that appear to be drawn from the earlier *Still Life with Fruit Dish on a Table* (1915): the turned table/chair legs, a schematic bunch of grapes, the horizontal architrave on the wall, the picnic items, the transparency of the glass and, in the metal construction, the black, white, brown and blue patterning of the latter painting. In *Bottle of Anis del Mono and Fruit Bowl with a Bunch of Grapes*, the imaginative procedures of *bricolage* re-emerge in the metal plate nailed into the wood of the fruit bowl, and the two vertical planks fitted over the compotier to construct the bottle and fruit. As *bricoleur*, Picasso builds his still life structure by "fitting together the remains and debris of events".[4] In addition, the reverse collage effects of a trellis pattern on the bottle of *maraschino* and the bunch of grapes etching on the surface create a painterly *bricolage*. This technique also provides the inspiration for *Violin and Bottle on a Table*, developing the earlier still lifes: *The Snack* and *Bottle of Bass, Glass and Newspaper*. The wooden structure fans out into a 180-degree arc across the pictorial plane, as if the objects being proffered are literal ones, but, of course, they are illusionary – evidence of the skilful practice of the *bricoleur*, who Levi-Strauss believes uses "all the heterogeneous objects [in] his treasury. By his craftsmanship [the *bricoleur*] constructs a material object which is also an object of knowledge".[5]

The intimate relationship between these works and Picasso's large painted metal constructions of *Violin* and *Guitar* (see Chapter 14) is not simply a formal coincidence. Both of these works were later shown together in the Exposition Surréaliste d'Objets at the Galerie Charles Ratton in May 1936 and, in particular, hanging among various tribal artefacts and masks on the walls. *Violin* demonstrates Picasso's continuing interest in tribal art, and the colour of this construction is reminiscent of the Grebo masks, whose savage and magical status had fascinated the artist in 1912. The striking anthropomorphic affinity to a masked harlequin and the bold diamond pattern, signifying this *commedia dell'arte* character, indicates that it is highly likely that he created this construction at the same time as the famous *Harlequin* painting. Whatever their structural or technical relationship, the "savage mind" and application underpinning both works imply that *art nègre* had once more become of great importance to the artist. The exorcist character of the Harlequin, depicting a primitivized mask-head of a grimacing/grinning harlequin, who grasps a palette showing the artist's profile, was, it has been suggested, triggered by Eva Gouel's illness and final demise on 14 December 1915. Picasso's cursed mentality is reinforced by the rudimentary design of flat, collage-like planes, which are awkwardly arranged on top of one another and add to the out-of-kilter design of Harlequin's suit, head and body. The overall, metronomic quality of Picasso's *Harlequin* is suggestive of a ticking timepiece, a grim harbinger signalling Eva's tragic fate and the horrific events of the First World War. The strange and eerie code to this phase of Picasso's work can be seen in the *Man Leaning on a Table* (see page 93), which incorporates elements of the *Still Life in a Landscape*, and the rather witty, meretricious and surreal *Man with a Bowler Hat* (perhaps inspired by Giorgio de Chirico's *The Child's Brain*, 1914). Both of these works pre-empt Picasso's pseudo-architectural costume designs for the French and American Managers, created for the ballet *Parade* in 1917 (see Chapter 11). *Man Leaning on a Table* went through many changes and was, in all likelihood, started before Eva Gouel's death and possibly painted over the entire period that she was terminally ill. As a result of Eva's ill health and eventual death, *Man Leaning on a Table* is less figurative, more complex and mournful-looking than earlier works, so the dark L-shaped section near the top of the composition, represented by two tiny circular, watchful eyes, strongly recalls the black mask-like countenance of Picasso's earlier *Harlequin*.

If this monumental work is a companion self-portrait to the Harlequin figure, as historians have suggested, then it indicates that the painting was created at a time of crisis and self-analysis for Picasso. The painting was also executed during one of the bloodiest and extended battles of the First World War at Verdun, in which thousands of lives were claimed. Although *Man Leaning on a Table* is clearly not a painting about war, the numerous pointillist dots on Picasso's canvas appear like markers or badges for lost and wounded friends, and the countless, anonymous dead soldiers on the front lines. As we can see, a pacifist stance is often apparent in his works. When Pierre Daix asked Picasso whether he was aware of the newspaper clipping about the Balkan War in his 1912 *papier collé Glass and Bottle of Suze*, the artist stated, "Oh yes, I found that in a newspaper, and it was my way of showing I was against the war".[6]

4 Claude Lévi-Strauss, La Pensée Sauvage, Plon, Paris 1962. Translated as *The Savage Mind*, Weidenfeld and Nicholson, London, 1966. Quotations taken from pages 17 and 20.

5 Ibid.

6 Pierre Daix, Picasso and Braque a Symposium, MOMA, New York, 1992, p. 74–76.

Painter and His Model, *1914*

Oil and crayon on canvas, 58 x 59.9 cm (23 x 23.5 in).
Musée Picasso, Paris

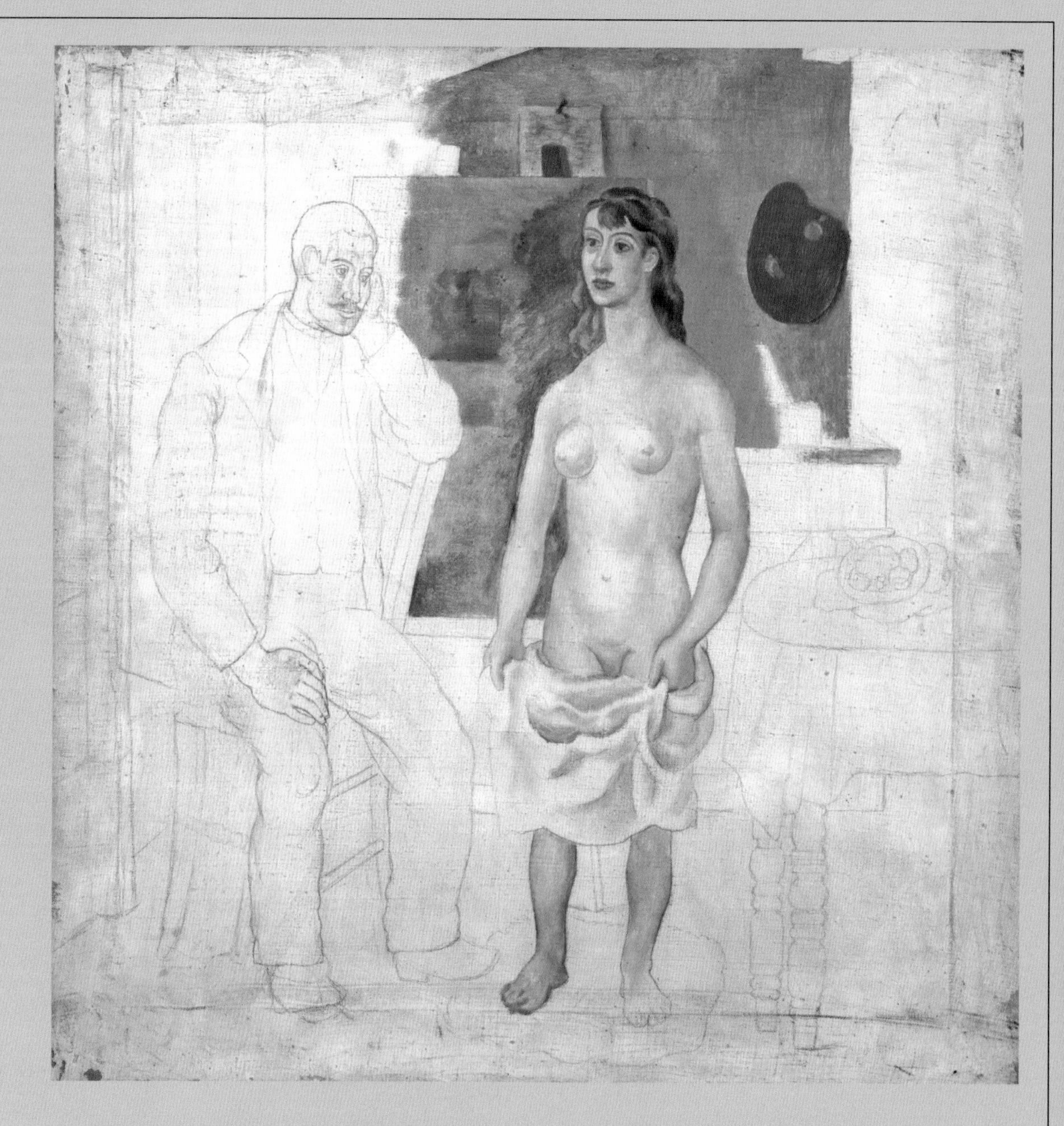

The most fascinating of Picasso's naturalistic works is perhaps a small oil painting that the artist created in 1914, controversially entitled *Painter and his Model* (see right). Because of its studio setting, Kenneth E. Silver places the subject as an artist (even Picasso himself) and his model. To support his claim, he has identified a study of a *Bather*, from the same year as the painting. Silver links the painting and drawing to Gustave Courbet's "great machine", *The Painter's Studio* (1854–5), in which the model turns toward the painter and cusps her breast with her hand. On closer inspection, it becomes clear that the earlier study is actually a sketch of Picasso's "secret love" Gaby Depyre (whom Picasso probably met in January or February 1913, and at the time of Eva's operation), produced at least a year later than the 1914 painting. Furthermore, as John Richardson points out, the seated figure is a "Cézannesque cardplayer type", who represents the Midi and is a companion to the male figures in cafés – café dreamers and cardplayers – whom the artist had consistently portrayed during the previous three summers in the south of Avignon. Richardson also suggests that the picture is allegorical, and represents "the two great nineteenth-century masters [Cézanne and Ingres], who preside over this period of change".[7]

The painting is fascinating for a number of reasons, especially its apparently unfinished state, which acts like an inventory or a record of Picasso's stylistic progress in recent years. The Cézannesque figure reveals the guiding influence of the French master, who opened up new paths to Cubist adventures in painting. Indeed, the palette behind Picasso's female nude and the small painting nailed to the wall may be a reference to Braque's Cubist painting *Violin and Palette* (1909), in which a *trompe l'oeil* nail holds up the painter's tool at the top of the composition. Meanwhile, the still life, tilted upward and forward on a table, is another nod in the direction of Cubism. The seated male is a further reminder of the numerous drawings that Picasso executed in Avignon during the summer of 1914, depicting a figure at a table, who is sometimes seen playing cards or resting his elbow on a chair or a table. More importantly, these drawings inform us of a practice that would define the artist's work over the coming years, for both the sketches and the partly naturalist painting are precursors of the Classicism and Cubism that Picasso would develop in tangent in his art practice. There is good reason to believe that the timing of Picasso's venture into this new form of Classicism was influenced by the outbreak of the First World War. There is no doubt that contemporary ideology was seeking some sort of order and sobriety, particularly through the myth of France as a nation steeped in Latin traditions and civilizing values, often championed by right-wing writers and politicians as an antidote to Modernism, which they perceived to be nothing less than a foreign invasion from the Left. This trumpeting *rappel à l'ordre* ("call to order") applauded by the chauvinistic press, is usually touted as an explanation for Picasso's supposed *volte face* in employing classical styles, or as an obedient reaction to a volatile political and social atmosphere. However, although these factors undoubtedly had an impact on Picasso's art, they do not account for the coherent sequence of Cubist drawings, paintings, *papiers collés* and constructions that he produced in the lead-up to showcasing his classical imagery in the ballet *Parade* in 1917. We know that Picasso was a pacifist and abhorred war or violence of any kind, which suggests that his views were more complex than they first appear. As Richardson has demonstrated, however, beyond the circumstances and horror at the looming possibility of War, there is little evidence whatsoever in correspondence or statements by the artist or his friends and companions "as to where he stood ideologically".[8]

7 John Richardson, *A Life of Picasso: Vol. II*, p. 341.
8 John Richardson, ibid, p. 343.

Above left

Harlequin, *1915*

Oil on canvas, 183.5 x 105 cm (72 x 41.5 in). The Museum of Modern Art, New York

Picasso's magisterial *Harlequin* was painted amid the turmoil of war and the threat of death, injury and illness. As the War raged on, his lover Eva became gravely ill and would die in the winter of 1915. His great friend Apollinaire was also recovering from a head wound. In this context it is not hard to imagine this grinning/glowering Harlequin as a grim reaper.

Above right

Still Life in a Landscape, *1915*

Oil on canvas, 62 x 75 cm (24.5 x 29.5 in). Meadows Museum Dallas

Many of Picasso's still-life subjects made during the wartime mix pre-war Cubist and naturalistic styles, and often mimick Baroque traditions of still-life painting. Thus, *Still Life in a Landscape* uses dots and passages of highly coloured "rococo" fakery, and combines these with playful and witty Cubist tricks, spaces and inventions.

Above left
Bottle of Bass, Glass and Newspaper, *1914*
Painted milk tin, sand wire and paper, 20.5 x 14 x 8.5 cm
(8 x 5.5 x 3.3 in). Musée Picasso, Paris

This work was created using a tin milk can, textured with sand and painted in red, blue, grey, black and white, and pinned with wire and nails at the base. The label on the "bottle" depicts the letters "Bass", surrounded by the red diamond-shaped trademark for pale ale, a popular drink in France.

Above right
Violin, *1915*
Painted sheet metal and wire, 100 x 63.5 x 18 cm (39.5 x 25 x 7 in).
Musée Picasso, Paris

Picasso's sheet-metal construction of a *Violin* was made around the same time as the *Harlequin*, and its patterned paintwork and anthropomorphism recalls the head of a masked/costumed figure. Moreover, the rudimentary cut and arranged metal sections are highly evocative of the earlier *bricolage* methods that Picasso used in his pre-war Cubist sculptures.

Right
Man Leaning on a Table, *1915–16*
Oil on canvas, 200 x 132 cm (78.5 x 52 in).
Private Collection

This is perhaps the greatest of Picasso's wartime paintings. Photographs of the work in the artist's studio in the summer/autumn of 1915 show that it was originally a more decorative painting, but that it acquired a darker countenance after his lover Eva died in December 1915 and a clandestine affair with Gaby Depeyre collapsed in the spring of 1916.

By the beginning of the First World War, Picasso's search for new innovations in art resulted in dramatic shifts from one style to another. His work swung increasingly between Cubist, Realist, and Neo-Classical styles, and these sudden stylistic changes were exacerbated by his creative involvement with the Ballet Russes and the circumstances surrounding the War in Europe. As André Breton and his Surrealist entourage courted Picasso as the supreme leader of the French avant-garde, the artist's continued commitment to creating a magnificent memorial to his great friend Guillaume Apollinaire saw the creation of radically new types of monumental sculpture.

Section 3: 1917–1928

Chapter 11

The Ballet Russes: *Parade*, Jean Cocteau and the Influence of Guillaume Apollinaire, 1917

Sponsored by high society, *Parade* was organized as a benefit for the *mutilés de guerre* (war victims) at the Théâtre du Châtelet in Paris on 18 May 1917, and it signalled Picasso's entrance into the very public and bourgeois institutions of ballet and theatre in the Ballets Russes. Serge Diaghilev (see page 58) had formed the Ballets Russes as an extension to major exhibitions and theatre productions in Russia and France, beginning at Théâtre du Châtelet in May 1909. Diaghilev, who constantly sought to re-invent his productions with radical dance techniques, music, costume and theatrical design, had previously shocked all of Paris with the distinctly "primitive" rhythms of Igor Stravinsky's *Sacre du printemps* (*The Rite of Spring*) at the Théâtre des Champs-Élysées in 1913, and one of the most important theatrical works of the twentieth century. Jean Cocteau had desperately tried to persuade the leader of the Ballets Russes, Diaghilev, to stage his play in Paris, and the rather mercurial Cocteau was eventually ordered to astound him with his art direction. According to the Salon Cubist Jean Metzinger, this was "the first time [Picasso's] Cubism had to face the crowd".[1] *Parade* coincided with the bleak carnage of the First World War, where battles raged on the Western Front and senseless slaughter, horror and mutinies prevailed. *Parade's* narrative was intended to bring Modernism into line with the current ideology of a public seeking the order, myth and flummery of a "True France". Yet the Parisian first-night audience received the ballet in uproar, with whistles from detractors and applause from supporters at times drowning out the voices of the players with shouts of "Boches" (Huns) and "météques" (foreigners). The ballet's scenario and its Cubist elements, despite the archaic allusions presented by Picasso's drop curtain (see page 96), were perhaps seen as equivalent to a foreign invasion: some of those present, including troops from the Front, were seemingly in no mood for such Modernism.

Picasso's drop curtain, which intimated a loosely classical or Latin theme, was markedly different from the rest of the *Parade* production. It depicted a winged horse (Pegasus) tending its foal and a group of *commedia dell'arte* characters dining in an archaic setting. This congregation of circus players, as depicted on the overture curtain, is evocative of the poems "Spectacle" and "Les Saltimbanques" sent by Apollinaire to Picasso in 1905, which explored the arts of magic and illusion as their main themes.

When Erik Satie's solemn prelude had died down and the drop curtain finally lifted, the audience was treated to a more contemporary spectacle. Jean Cocteau's scheme of a modern metropolis accompanied Satie's beautifully brash score of ragtime, folk music and cabaret songs, whereas Picasso's lyrical curtain for the ballet, Cubist-futurist decor and Manager costumes complemented the poetic imagery of Apollinaire's "Zone" (December 1912). "Zone" opens with an unpunctuated eulogy celebrating the city, its dwellers and the modern media as an actual form of poetry: "You read handbills catalogues advertisements that | Sing out loud and clear | There is where poetry is this morning and for prose there are newspapers".[2] Apollinaire's enthusiasm for the modern metropolis – the celebrated theme of *Parade* – was further emphasized in his programme note "Parade et L'Esprit Nouveau". Francis Steegmuller, Cocteau's biographer, has argued that it was either Misia Sert, Cocteau or Picasso himself who asked Apollinaire to write the programme note for *Parade* during the preparation of his own Cubist-costumed play, *Les Mamelles de Tirèsais*, which would be performed on 24 June at the Conservatoire Maubel in Montmartre. Apollinaire wrote his note after attending some of the ballet's rehearsals and the text appeared first in the newspaper *Excelsior* on 11 May, then a week later in the actual programme of *Parade*. Apollinaire made special mention of "the fantastic constructions representing the gigantic and surprising figures of the Managers". The poet reflected, "Picasso's Cubist costumes and scenery bear witness to the realism of his art. This realism – or Cubism, if you will – is the influence that has

1 Francis Steegmuller, *Cocteau: A Biography*, Boston, Nonpareil, 1986, originally published 1970, p. 176.
2 Guillaume Apollinaire, *Zone*, translated by Samuel Beckett, The Dolmen Press, Dublin, Calder and Boyars, London 1972, p. 23.

most stirred the arts over the past ten years".[3]

Apollinaire was the "impresario of the avant-garde"[4], according to Roger Shattuck, and his influence among young Parisian artists and writers at this time was immense. However, his programme note for *Parade* is more renowned today for its use of the expression "surréalisme" (super-realism) and for the propaganda that the text created in avant-garde circles. Apollinaire's use of the concept is influential both in terms of the context of the ballet and Picasso's contribution to the performance, for it was the interplay between Léonide Massine's choreography and the artist's Cubist sets and costumes that created "une sorte de surréalisme". Apollinaire appears to have developed this idea in two letters to Léonide Massine and Paul Dermée in March and May 1917. Here the poet again used the term "surréalisme" and in a previously unpublished text entitled "Le Cubisme et La Parade". Picasso was presented as the pioneer of Surrealism, his Cubism signifying a new realism in opposition to superficial and transient forms of art. As Picasso's dealer Daniel-Henry Kahnweiler would later insist, it was Picasso who actually invented the concept of "surréalisme" and Apollinaire who adopted it as a fundamental aesthetic idea describing all forms of artistic expression.

Admiration for the poet Apollinaire, himself a *mutilé de guerre*, who had suffered a head wound and its trepanation (see page 56) – made him the perfect choice to write a preface for the ballet. The undoubted inspiration of his poetry in relation to the design for the *Parade* drop curtain acknowledges the importance of his literary genius for Picasso and Cocteau in their conceptualization of the ballet. Moreover, Picasso's Managers could almost have taken their cue from Apollinaire's imagination; they were modelled on precisely the kind of sculpture that the poet championed in his writings. "What sculpture will pursue through the streets its terrified admirer," he wrote.[5] Apollinaire's poetic sense of animating the inanimate forms a direct connection with the actions of Picasso's Managers, which were the incarnation of, literally and metaphorically, the towering city. Picasso knew his friend's work intimately and Apollinaire's artistic choices in his text *Méditations esthétiques* (1913) corresponded to a decision to reproduce a Cubist portrait by Picasso for the frontispiece of his volume of poetry *Alcools* (see page 53). The drawing is important not only for presenting a remarkable likeness of Apollinaire, but also for the conceits that Picasso would employ in his Managers: a Cubist portrait amusingly described by a series of stovepipes, accompanied by a tousled lock of hair that, without doubt, belonged to Apollinaire.

Although Picasso's biographer John Richardson has suggested that the assemblage of the Manager figures was adopted from the "caricatures of the uncouth giants Fafner and Fasolt, the builders of Valhalla in Wagner's *Ring*",[6] other connections can be drawn between the Managers and Apollinaire's aesthetic ideas. Apollinaire had previously championed Picasso's use of new materials in *Méditations esthétiques*, and recognized his Synthetic Cubist collages and construction techniques as the ultimate sign of creativity in the human imagination.

The photograph taken by Picasso of *Guillaume Apollinaire in Picasso's studio at 11 Boulevard de Clichy* illustrates the poet's particular custom of sucking on a pipe, and it may well have been a source for paintings such as *Man with a Pipe* (1911, see page 99), which extract numerous elements from the photograph of Apollinaire. If *Man with a Pipe* actually is a portrait of Apollinaire then it is surely one of the key sources for the Managers. Another example of Picasso associating Apollinaire with Cubist motifs is to be found in his still life *Violin, Wineglasses, Pipe and Anchor* of May 1912 (see page 99), where the allusion to Apollinaire's pipe coincided with the inaugural edition of the poet's periodical *Les Soirées de Paris* in November 1913. The stencilled letters, disconnected words and chance phrases of Picasso's painting create a simultaneous vision of the sights and sounds of a café scene, a depiction that pre-empts Apollinaire's experiments with poetic language in "Zone".

It is worth remembering that Apollinaire was the first person to promote Picasso's Cubist sculpture in *Les Soirées de Paris* with the reproduction of five recent relief works in November 1913. It is not hard to imagine that Picasso associated Apollinaire with Cubist sculpture and the towering figures of the Managers. The poet's fundamental presence – whether openly acknowledged or unconsciously absorbed by Picasso or Cocteau – was behind the whole creative process of *Parade*.

---

3 *Guillaume Apollinaire: Chroniques d'art*, 1912-1918, Textes réunis avec préface et notes par L.-C. Breunig, Éditions Gallimard, Paris 1960, "1917: Parade et L'Esprit Noveau", p. 532–34. Trans in *Apollinaire on Art: Essays and Reviews*, ed., L.-C. Breunig Susan Suleiman, translated by Viking Press, New York, 1972, "Parade", pp. 452–53.

4 Roger Shattuck, *The Banquet Years: The Origins of the Avant-Garde in France, 1885 to World War I*, Jonathan Cape (revised edition), London 1969, "Guillaume Apollinaire, 1880–1918: The Impresario of the Avant-Garde", Chapter 9, p. 253–297.

5 Apollinaire. *Oeuvres en prose complètes*, vol. 2, eds., Pierre Caizergues and Michel Décaudin, Paris 1991, p. 597.

6 John Richardson, *A Life of Picasso, Vol. III: The Triumphant Years, 1917–1932*, Alfred Knopf, New York, 2007, Chapter 3, "Parade", p. 34.

Drop curtain for *Parade, 1917*

Glue-paint on canvas, 16.4 x 10.5 m (64.5 x 41.3 in).
Centre Georges Pompidou, Paris

Jean Cocteau's synopsis for the ballet *Parade* is simple: it tells of a travelling circus group that takes to the streets of Paris. An itinerant group serves as the *Parade* – a Chinese conjuror, two Acrobats and a little American girl. Three Managers, one American and one French seek to court publicity, attempting to make the crowd comprehend by the most crass and extraordinary means the appeal of the show happening within. Yet not a soul enters. The Managers, exhausted by their efforts to cajole and convince the watching public, eventually collapse upon one another. Their failure leads the other players to make one final effort to explain to the crowd that the real show is actually going on inside. Cocteau's ballet presents a significant allegory of how the audience has recognized modern art but has failed to understand its true purpose. This time-honoured concept of the superficial aspects of life versus the meaningful creative work of poetry was especially relevant to Cocteau, Picasso and Apollinaire. Cocteau's rather dramatic account of the opening night of *Parade* as "the greatest battle of the War" (the French army had lost 140,000 soldiers in just two weeks and Russia was in the paroxysms of a revolution) and the rather egregious gimmickry of his scenario is often criticized by historians.[7] Nevertheless, the ballet's opaque modernist structure was pivotal to Cocteau's thinking throughout his life and work, and so it should not be underestimated.

7 Letter from Jean Cocteau to his mother, March 16, 1917, in Jean Cocteau, *Lettres à sa mère*, Paris Gallimard, 1989, p. 309.

Above

Project for the curtain of *Parade*, *1917*

Watercolour and lead pencil, 27 x 39 cm (11 x 15 in). Musée Picasso, Paris

This study for the drop curtain is part of a magnificent sketchbook filled with studies for the Ballets Russes production and with various harlequin figures that recall Picasso's Rose Period paintings.

Above left

Design for an Acrobat's costume, *1916–17*
Watercolour and pencil, 28 x 20.5 cm (11 x 8 in).
Musée Picasso, Paris

Picasso's costume design for the acrobat was adapted from circus vestments of the period, and most probably was taken from a contemporary photograph that Picasso owned of a female act entitled *Les Soeurs Ethair*. This type of realism was not uncommon in Ballets Russes productions.

Above right

Study for the Chinese Conjuror's costume, *1916–17*
Pen and ink, 28 x 19 cm (11.2 x 7.5 in). Musée Picasso, Paris

Picasso's costume design in brilliant red, yellow and black is of the type often worn by real Chinese conjurors, such as the famous contemporary magician Chung Ling Soo. The costume design was a great success and was used repeatedly in subsequent repertory programmes for *Parade*.

Above left
Man with a Pipe, *1911*
Oil on canvas, 90.7 x 71 cm (36 x 29.5 in). Kimbell Art Museum, Fort Worth

Picasso's Cubist painting represents the subject of a man smoking or holding a pipe, which recurs constantly during the Cubist era and would become a feature of his French Manager costume-assemblage designed for the ballet *Parade* in 1917.

Above right
Violin, Wineglasses, Pipe and Anchor, *1912*
Oil on canvas, 81 x 54 cm (32 x 21.5 in). National Gallery, Prague. Musée Picasso, Paris

Picasso's painting is an appropriation of Braque's use of stencilled letters, pyramidal forms and oval canvases, and full of puns and references to current places and people in his life. It is embellished with letters and objects that are a nod in the direction of Apollinaire's new periodical *Les Soirées de Paris*.

Chapter 12

Cubism, Classicism and *Commedia dell'Arte*, 1918–21

During 1918–20, Picasso's life was intimately associated with the Ballet Russes and the Parisian *beau monde*. His private circumstances had changed radically after marrying the dancer Olga Koklova in 1918, daughter of a Russian imperial army officer, whose status demanded bourgeois comforts and a high society lifestyle. Picasso's love for Olga, and his involvement with the Ballets Russes, gave Picasso's work a new lease of life, and a burgeoning dialogue between art, dance and music, as well as stimulating a series of *Maternités* (mother-and-child works) inspired by the birth of Paulo, and executed at Fontainebleau in the summer of 1921 (see Chapter 13). As Cécile Godefroy has rightly argued, Olga became Picasso's subject and muse because of her presence as a dancer. Notably, between 1911 and 1917, the Russian ballerina had danced in nearly 30 Ballets Russes productions, 15 of which were premières.

Picasso had a relatively comfortable wartime existence and although his career and financial circumstances had suffered little, the First World War had altered many of his pre-war friendships and his art. Meanwhile, Cubism's validity and status within the post-war art world was under threat. Picasso's old Cubist compatriot, Georges Braque (who had been badly injured in the trenches), bitterly complained to the dealer Daniel-Henry Kahnweiler about Picasso having created a new genre of painting that was Ingresque – an acidic reference to the French society painter Jean-Auguste-Dominique Ingres's portraits of upper-class ladies surrounded by the trappings of their bourgeois existence and beautifully dressed in all their finery.

Picasso's Cubist work was set against a backdrop of dissension and effusiveness towards his early bohemian life and achievements as a radical avant-garde artist at Bateau-Lavoir. The heterogeneous production of the Cubist ethos remained a vital characteristic of Picasso's post-war practice and the subject of the bohemian world of the café environment was ideally suited to assemblage works, such as *Fruit Bowl and Guitar (with a Fluted Glass)* of 1919, made from discarded cardboard packaging. Here the *bricolage* assembly techniques or hobbyist tricks of Picasso's early Synthetic Cubist works remained, but were now superseded by ever more complex projects, and inspired perhaps by his experiences of working for the theatre and ballet. For instance, *Guitar and Table Before a Window* (see page 103), *Fruit Bowl and Guitar* and the sketches for these sculptures – with diagrams and instructions noting the piecemeal assembly of parts – were vital to the perspectives and folding sections of Picasso's later sheet-metal sculptures, such as the famous *Woman*. The studies for *Fruit Bowl and Guitar* clearly demonstrate Picasso's move away from the earlier frontal effects of Cubist wall-relief assemblages toward more complex, perspectival spaces with planes fanning out from the construction, which encouraged the viewer to examine the work from multiple angles. One can explore the sculpture more fully in the round, whether by gazing from above and below, or right through the piece, as if it were a pop-up structure, which could easily be flattened into two dimensions. Picasso's new concept and execution of constructed sculpture demonstrates his continued interested in cubistically operated set pieces, such as the one for *Pulcinella* in 1920. With its abstracted and interlocking Cubist panels for the centre stage and simple semantic signs for the theatre curtains, the design pays homage to Picasso's love of paper cut-out toys, children's theatres, pop-up books and his most contemporary Cubist sculptures, which also make reference to the theatrical scenery used by travelling troupes and *commedia dell'arte* players.

Similarly, in the summer of 1919, while holidaying at Saint-Raphaël, Picasso executed a number of beautifully tranquil Cubist pop-up still-life paintings in gouache, watercolour and oil, representing a compotier and a guitar on a highly ornate table, and positioned before an open window with a sea view. Elegant and candy-coloured, *Still Life in Front of a Window at St. Raphaël* (see page 104) displays bourgeois comforts aplenty while simultaneously alluding to the Cubist still-life assemblages of Picasso's pre-war era in its cut-out and slotted-together elements. If there is any doubt about the diversity and complexity of Picasso's art at this time, we need look no further than at drawings from this period, which reveal strikingly different aspects of his life: his nostalgia for an earlier bohemian lifestyle and his bourgeois domestic circumstances with Olga at rue La Boétie. Here the organized and fashionable apartment (including Cubist relics and tribal artefacts from his recent past) contrasts with the clutter and chaos of his upstairs studio, which Picasso gathered and created to make himself feel at home. Picasso only allowed his old friends who had gone to rue Ravignan to visit him there. No one was allowed to clean up Picasso's mess – even the cigarette butts – and Olga herself never went up to Pablo's studio; he went down to Olga's floor.

Three Musicians, *1921*

Oil on canvas, 200.5 x 223 cm (79 x 88 in).
Museum of Modern Art, New York

Three Musicians drew upon a wide range of motifs for its subject-matter, in particular Picasso's wartime interests in *commedia dell'arte*, theatre and circus acts, and it translated into a commemorative painting. The impact, mood and nostalgia of *Three Musicians* can be associated with the campaign for a monument to Guillaume Apollinaire. It is a sorrowful work that has an air of transience, meditation and mourning. Peter Read has suggested that *Three Musicians* evokes Apollinaire's "The Musician of Saint-Merry" in *Calligrammes*, where the music and poetry of an anonymous flautist entices a number of spellbound women to pass over, into the place of the dead. Theodore Reff sees the work as a *memento mori* to Picasso's two lost friends (Apollinaire, who had died in 1918, and Max Jacob, who had retired to a Benedictine monastery). However, Elizabeth Cowling forcefully argues that these fictional musicians represent real people from the world of music and theatre: Erik Satie (as the ill-tempered and mischievous Harlequin), Manuel de Falla (as the celibate and deeply religious monk) and Igor Stravinsky (as the radical composer). Picasso's designs for plays at the time, such as *Le Tricorne* (*The Three-Cornered Hat*) and *Cuadro Flamenco*, also dealt with traditional folkloric themes, including peasant songs and dances; their guitarists, fiddlers and flautists lent a distinctly Spanish coloration to the painting, helping the artist to develop the idea of performing musicians on a stage. Theatre became inextricably intertwined with Picasso's Cubism, and his ventures into the theatrical milieu gave birth to, and were influenced by, fascinating and complex visual arts in two and three dimensions. The large canvas that Picasso painted for *Three Musicians* developed from the gouaches of *Pulcinella and Harlequin* (see page 102), executed in the summer of 1920, and translated the *commedia dell'arte* leitmotifs on an epic scale, which would further his contemporary Cubist painting.

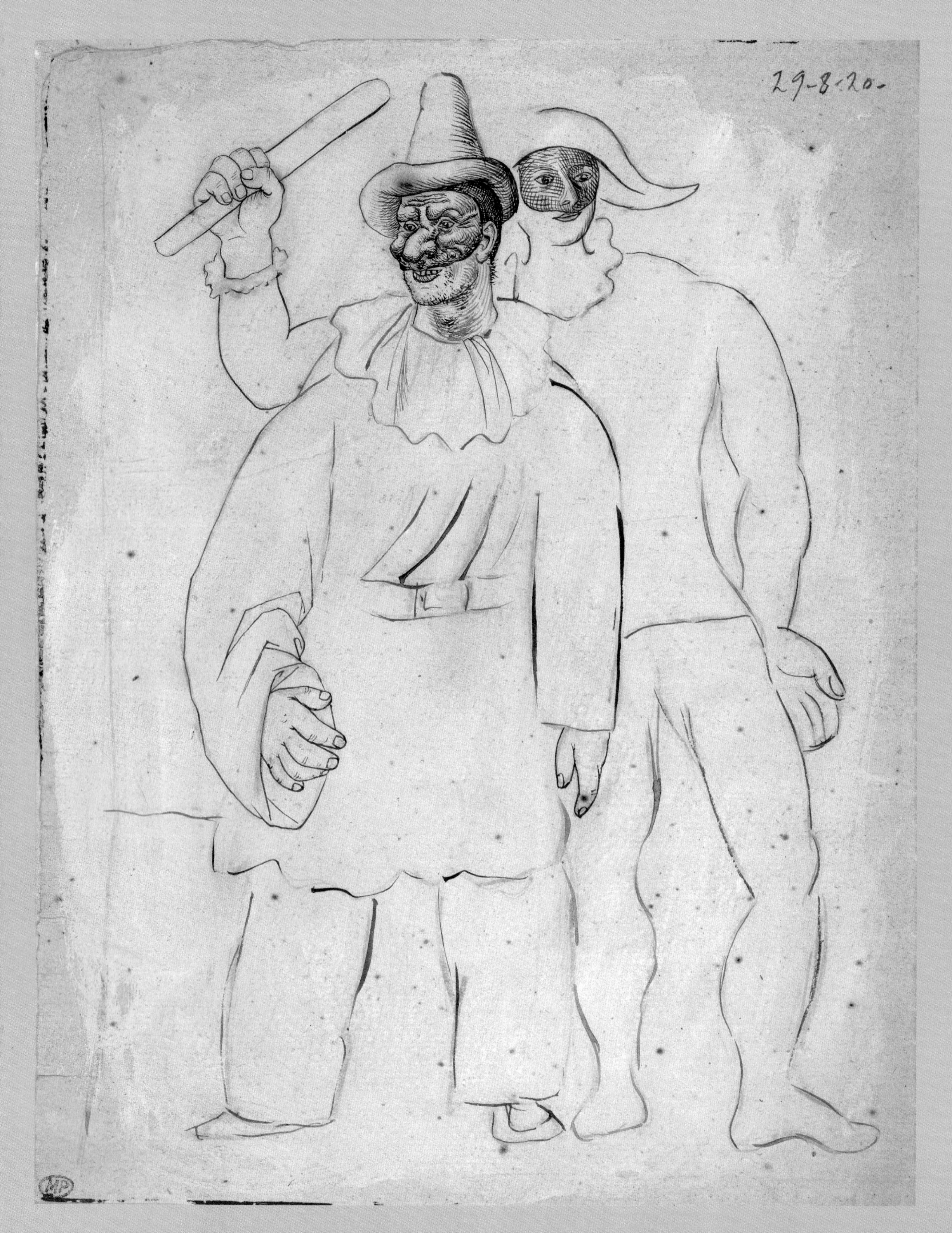
29-8-20.
MP

Opposite
Pulcinella and Harlequin, *1920*
Gouache and ink, 27 x 21.4 cm (10.6 x 8.4 in).
Musée Picasso, Paris

The theatre was a major influence on Picasso's work from 1917 onwards, and his collaboration with Diaghilev's Ballet Russes would see him involved in a production of *Pulcinella* in 1920. Pulcinella and Harlequin are two *commedia dell'arte* figures that are precedents for two figures in the *Three Musicians*.

Above left
Guitar and Table Before a Window, *1919*
Construction of painted cardboard, paper and crayon strokes
12 x 10.5 x 4 cm (4.7 x 2.7 x 1.5 in). Private Collection

This cardboard construction combines naturalistic and Cubist elements, and bears similarities to the drop curtains used in traditional theatre and ballet. The fragile piece appears hastily constructed and reveals a desire by the artist – a natural sculptor – to demonstrate the work of the hand.

Above right
Study for Guitar and Table Before a Window, *1919*
Gouache and pencil on paper, 34 x 23.5 cm (13.5 x 9.5 in).
Musée Picasso, Paris

This study for Picasso's 1919 construction shows that the art of toy models was not lost on the artist. The piecemeal arrangement suggests that pop-up books and children's theatres were sources of invention for his *commedia dell'arte* set pieces.

Picasso

Opposite

Still Life in front of a Window at St. Raphaël, *1919*

Gouache and pencil on paper, 31 x 22 cm (12.2 x 8.6 in).
Berggruen Collection, Berlin

This beautiful, elegant gouache is one of a number of French window scenes looking out to sea, executed while holidaying at Saint-Raphaël in the summer of 1919. The work suggests that bourgeois comforts were plentiful for the artist during the period.

Above

The Artist's Studio at rue la Boétie, *1920*

Pencil on grey paper, 62.5 x 48 cm (24.6 x 18.9 in).
Musée Picasso, Paris

As opposed to the bourgeois décor of the dining room at rue la Boétie, this drawing shows the clutter that visitors to Picasso's studio often described. Musical instruments, canvases, frames, palettes, paints, brushes, cigarette boxes and wine bottles can be seen strewn around the cramped-looking room.

Chapter 13

Dreamers, Readers and Bacchantes: Picasso and Painting in the early 1920s

Picasso painted the minute yet exquisite *Bathers* (see page 110) while holidaying in Biarritz in 1918. This highly unconventional painting depicts a young female caught in revelry, disrupting the peaceful tranquillity of a calm Mediterranean scene. As her companions sleep or relax – one wrings the seawater from her hair while another slumbers on the beach and dreams – the standing bather's twisted body is seemingly lost in the throes of ecstasy. The *Bathers*, created during the wartime period, does not ascribe to "call to order" idioms or post-war propaganda and codes rejecting irrationality, sexuality, excess and disharmony. Trying to classify the artist's painting at this time is almost impossible given that Picasso employed neo-classical, naturalist, realist and Cubist styles (often simultaneously). The artist had previously completed the melancholy and nostalgic *Three Musicians*, which signalled self-conscious allusions to the theatre, to the modern painting style of Cubism and themes of antiquity derived from poetry. Picasso's work now made direct reference to the antique in a number of related paintings that avoided simple historical or autobiographical interpretations. The First World War undoubtedly had an impact on the artist's works but neither this nor his recent *embourgeoisement* following his marriage to a Russian aristocrat, along with his entrance into polite society and a new theatrical milieu, were going to curtail Picasso's artistic continuum. The artist would continue to mix unorthodox definitions of Classicism, Naturalism and Cubism when painting the human figure. At this time, Picasso painted a number of contemporary yet timeless-looking figurative subjects such as *Woman Reading* and *Seated Woman* (see page 109) (both 1920), as well as *Reading the Letter*, *Large Bather, Mother and Child* and, most famously, *Three Women at the Spring* (see page 108) (all 1921), all of which make subtle allusions to the Arcadia of antique fresco paintings – "Pompeian fantasies", as Picasso liked to call them – which he saw in Naples and Pompeii during his Italian sojourn with Cocteau, Diaghilev and Massine in March 1917. *Reading the Letter* is part of this series of paintings that give the human figure a classical monumentality, a Romanesque countenance and gravitas. The painting may well be a neo-classical equivalent to the *Three Musicians*, with the contemporary clothed figures lost in contemplation of an intimate letter, appearing as if they have been quarried from the rock and stones around them. Their monumentality is enhanced by their fraternal synergy, earthy coloration and melancholic appearance. The work may be an elegy to lost friendships since reading letters in wartime Europe inevitably brought tragic news from the Front. The painting also alludes to Picasso's friendship with the poet Apollinaire (signified by the book and letter) and Georges Braque (who Picasso identified him with), both of whom shared his Cubist adventures and its discoveries.

In other paintings of the period, figures seem absorbed in reading, lost in thought or reflecting on things past. *Seated Woman* (1920, see page 109) recalls the Arcadian figure in *The Recognition of Telephus by Hercules* (a fresco Picasso saw in Naples), equating a Roman or Greek goddess with the modern woman by blending touches of contemporary style and character with those of generalized poses and references to antique garments and the world of classical antiquity. Drawings and antiquities in the Louvre and the British Museum seem likely sources for the Fontainebleau pastel studies that Picasso did of Olga in 1923 (see page 110), which merge painting and sculpture and, in the process, make reference to Greek statuary. Not surprisingly, these are related to *Three Women at the Spring*. Here there is little, if any, domestic narrative: the seated women – like many similar paintings of this genre – stare into nothingness, lost in a world of contemplation, crammed into claustrophobic spaces and sombre settings that intimate an air of melancholy, introspection and transience. Others can be understood within the context of the birth of Picasso's son (Paulo) on 4 February 1921, and undoubtedly the source of the Grecian Mother and Child paintings, depicting a statuesque goddess contemplating her playful offspring, and presumably espousing the values of *fécondité et maternité* (fecundity and maternity) in the post-war era. Picasso's attraction to the allegorical theme of "La Source" should also be viewed in terms of imagery associated with Mediterranean types, such as the Catalan Aristide Maillol's sculptures *The Mediterranean (Woman)*, 1905 (see page 110) and *Grief* (1921, exhibited in the Jardin des Tuileries, Paris); the neo-classical paintings of Nicolas Poussin and renowned antique and Renaissance representations of pensive or mourning women.

Like many of Picasso's neo-classical paintings, *The Pipes of Pan* (1923, see page 111) gives the music-loving pair a simple costume and setting: a theatrical backdrop of blue skies, ocean and plain walls, and stone blocks painted in earthy colours, which draw upon his imagery of *saltimbanques* (acrobats) in 1905–6. In doing so, *The Pipes of Pan* illustrates Picasso's concept of an ageless classical youth by evoking the archaic instrument and setting his elegy in a scene of timeless, Mediterranean calm that merges tradition and modernity with longing and memory. Oblivious to their surroundings, Picasso's classical types are lost in musical reverie and perhaps transfixed by the archaic sounds of a mysterious and haunting lyricism of a long since vanished past.

The theatricality of *The Pipes of Pan* appeared slightly earlier in the Bacchanalian *The Race* (*Two Women Running on the Beach*) of 1922 (see page 111), and the Dionysiac *Bullfight* of 1922–23, which both introduce something of a Nietzschean spirit into Picasso's rather tranquil and meditative classicism. Derived from ancient Cretan culture, *Bullfight* dispenses with traditional blood and gore to reveal a Spanish *corrida* – a matador and a beast erotically entwined in a post-coital embrace – in a scene full of theatricality and Dionysiac ecstasy. In the small yet powerful gouache better known as *The Race*, two delirious and pneumatic-looking bathers tear along an otherwise peaceful beach, framed by calm lapis lazuli skies and water. With their heads flung back in explosive reverie – breasts exposed to the elements and hair blowing in the wind – these crazed maenads are lost in the kind of Dionysiac abandon that is typical of classical and Renaissance subjects. Although Poussin's *Bacchanal before a Herm* (c.1634) has been sighted as a point of reference for *The Race*, Titian's *Bacchus and Ariadne* (1520–22, see page 111) was probably a more likely source for the running figures (the god Pan – wreathed in snakes – energetically strides across the Venetian landscape), and possibly derived from a Roman sculpture of the *Laocöon* (c.160–130 BC, discovered in 1506), which depicts a powerfully muscular figure grappling with a huge reptile, and is on display in the Vatican Museum. Picasso probably saw Titian and Poussin's Bacchanalian subjects in the National Gallery when working on *Le Tricorne* in 1919, and the theatricality and manic, balletic energy of Picasso's *The Race* was perfectly adaptable as a piece of scenery. Notably, in 1924, Picasso allowed Diaghilev to have the painting copied on to a front cloth for *Le Train Blue*, and subsequently it was regularly used for Ballets Russes performances. The Race subverted the themes of the Ballets Russes by imagining trained ballerinas shedding their scanty attire and abandoning themselves to Dionysiac hysteria and orgiastic reverie. This theme of the females lost in a bacchic dance thus fostered and secured Picasso's relationship with the Surrealists.

Three Women at the Spring, *1921*

Oil on canvas, 204 x 174 cm (80.5 x 68.5 in). The Museum of Modern Art, New York

Three Women at the Spring (1921, see left) is monumental in every sense of the word. Its sombre, melancholy and thoughtful figures, fashioned in the form of three enormous Greek goddesses, muses or fates, appear to contemplate the unknowable. More sculpture than painting, the women in this spellbound group are enormous and dense, as sturdy as the columns of a classical temple, their moulded flesh coloured in tones of terracotta, black, brown and white, suggestive of ghostly figures drawn from a mythical world. These maternal-looking women, apparently drawing water from a spring, are borrowed from the artistic theme of "La Source", in which civilization derives its spiritual life and salvation from a fountain of water, symbolized by the jug-bearing females. The sanguine nature of the work imitates cartoon compositions used by High Renaissance artists and the painting alludes to the eternal nature of well-springs, streams, rivers and fountains as sources of replenishment, fertility and life. However, the environment is parched and littered by empty vessels (only the merest suggestion of water runs through the hand of the central figure), and nothing grows or flourishes in the solemn, sterile and decaying environment so reminiscent of ancient frescoes and statuary. If this is the artist's version of Arcadia, it inverts traditional iconography in favour of a barren and desolate interior: a mausoleum containing funerary objects (jars and jugs), which perhaps hold the ashes or spirits of the dead souls from the immediate aftermath of the First World War.

Above

Seated Woman, *1920*

Oil on canvas, 92 x 65 cm (36 x 25.5 in). Musée Picasso, Paris

Picasso's *Seated Woman* is part of an important series of seated female figures seemingly lost in *pensée* (thought). Her pose is reminiscent of antique and statuesque frescos that the artist saw when visiting Naples to help garner inspiration for the setting of the ballet *Parade* in 1917.

Above left
Bathers, *1918*
Oil on canvas, 27 x 22 cm (10.5 x 8.5 in). Musée Picasso, Paris

Picasso's *faux-naïf* painting looks similar in style and coloration to Henri Rousseau's *Football Players* (1908), which is held in the Solomon R. Guggenheim Museum in New York. The strange anatomies and contorted poses of the female bodies give the work a "surreal" and frenzied atmosphere.

Top right
Portrait of Olga, *1923*
Pastel and black chalk, 104 x 71 cm, (49.9 x 27.9 in). Musée Picasso, Paris

Olga appears in numerous guises in Picasso's work. As well as being featured as a dancer, she appeared dressed in elegant finery in neo-classical portraits, which emphasized her beauty. This large pastel work is part of a series of portraits and imagined figure drawings that show, with meticulous accuracy, individual subjects in thoughtful disposition.

Above right
The Mediterranean (Woman),*1905, Aristide Maillol*
Stone, height 116 cm (45.5 in). Oskar Reinhart Collection, Winterthur

It is likely that Picasso saw Maillol's heftily built *Mediterranean (Woman)* since the artist visited him at Villeneuve-Saint-Georges, in Paris, as early as 1900. Picasso certainly viewed *Woman* when it was exhibited at the October 1905 Salon, and held up as a superb example of French avant-garde classicism.

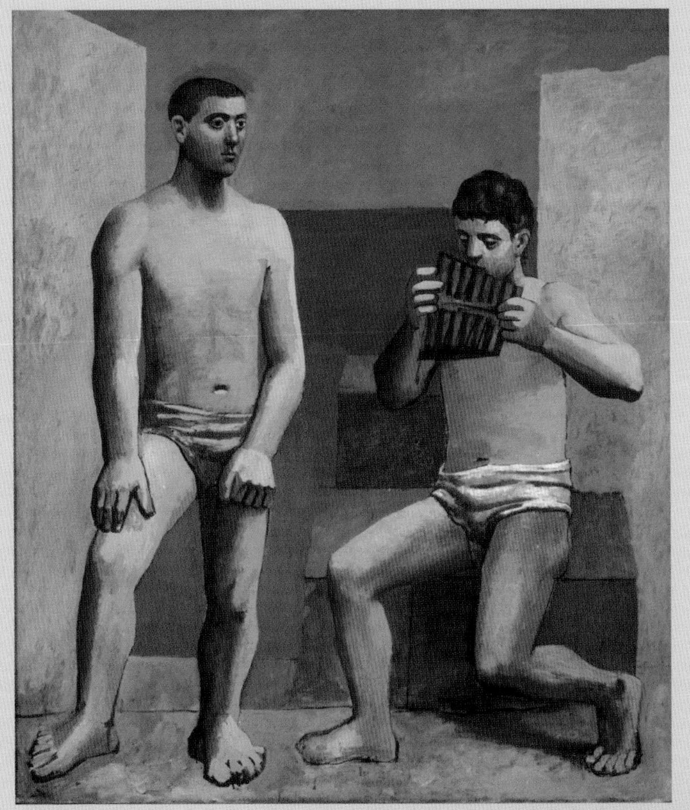

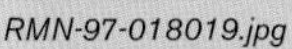

RMN-97-018019.jpg

RMN-97-018230.jpg

Above left

The Pipes of Pan, *1923*

Oil on canvas, 205 x 174 cm (80.5 x 68.5 in). Musée Picasso, Paris

Picasso's *Pipes of Pan* was executed in the summer of 1923, when the artist and his family were on holiday in Antibes. There are many studies for this work, and it seems the painting went through many "classicizing" stages before Picasso settled on a scene of two Mediterranean "types" – singer and musician – plying their art before blue waters.

Above right

The Race (Two Women Running on a Beach), *1922*

Gouache on plywood, 32.5 x 41 cm (13 x 16 in).
Musée Picasso, Paris

The plump figures of Picasso's *The Race* are sisterly companions to the artist's depictions of dormant mothers lying on a beach, such as *Family by the Sea* (1922) in the Musée Picasso in Paris, but here they are transformed into free-flowing, joyous maenads.

Left

Bacchus and Ariadne, *1520–22*

Oil on canvas, 172 x 190.5 cm (67.5 x 75 in).
National Gallery, London

Titian's painting was probably a source for Picasso's *The Race*, and typical of mythological subjects depicting Bacchus (God of wine) as the cause of riotous behaviour. The cloud pattern in *The Race*, projected on to the deep blue sky, appears to mimic the ring of stars above the clouds in Titian's painting.

Chapter 14

Picasso and Surrealism: *La Révolution Surréaliste* and the Crisis in the Painting, Collage and Sculpture of 1924–26

Although Picasso's experiments in *Les Demoiselles d'Avignon* (1907) had, to a degree, pre-dated the Surrealist fascination with such concepts, *La Danse* of 1925 (see page 114) announced a new, expressive and disturbing return to the subjects of savagery and hysteria. Prior to the creation of this dramatic painting, Picasso executed a sheet metal sculpture *Guitar* (see page 115), a powerhouse in the art of cutting, bending and folding a single sheet of metal into a twisted anthropomorphic female figure, whose clothing appears to have been torn asunder by a bewitched lover, or, like Venus, born without her flowing finery. Using the established metaphor of woman as guitar, Picasso paradoxically signifies the curvaceous female/guitar by crudely cutting out her frame in the same aggressive manner of his pre-war constructions. Flamboyantly displaying her fluttering gender, she flaunts her sexuality yet is forced to reveal her vulnerable nature. Picasso's ghostly, *grisaille* palette suggests that she may even be a private funerary monument to his great friend Apollinaire, since the artist had previously agreed to create a tomb for the poet in Père Lachaise cemetery in Paris. Whatever the circumstances, Breton – who had much to gain from an alliance with the most famous avant-garde artist of his generation – proudly proclaimed Picasso to be one of his own, and to prove so chose his strange and foreboding *Guitar* for the first issue of *La Révolution Surréaliste* on 1 December 1924. Like a spectre, Picasso's construction was situated within the pages so as to emphasize the eerie nature of Pierre Reverdy's text ("The dreamer among the ramparts"), as if it were a product of the haunted, Surrealist imagination.

Picasso never aligned himself wholeheartedly with Surrealist ideologies and imagery: he was far too shrewd and independent to sign up to a series of doctrines and manifestos based on a "cult" of insanity. However, in July 1925, Breton reproduced *Les Demoiselles d'Avignon* alongside *La Danse* in *La Révolution Surréaliste*, another indication that Picasso was happy to do so to reinforce and retain his status as leader of the avant-garde. When Breton saw the painting, he wrote obsequious letters to Picasso, begging permission for the work to be reproduced in *La Révolution Surréaliste*. Flattered no doubt by Breton's attention and enthusiasm for the painting, Picasso agreed. *La Danse* takes its subject from a balletic Three Graces (the handmaidens of Venus), but the left-hand dancer has a horrendous grimace – her mouth looks like a man-trap – while her frenzied body appears to be contorted in a series of agonizing twists and turns. The Dancer appears to be in the throes of ecstasy or "la grande attaque hystérique" ("the major hysterical fit"), to use the phrase of Jean Martin Charcot (Freud's tutor at *La l'sapêtrière* hospital during 1885–86). The central dancer holds her arms wide open, in the symbolic religious stance of a crucified figure, thus evoking a *danse macabre*, whereas the third, half in darkness and half in light, recalls the Surrealist notion of a *femme fatale* made flesh, or "the being who casts the greatest shadow or the greatest light within our dreams", according to Charles Baudelaire.[1] It can be no coincidence that death's shadow, represented by Picasso's silhouette thrown against the window, emerges from the gloom like a terrifying omen.

Death was very much on Picasso's mind in the spring and summer of 1925, because two of his friends Ramon Pichot (the oldest and closet) and Erik Satie had passed away in March and July respectively under the most appalling and distressing of circumstances. Satie, who was attended to by Picasso at the end, died of pleurisy complicated by his terminal cirrhosis, and apparently left behind nothing but a wretched, filthy apartment across from a house emblazoned with the words, "this house is haunted by the devil". Picasso also executed a number of mysterious-looking still-life compositions in 1925 based on a ram's head, which may well commemorate Satie's sad demise in terms of a Spanish *memento mori*. Pichot's death was exacerbated by syphilis, tuberculosis and heart problems. As Gertrude Stein remembers, Pichot was known for his "wonderful religious Spanish dance ending in making of himself a crucified Christ upon the floor".[2] According to Roland Penrose, Picasso hated the title because "the painting is above all connected with the misery on hearing of the death of his old friend". He exclaimed: "It should be called The Death of Pichot".[3]

Of course, another notable presence behind the painting is that of Olga Koklova, as she often appears on the left in Picasso's sketches for *Three Dancers*. Pierre Cabanne has claimed Picasso's relationship with Olga had begun to deteriorate by 1925

1 *La Révolution Surréaliste*, no. 1, 1 December 1924, p. 17.
2 Gertrude Stein, *The Autobiography of Alice B. Toklas*, Harmondsworth, Penguin Books, 1966, p. 117. First edition: New York, Harcourt, Brace, 1933.
3 Elizabeth Cowling, *Visiting Picasso: The Notebooks and Letters of Roland Penrose*, Thames and Hudson, London, 2006, p. 276.

(although he shows no real evidence for the fact), and that *La Danse* suggested some "psychic ailment".[4] In Picasso's view, Olga had become violent and tyrannical, apparently losing her mind at times, and she perhaps represents the fantasies of Picasso (and his biographers) about a supposedly monstrous, grimacing female with gnashing teeth threatening eyes, a ravaged body and countenance.

If *La Danse* conveyed a certain amount of anxiety and uncertainty regarding his marriage to Olga, then the collage *Guitars*, which followed in the spring of 1926, was simply pure malice and spite directed at the little ballerina for her supposed instability, but, more equally, his own "terrible rages". It would be wise not to accept unquestioningly all the things that have been said about Olga Koklova, for historical evidence is simply not there to substantiate these claims at present. In fact, we know very little about her relationship with Picasso, let alone her own career as a dancer. What information we have derives from Picasso himself and his adoring biographers Roland Penrose, Pierre Cabanne and John Richardson, following the artist's complete break with Olga in 1935, so this subject often lacks objectivity.

Most scholars agree that by 1926 Picasso's marriage to Olga was in a state of decline, and that the large nail and hessian *Guitar* was something akin to a death wish directed at his wife. As Lydia Gasman has argued, Olga is symbolized by the filthy-looking piece of hessian on to which Picasso unleashed his rage in his countless stabbings of six-inch nails, fired into the coarse cloth so as to cause the maximum amount of injury. The other shirt-tail work is possibly an interpretation of the artist's own (rather dramatic) crucifixion, his shirt dirtily pinioned with a rope, nails, a hook and a wooden baton, which passes right through the body of Picasso's musical instrument. Equally, this strange "musical instrument" could be interpreted as a self-referential *memento mori* to his lost friendship with Erik Satie (whose soiled bedding and clothing the painter Léopold Survage and Picasso changed when his pleurisy took hold). Louis Aragon discussed the *Guitars* in "La peinture au défi", which he wrote for an exhibition of collages at the Galerie Goemans in March 1930. In doing so, he claimed that, "The principle of collages admits that painters had passed from white to black magic. I was too late to go back. The new magicians had reinvented incantation".[5] Aragon went so far as to suggest that Picasso was involved with black magic and voodoo.

As a regular and privileged visitor to Picasso's studio, Breton was well aware of the artist's belief in magic and the occult, and he would go on to discuss this phenomenon in his text *L'art magique* in 1957. Breton was naturally fascinated by what he saw as the sadistic and delirious character of Picasso's shirt-tail *Guitar* and, like the earlier sheet-metal *Guitar* of 1924, it too became an emblem of his publication *La Révolution Surréaliste*. It was given the accolade of being reproduced on the centre page of its seventh issue on 15 June 1926 and, in light of Breton and the Surrealists' interest in the fetishistic qualities of Picasso's collages, the 1926 Guitars must surely have been viewed as incantatory objects associated with primitive sorcery and magical rites.

The cannibalization of the finery of Olga (Picasso would rather cruelly call her the "old Chiffon"), including discarded fragments of tutus and buttons appropriated from her sewing box, shows an acute awareness of the laws of sympathetic magic. Picasso's miniature Guitars (see page 115) are not only vaginal-looking, but the penetration of nails and string nails into their cardboard ground celebrates a sadistic attack on objects of love or hate. Their execution with needles and string, buttons, nails and tulle suggests a certain type of magic, voodoo, in which, "the magician… infers that whatever he does to a material object will affect equally the person with whom the object was once in contact [and where] the garment by itself is enough to give the sorcerer a hold upon his victim," as James Frazer writes in *The Golden Bough*.[6]

Picasso's friendship and involvement with the Surrealists, who were themselves fascinated by "primitive" sorcery and occult objects, undoubtedly further stimulated the artist's highly superstitious nature. In return Breton, Aragon and their Surrealist company eulogized the magical potential of Picasso's 1926 *Guitars*: collage had a dark side and they instantly saw its conception and importance in the context of black magic. As Picasso explained to Roland Penrose, he had originally "thought of embedding razor blazes in the edges of the picture so that whoever went to lift it would cut their hands".[7]

Second Manifesto of Surrealism, *1930*

Surrealism as an idiom or movement is not easy to define, but the term is most commonly used to describe a fascination with the unconscious, dreams and desire. In the *Second Manifesto of Surrealism* (1930) André Breton defined the Surrealist project as a salvaging of the secret realm of the dream: "We are not afraid to take up arms against logic […] to swear that something we do in dreams is less meaningful than something we do in a state of waking."[8] The Surrealists' investigations into irrationality, madness, delirium and desire were driven by, and symptomatic of, a long history of psychoanalytical theory, in particular the work of Sigmund Freud. He was fascinated by unusual and disturbing "pathological" states, which he believed were manifested in the form of anxiety, neurosis and taboos hidden within the repressed psyche, and that these symptoms were essentially an outcome of the endless pursuit of and struggle with one's desires and fantasies. Whereas Freud attempted to harness the undirected stream of the subconscious or "cure" pathological states, the Surrealists celebrated the "dream state" as the purest declaration of mankind's creative freedom. Breton's *La Révolution Surréaliste* of 1 December 1924 (see page 125) therefore contained a plethora of images, objects and literary experiments that were an attempt to explore the hidden territory of the subconscious. The overall choice of works by Breton for *La Révolution surréaliste* clearly demonstrates the Surrealist's fascination and familiarity with Freudian psychoanalysis, through its conflation of ideas on desire, madness, primitive mentality and delirium.

---

4 Pierre Cabanne, *Picasso: His Life and Times*, 1977, William Morrow and Co, New York, 1977, p. 244.
5 Louis Aragon, *La peinture au défi*, reprinted in Les Collages, Herman, Paris, 1965, p. 47 and 49.
6 James George Frazer, *The Golden Bough: A Study in Magic and Religion*, Macmillan and Co. Ltd, 12 vols., London, 1949 [first edition: 1890–1915], Chapter III, "Sympathetic Magic", p. 43–44.
7 Roland Penrose, *Picasso: His Life and Work*, 1958, p. 232.
8 André Breton, "Second Manifesto of Surrealism 1930", in *Manifestoes of Surrealism*, translated from French Richard Seaver and Helen R. Lane, Ann Arbor Paperbacks, The University of Michigan Press (First edition 1969), 1972, p. 128.

Left
La Danse, *1925*
Oil on canvas, 215 x 142 cm (85 x 56 in).
Tate Gallery, London

Guilt, regret and grief appear to be behind the subject of Picasso's most important painting of 1925, *La Danse*. Ramon Pichot had been one of Picasso's most loyal supporters during the burgeoning years of his artistic career, and had visited his sick bed just before Christmas, in December 1924, only to die on 1 March 1925.

Opposite top left
Guitar, *1924*
Painted sheet metal, tin box and wire, 111 x 63.5 x 26.6 cm (43.7 x 25 x 4.1 in). Musée Picasso, Paris

This magnificent sheet-metal sculpture marks a return to the Cubist facture and *bricolage* techniques of Picasso's pre-war work. It is closely related to the 1915 *Violin*, which is also made from sheet-metal, although this is a more open form of relief sculpture.

Opposite right
Guitar, *1926*
String, nails, ink and oil-painted cardboard, button, pieces of cloth, 24.7 x 12.3 cm (9.7 x 4.8 in). Musée Picasso, Paris

One of a group of miniature assemblage relief works that Picasso created during the spring of 1926, which were photographed in his studio alongside a portrait of Olga Koklova. These appear to have been associated with Olga, who Picasso often drew absorbed in the domestic activity of sewing.

Opposite below left
Guitar, *1926*
Gauze, string, button and crayon strokes on cardboard, 14 x 10 cm (5.5 x 3.9 in). Musée Picasso, Paris

Made with a torn section of blue tulle, and with strings pulled through the cardboard backing, this tiny work is an explicit representation of female genitalia. This makes the manufacture of the works with scraps pilfered from Olga's garments and the ballerina's sewing box seem particularly derogatory.

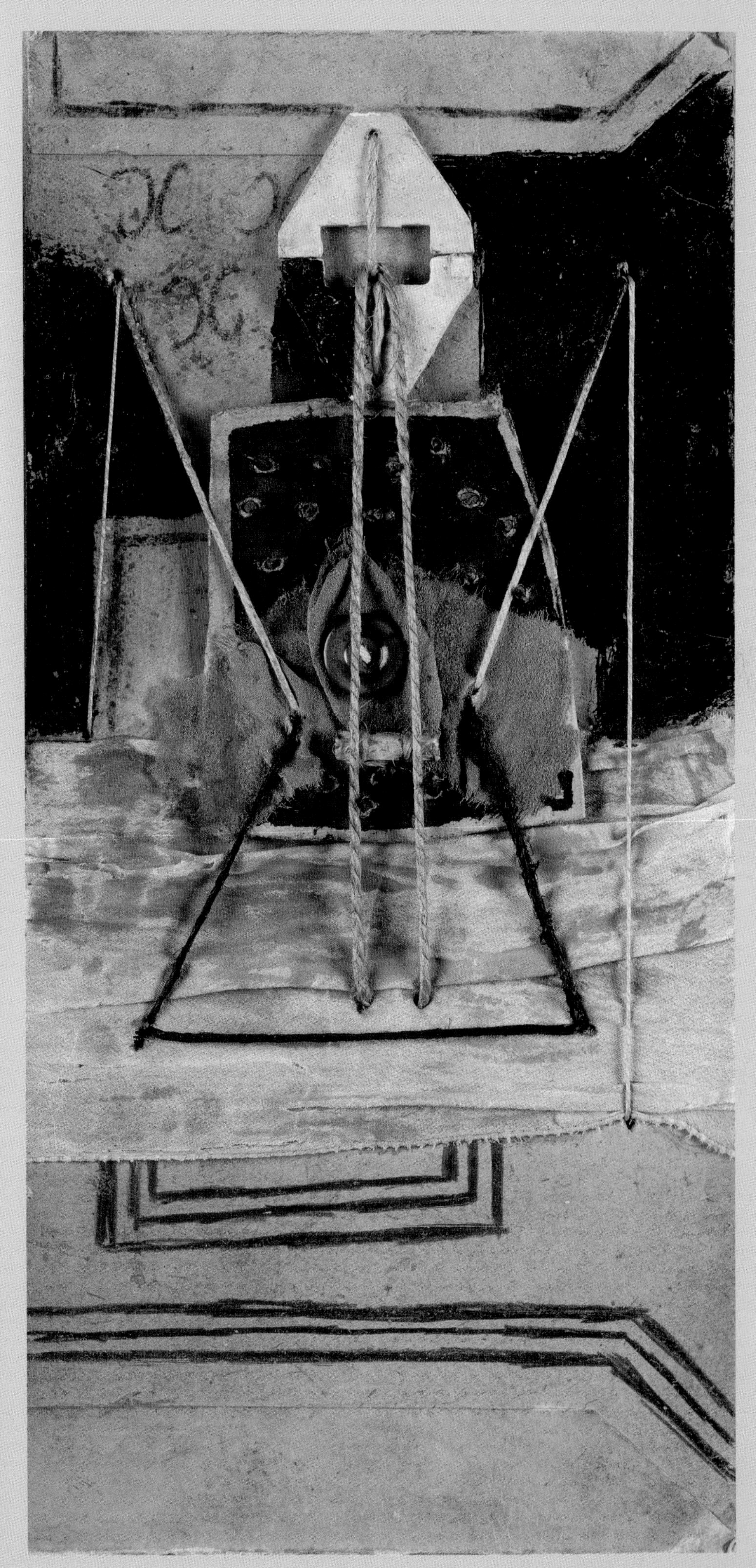

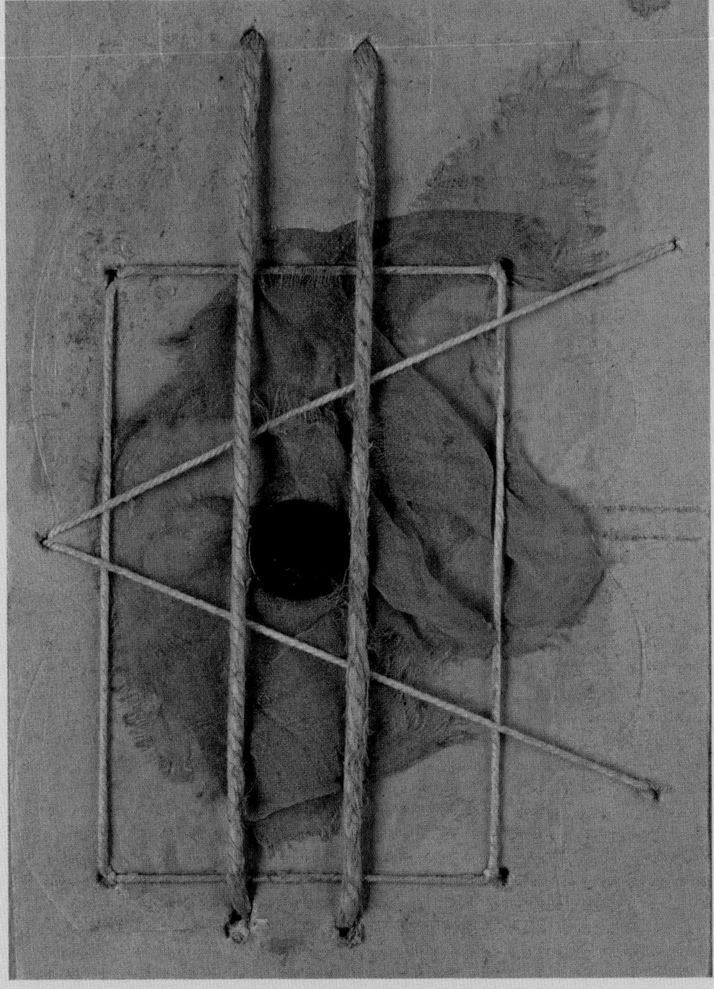

Chapter 15

Drawing and Sculpture: the Ballet *Mercure* and Picasso's Monument to Guillaume Apollinaire, 1924–28

Mercure was the sixth and final major work that Picasso would create for the theatre, and its creation was largely his own. The first performance, produced and organized by Etienne de Beaumont under a title borrowed from Apollinaire's periodical *Les Soirées de Paris,* took place at the Théâtre de la Cigale, Paris, on 15 June 1924. Picasso created the curtain, sets and costumes; Erik Satie penned the musical score and Léonide Massine drafted and choreographed the ballet's scenes. Despite John Richardson's claim that *Mercure* was an in-joke directed at Cocteau, Beaumont, Diaghilev and the Surrealists, Picasso's costume and set designs for the ballet *Mercure* amounted to much more than the admonishment of polite Parisian society. According to Richardson, Louis Aragon was first to recognize Mercure as a "major milestone" with regard to theatre and ballet. In *Le Journal Littéraire* on June 1924, Aragon exclaimed that *Mercure* was something of a revelation in style and conception for Picasso, and one that owed absolutely nothing to Cubism or realism, transcending both idioms entirely.

To Aragon and the Surrealists the designs and sets for *Mercure* might have appeared to take the form of a completely new direction in Picasso's sculptural oeuvre, but this is not entirely true. To represent the ballet's tableau scenes, Picasso assembled three movable decorations from bent or twisted rattan, laid at angles on to cardboard with bits of wood and wicker, and illustrated these with schematic figures and animals. However, Picasso's adaptation of this free-flowing line can be traced back to the 1907 doodles of animals that he created for Apollinaire's volume of poems *Le bestiaire ou Cortège d'Orphée* (see page 49). The artists also devised numerous line drawings during 1917–18: a dancing harlequin holding a bat; various drawings of animals and a series of pencil sketches executed in 1920, representing a horse and a trainer.

The *Mercure* decorations are connected technically and thematically with the drawings that Picasso made at Juan-les-Pins for Balzac's *Le Chef d'oeuvre inconnu* (*The unknown masterpiece*) in the summer of 1924. The latter replicate the shaped and twisted effects of the bent rattan in the set pieces and demonstrate that Picasso continued to search for the development of an open type of constructed sculpture. In formulating ideas for *Mercure*, Picasso also looked back to the geometry of pre-war graphic experiments where lines intersect, creating grid-like, transparent patterns or structural armatures that render line drawings in sculptural terms. In relation to studies for the Cubist *Head of a Woman* (*Fernande*) of 1909, Picasso actually claimed that he originally "had the intention of doing them in wire".[1]

This concept is essential to the constructive "language" used in the *Mercure* set pieces, and although it is unlikely that Picasso was thinking in theatrical terms in 1912–14, he must have later perceived that the constructive "syntax" of his pre-war Cubism could easily be adapted to stage design. This has led certain authors such as Werner Spies to underplay or to ignore the important material and constructional relationships between Picasso's early Cubist sculpture and his later theatrical costumes and set designs. Spies's definition of how the *Mercure* sets relate to Picasso's earlier sculpture is inconclusive when he claims that the linear designs Picasso created for *Mercure* were not totally three-dimensional in aspect, and that these stage décors essentially remained "flat" and entirely bound up with the picture plane. Yet Picasso's tableau objects were, according to his interpretation, truly sculptural, as he understood the term, and became the antecedents for the open-work construction techniques used in the 1928 wire models (see page 120), which are often described as "drawings in space".

Designed for Apollinaire's tomb, the maquettes, with their transparent weightlessness and airiness, could only have been transposed by the patterned or linear effects in two and three dimensions; effects which, it has been observed, evoke Apollinaire's description in *Le Poète assassiné* (1916) of a memorial sculpture erected (prophetically) as "a statue of nothingness, of the void [and] filled with his ghost".[2] The initial studies for the monument were probably rejected as unacceptable by the commissioning body. André Billy described the bathers series as "a bizarre, monstrous, mad and incomprehensible thing, almost an obscenity, apparently sprouting genitals from various places".[3] Certain drawings from these sketchbooks, particularly the androgynous *Bather* (see page 120) of 1927, portraying "surreal" and androgynous bathers bursting with erotic forms, frolicking on the beach, or unlocking a door of secrets to a small cabin, could easily have been considered as pornographic. They coincided with Picasso's

1 Roland Penrose, *The Sculpture of Picasso*, New York, 1968, p. 19.

2 Werner Spies, *Picasso on the Path to Sculpture: The Paris and Dinard Sketchbooks of 1928 from the Marina Picasso Collection*, Prestel-Verlag, Munich and New York, 1995, p. 10–11.

3 Paul Léautaud, *Journal littéraire*, Paris, 1956-63, vol. IV, p. 164, entry for 14 December 1927.

clandestine affair with the young Marie-Thérèse Walter. Inspired by seeing her on the beach, the drawings make reference to their secret passions within the privacy of a locked cabin and to Picasso's desire for his lover's sensual body. Here, sexual metaphors of keyholes and of unlocking secret doors go hand in hand with erotic references to phalluses and bodily apertures.

When designing a monument to his great friend, Picasso certainly did not forget the mythological character Hermes/Mercury, magician and god of the Underworld, whose cult was marked by a huge priapic phallus. From the artist's bathing cabin appear ghostly apparitions: figures created from stones and scoured bones, standing before the entrance to a traditional-looking tomb. Picasso, unsurprisingly, sought to celebrate and mourn Apollinaire through the creation of a funerary monument whose imagery was inspired by shared interests and metaphysical questions concerning sex, magic, life and death. What finer tribute could there be than that of an encoded image of Hermes/Mercury, philosopher, inventor of languages, god of fertility and messenger from the living to the dead, presiding over Apollinaire's tomb? Indeed, the second Greek treatise of the *Corpus Hermeticum* actually provides a model for the syntax, spatial relationships and constructive play of Picasso's radical wire maquette constructions: "The things you call 'full' are empty of air since they are crowded with these other bodies and have no place to take in the air. Therefore, the things that you call 'empty' must be named 'hollow' rather than 'empty,' for in their substance they are full of air and spirit".[4]

The suggestion that Picasso's memorial sculpture to Apollinaire has its conceptual origins in theatrical projects, with sculptural techniques derived from Cubist construction, as well as ideas and themes taken from ancient philosophy, literature and mythology, leads to one logical conclusion: Picasso's involvement with the theatre stimulated solutions to the problems of working in three dimensions, and helped to increase Picasso's range of plastic expression during 1928.

The ballet *Mercure*, unlike *Parade*, offered little in terms of a conventional story, but instead presented various aspects of Mercury's mythological character: messenger to the gods, god of fertility, cunning thief, philosopher, magician and the henchman who accompanies souls down to the Underworld of Hades. The ballet, studied with an array of characters from Greek and Roman mythology, opens with a 30-second introduction and a tableau representing Night. It is a love scene between Venus and Apollo, set amid the signs of the zodiac. At the end of scene one, Mercury, in a fit of crazed jealousy, kills Apollo only to resurrect him with his magic wand. In the second tableau scene, Mercury steals and makes off with the pearls of the bathing Three Graces, hotly pursued by Cerberus. The third and final tableau depicts a feast at the home of Bacchus with Mercury, Pluto, Proserpine and Pulcinella in waiting. With the aid of Chaos, Pluto kidnaps Proserpine and carries her off to the Underworld.

4 *Hermetica*: the Greek *Corpus Hermeticum* and the Latin *Asclepius*, translated by Brian P. Copenhaver, Cambridge University Press, 1992, p. 11.

Left
Design for the Curtain for *Mercure*: Harlequin Playing the Guitar and Pierrot Playing the Violin, *1924*
Pastel on grey paper, 25 x 32 cm (9.8 x 12.6 ins).
Musée Picasso, Paris.

This colourful pastel drawing on grey paper represents Picasso's beloved commedia characters, Harlequin and Pierrot, playing musical instruments. Picasso created the drawing for the drop curtain for the ballet *Mercure* on 18 June 1924, and as part of a series of "Soirées de Paris" organised by Count Etienne de Beaumont.

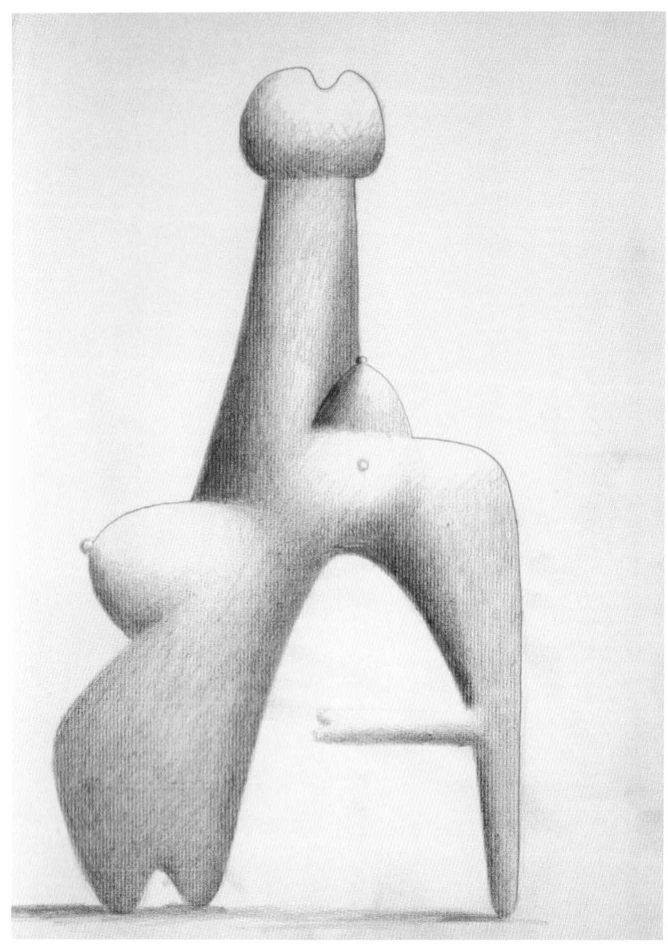

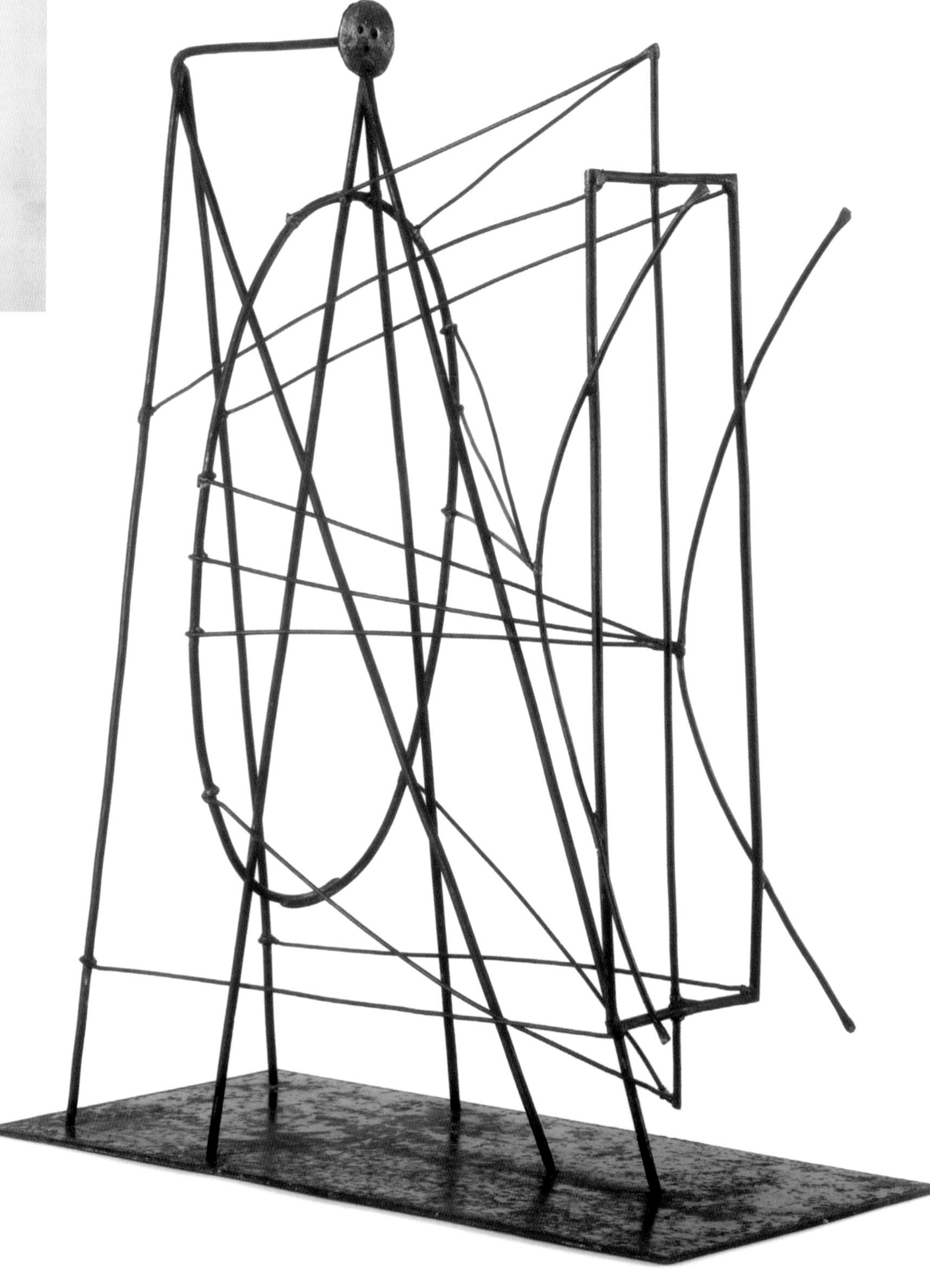

Above

Bather, *1927*

Pencil, 30.5 x 23.2 cm (12 x 9 in). Musée Picasso, Paris

This drawing is probably inspired by Picasso's affair with Marie-Thérèse Walter, and relates to a sketchbook filled with erotic drawings. Here the figure metamorphoses into a priapic phallus sprouting breasts and taking the form of a monumental sculpture.

Right

Figure (Design for a Monument to Apollinare), *1928*

Construction in wire and sheet iron, 59.5 x 18.5 x 40.8 cm (23.4 x 7.2 x 5.3 in). Musée Picasso, Paris

Picasso created this metal montage with the help of fellow Spaniard and sculptor Julio González, who taught him the art of welding. The construction was inspired by his young love, Marie-Thérèse Walter.

Gallery 2

Special documents, photographs and illustrations

Above

Programme for the Ballets Russes, *1917*

Gouache and pencil, 20 x 27 cm (7.8 x 10.6 in). Musée Picasso, Paris

Picasso was inspired by the burgeoning dialogue between art, dance and music in the sphere of the theatre. His involvement with the Ballets Russes gave his art a new lease of life, as seen in his designs for the ballet *Parade*.

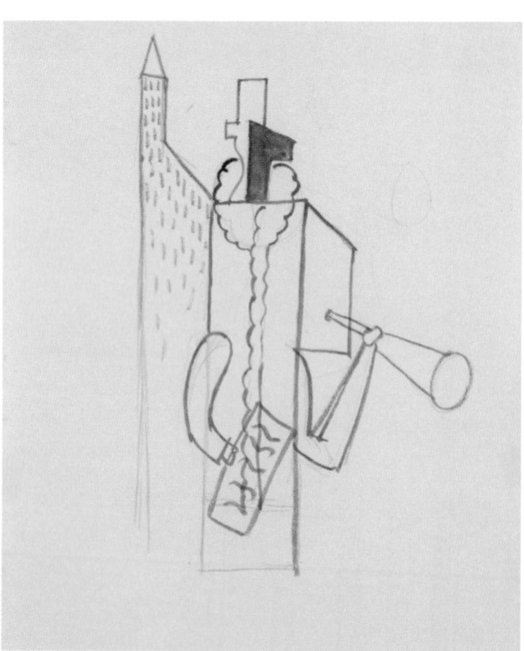

Left
Design for the Manager costume for Parade, *1916–17*
Watercolour and pencil, 28 x 20.5 cm (11.2 x 8.1 in). Musée Picasso, Paris

Picasso's Cubist-futurist design of the Manager costume for Parade complemented the imagery of Apollinaire's "Zone" (December 1912), which opens with a eulogy celebrating the city, its dwellers and the modern media as a form of poetry.

Above
Study for the set of Parade, *1916–17*
Pencil, 22.5 x 28 cm (8.9 x 11.2 in). Musée Picasso, Paris

This sketch presents a cubo-futurist cityscape, and closer in style to Picasso's Cubist paintings at this time.

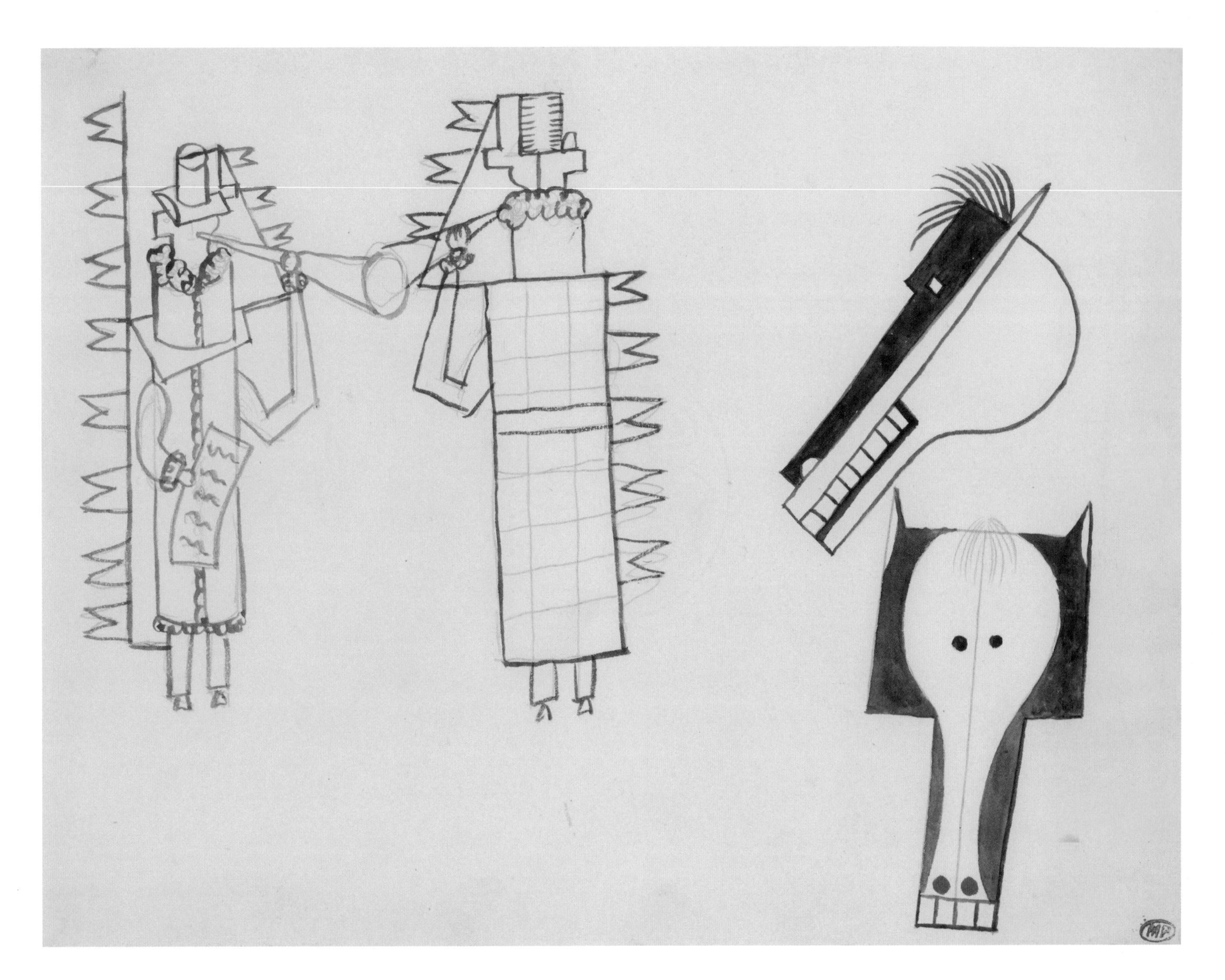

Above
Design for the Manager costume for Parade, *1916–17*
Gouache and pencil, 20.5 x 28 cm (8.1 x 11.2 in).
Musée Picasso, Paris

When Apollinaire wrote the programme note for Parade after he had attended some of the ballet's dress rehearsals, he made special mention of the 'fantastic constructions representing the gigantic and surprising figures of the Managers.

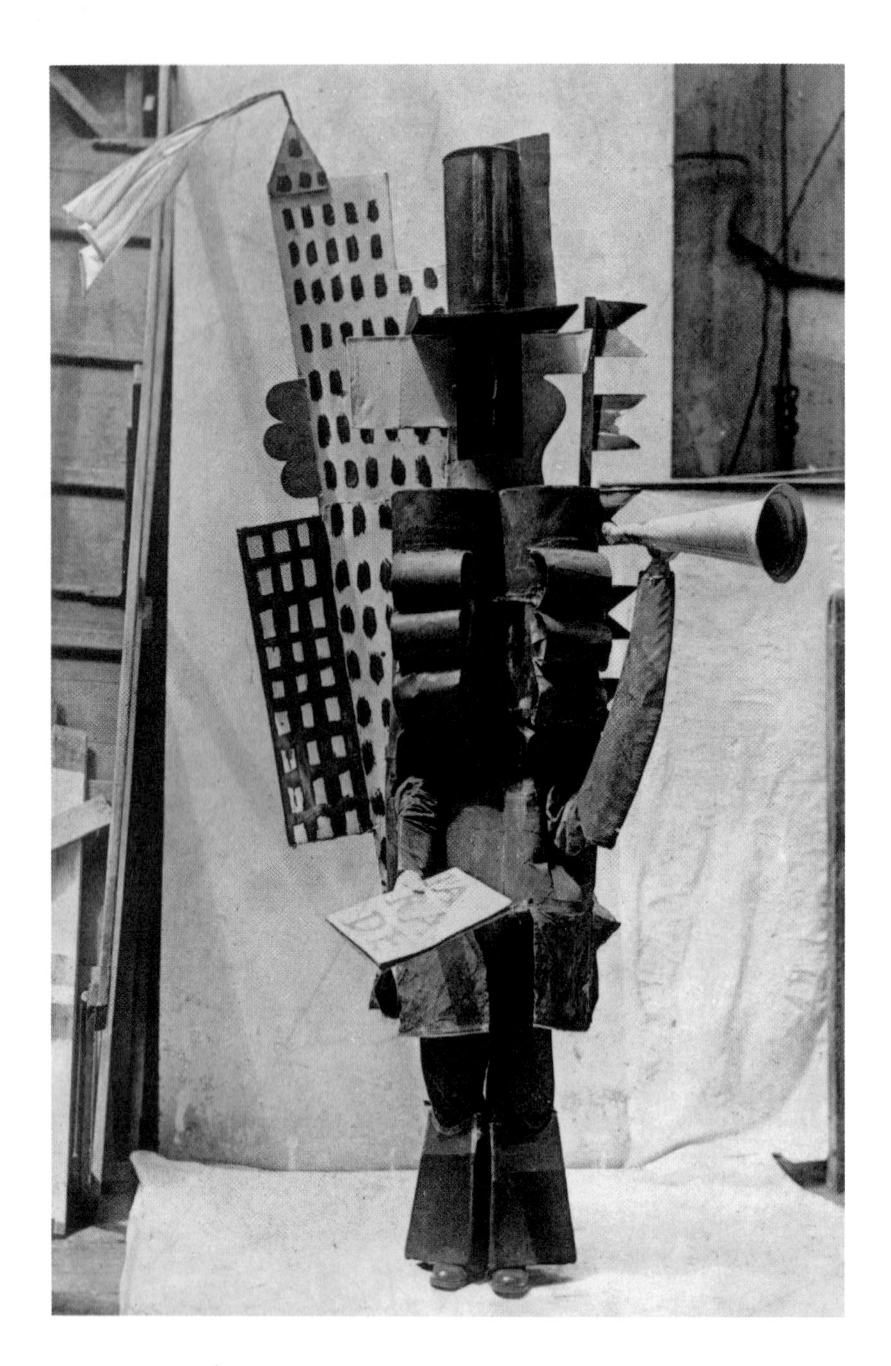

Above

Statkewickz as the American Manager in the first performance of Parade

Photograph, Museum of Modern Art, New York

This photograph depicts the Manager as a towering figure, wearing an assemblage of motifs from the city. As Apollinare wrote in his programme note for *Parade*, "Picasso's Cubist costumes and scenery bear witness to the realism of his art".

Above

Portrait of Raymond Radiguet, *1920*

Illustration, 11.6 x 10 cm (4.5 x 3.9 in). Musée Picasso, Paris

Raymond Radiguet was a young French novelist and poet, who joined leading artists in the Cubist circle such as Guillaume Apollinaire, Max Jacob, Erik Satie and Jean Cocteau. The drawing became the frontispiece of Radiguet's *Les Joues en feu*, 1925.

Le Monde entier parle du

MANIFESTE DU SURRÉALISME

POISSON SOLUBLE

par

ANDRÉ BRETON

Qu'est-ce que le Surréalisme ?

KRA, ÉDITEUR
6, Rue Blanche

Le volume : 7 fr. 50

Nº 1 — Première année 1er Décembre 1924

LA RÉVOLUTION SURRÉALISTE

IL
FAUT
ABOUTIR A UNE
NOUVELLE DÉCLARATION
DES DROITS DE L'HOMME

SOMMAIRE

Préface : J.-A. Boiffard, P. Eluard, R. Vitrac.
Rêves : Georgio de Chirico, André Breton, Renée Gauthier.
Textes surréalistes :
Marcel Noll, Robert Desnos, Benjamin Péret, Georges Molkine, Paul Eluard, J.-A. Boiffard, S. B., Max Morise, Louis Aragon, Francis Gérard.
Le rêveur parmi les murailles : Pierre Reverdy.

Chroniques :
Louis Aragon, Philippe Soupault, Max Morise, Joseph Delteil, Francis Gérard, etc.
Notes.
Illustrations : Photos Man Ray.
Max Morise, G. de Chirico, Max Ernst, André Masson, Pablo Picasso, Pierre Naville, Robert Desnos.

ABONNEMENT, les 12 Numéros : France : 45 francs Etranger : 55 francs

Dépositaire général : Librairie GALLIMARD
15, Boulevard Raspail, 15
PARIS (VIIe)

LE NUMÉRO : France : 4 francs Étranger : 5 francs

Above

Cover of the first issue of the of La Révolution Surréaliste, *1924*

Manuscript. Musée Picasso, Paris

Although Picasso never aligned himself fully with the Surrealist movement, its leader André Breton proclaimed the avant-garde artist as one of his own. He selected Picasso's new metal *Guitar* for the first issue of *La Révolution Surréaliste* on 1 December 1924.

Previous pages
Mercure, *1927*
Photograph

Russian-American dancer and choreographer Leonide Massine (1896–1979), centre, plays the title role in the ballet Mercure at the Prince's Theatre, London. Also dancing are Vera Petrova as Venus and Boris Lissanevitch as Apollo. Music by Erik Satie and designs by Pablo Picasso.

Above right
Three Dancers, *1924*
Black pencil drawing, 27 x 21 cm (10.5 x 8 in). Musée Picasso, Paris

This 1924 sketchbook drawing is to be found in an album in the Musée Picasso, Paris, and related to a series of line drawings for the ballet *Mercure*. Picasso first used the technique of a free-flowing line to create animal drawings in 1907, and he adopted this technique when creating the wire sculptures for the set pieces of *Mercure*.

Right
Head of Man, *1930*
Pencil drawing,17 x 10.5 cm (6.7 x 4.1in). Musée Picasso Paris.

This is one of a number of sketchbook studies for Picasso's metal montage *Head of a Man* (1930), and showing the sculpture on a tall stool, which is supported by large cloven-hoofed legs.

Above
Picasso's Studio, *1936*
Photograph. Musée Picasso, Paris

This photograph of Picasso's studio contains artworks depicting both naturalistic and Cubist subjects. The rather haphazard state of the studio demonstrates Picasso's love of objects and detritus, which he often used in his collages, construction and assemblages.

Right
Picasso painting Guernica, *1937*
Photograph

Here Picasso paints his political mural, Guernica, in which he lent expression to his outrage at the cruelties inflicted on ordinary Spanish citizens under the rule of Franco, using the iconography of the bullfight.

Above
The Dream and Lie of Franco, *1937*
Etching and aquatint, 31.4 x 41.2 cm (12.3 x 16.2 in).
Musée Picasso, Paris

Picasso's most blatantly political work, condemning Franco, was a series of etchings entitled *The Dream and Lie of Franco* (January–June 1937), in which the tyrant is depicted as an ugly, vainglorious and cruel bigot.

Right
Picasso wearing a bull's head mask, *1949*
Photograph

This photograph depicts the avant-garde artist Picasso as he poses in a large bull head mask on a beach located in Golfe Juan, near Vallauris, in France.

20 mai 46

Left
Portrait of Françoise, *1946*
Pencil and charcoal with coloured crayon shading, 66 x 50.5 cm (25.9 x 19.8 in). Musée Picasso, Paris

This drawing portrays Picasso's young lover François Gilot and shows the influence of Henri Matisse. Gilot met Picasso as an art student in the spring of 1943, during the German occupation of France.

Above
Armoured horse and knight, *1951*
Ink, lavis, plume, 13.5 x 21 cm (5.3 x 8.3 in). Musée Picasso, Paris

This ink drawing presents an armoured knight on horseback from an array of multiple viewpoints. The drawing, representing a filigree web of lines, characterizes the precision and web-like patterns used in Picasso's late work.

PICASSO
ET NOTRE TEMPS
CONFÉRENCE
AVEC PROJECTION PAR
PAUL HAESAERTS
ALLOCUTION DE L'ABBÉ MOREL
VENDREDI 22 NOVEMBRE 1946 — 21 HEURES
GRAND AMPHITHÉATRE DE LA SORBONNE
PRIX DES PLACES 65 francs — Adhérents de Travail & Culture 40 francs
Billeteries : 5, rue des Beaux-Arts — 1, rue de Chateaudun — Maison de l'Université U. F. U. Place de la Sorbonne
Chez les Concierges de la Sorbonne — Chez Durand, 4, Place de la Madeleine

Above

Cover of Picasso et Notre Temps, *1946*

Original print, 75.5 x 52.7 cm (29.7 x 20.7 ins). Musée Picasso, Paris

This original print was produced for a conference held in the evening of 22 November 1946. Picasso, Haesaerts and Morel were all deeply involved with this conference at the Grand Ampithéâtre of the Sorbonne.

Right

Picasso and Miguel Dominguen, *1955*

Photograph. The Edward Quinn Archive

In this photograph, Picasso is pictured playing bull with the Spanish Matador Luis Miguel Dominguen, who was among the greatest bull fighters of the twentieth century. The avant-garde artist would design costumes for his good friend.

Above
Exhibition of ceramics at Vallauris, *1958*
Poster, 67 x 51 cm (26.3 x 20 ins). Musée Picasso, Paris

Here Picasso advertises a ceramics exhibition held at Vallauris. The brightly coloured and open design of the poster reflects the expressive nature of the artist's work in later years.

Right
Picasso in his studio at Vallauris, *1950s*
Photograph. Private collection

Picasso created bold and expressionist ceramic vases in his studio at Vallauris, storing objects and materials that he needed to create such artworks in Le Fournas, a large disused perfume factory.

Above
Long Live Peace, *1954*
Painting, dimensions unavailable. Musée d'Art et Histoire, Saint-Denis, France

Picasso's painting *Long Live Peace* articulates his pacifist beliefs, which led to his famous outcry for peace in the painting *Guernica*, shortly after the German bombing of the Spanish city.

Right
Picasso, Françoise Gilot and their son Claude, *1952*
Photograph. Private Collection

Picasso is shown here with his young lover Françoise Gilot and their son Claude. The couple met when Gilot was 21 and Picasso was 40 years her senior. They had two children and spent almost a decade together.

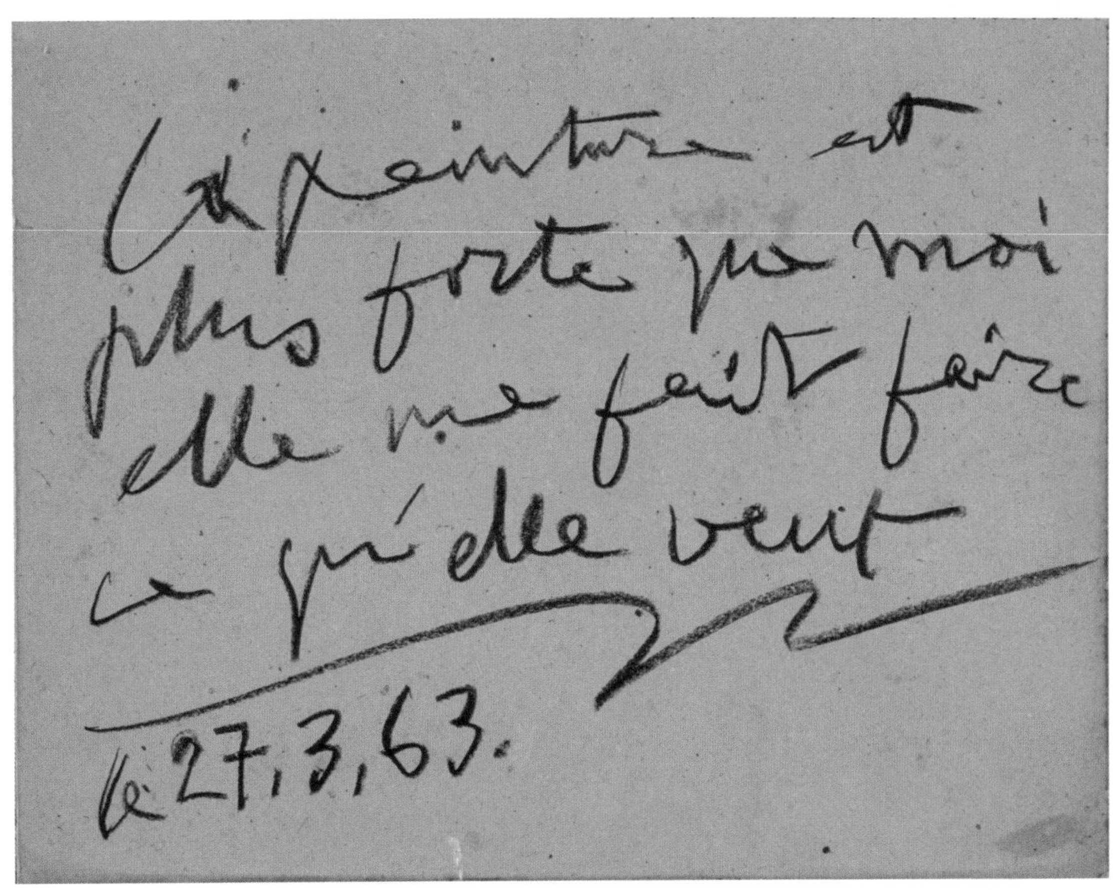

La peinture est
plus forte que moi
elle me fait faire
ce qu'elle veut

le 27.3.63.

Left
Picasso and Cocteau at a Bullfight, Vallauris, *1956*
Photograph, Private collection

Pablo Picasso at a bullfight in Vallauris, France, pictured together with his wife Jaqueline (left) and the French poet and artist Jean Cocteau (right). Behind them with a scarf is Picasso's daughter Maya.

Above
Carnet 56, troisième de couverture, *1963*
Craie de cire, 21 x 27 cm (8.3 x 10.6 in). Musée Picasso, Paris

Picasso's famous statement that: "Painting is stronger than me, it makes me do its bidding."

Above

Le Déjeuner sur l'herbe after Manet, *1962*

Graphite, 42.5 x 52 cm (16.7 x 20.4 in). Musée Picasso, Paris.

In this drawing, Picasso presents his own subversive interpretation of Édouard Manet's famous painting of a picnic scene, *Le Déjeuner sur l'herbe*, which was exhibited at the Salon des Refusés, Paris, 1869.

Picasso's work in the 1930s, 1940s and 1950s saw a resurgence of interest in tribal art and artefacts, as well as an obsession with bones and various aspects of the human and animal body. This interest resulted in a flurry of creations depicting strange anatomies that intimated bone beneath flesh in a work of art. Picasso's late work often involved the subjects of violence and destruction, war and peace, and climaxing in a number of large murals or monumental paintings such as *Guernica* (1937) and *Massacre in Korea* (1951): works that express universal types of suffering. Picasso was also deeply interested in works by Old Masters towards the end of his life, and measuring himself against their greatest achievements so as to establish his fame and, ultimately, to ward off thoughts of mortality and impending death.

4

Section 4: 1929–1973

Chapter 16

Comparative Anatomies: *Woman in a Garden*, 1929–32

Picasso's project for the Guillaume Apollinaire monument led to the creation of a number of important metal constructions between 1928 and 1932, which are closely associated with the commission. These were reproduced and discussed in André Breton's famous essay "Picasso in his Element" for the Surrealist periodical *Minotaure* in 1933, and elaborate on the theme of metamorphosis, sex, violence and death. They also confirm a resurgence of Picasso's fascination with tribal objects and sculpture, as well as his renewed interest in Surrealism in both its orthodox and dissident forms. Sketches showing the artist's morbid obsession with creating monoliths out of bones or stones reveal that Apollinaire's death still haunted Picasso at the time.

Elizabeth Cowling has shown that mammal and dinosaur skeletons specifically inspired Picasso's drawings and paintings, such as *Woman Sitting in a Red Armchair* of 1932 (see page 148), and the skulls, skeletons and bones in his sketchbook drawings can be viewed in terms of Christian symbolism, death and *memento mori*. This, she argues, may have affected Picasso's decision to paint many of his later metal montages in white, for instance *Woman in a Garden* and *Head of a Woman* (see pages 146 and 149), to resemble bleached bones. Studies for *Woman in a Garden*, unlike the construction itself, make explicit the skeletal nature of Picasso's metal montage. A sketchbook from February 1929 until 1930 gives the figure's body a ribcage created out of flat-boards supported by vertical struts. Others show the structure with organic elements such as the kidney shape, rounded belly and navel of the finished work. In *Head of a Woman*, the tripod legs and colanders imply a perforated cranium to suggest a skeletal structure. Furthermore, some studies for *Head of a Man* depict the head with a bone-like nose intended to be bolted on to the flat metal plate of the face, whereas others (see page 129) actually show the head supported by legs and arms made out of huge bones.

Alternatively, John Richardson suggests the work of sixteenth-century anatomical artist Vesalius's *De Humani Corporis Fabrica* (1543), as well as pagan mythology informed the genesis of *Woman in a Garden*. In particular, the work was inspired by Ovid's *Metamorphoses* and the theme of Apollo and Daphne – "a love-struck god chasing the terrified nymph through the woods".[1] Indeed, Picasso's choice of theme and approach to this sculpture strongly recalls Ovid's poetic imagery: "My soul would sing of metamorphoses | But since, o gods, you were the source of these | bodies becoming other bodies, breathe | your breathe into my book of changes".[2]

Naturally, therefore, Picasso built a sculpture to guard Apollinaire's tomb that was filled with a spiritual, magical and hieratic presence – a female figure who seems to be part-human, part-animal and part-vegetable: a beautiful and savage-looking idol – a nymph, a goddess or a *monster sacré* – with serrated teeth and spikes for fluttering hair.

With its fusion of organic and vaguely mechanical or modified Cubist construction techniques, *Woman in a Garden* could indeed be described as a kind of comparative anatomy – a sculpture of contrasting juxtapositions of the kind presented in the dissident periodical *Documents* during 1929–30. Even Picasso's tiny constructed *Head* (1928, see page 147), whose simple, tripod-like base pre-empts the table element in *Woman in a Garden*, is in accord with Bataille's illustrations of Siamese twins, whose split heads and truncated bodies revolt against the so-called natural body. Picasso's assemblage techniques suggest various types of comparative anatomy and once again mirror the ethnographic Surrealist practices used by George Bataille, Michel Leiris and Marcel Griaule in the periodical *Documents* throughout the period.

1 John Richardson, *A Life of Picasso Volume 3: The Triumphant Years 1917–1932*, Chapter 32, "Woman in a Garden", p. 382.
2 *The Metamorphoses of Ovid*. Translated by Allen Mandelbaum, San Diego, Harcourt Brace, 1993, p. 3.

Woman in a Garden, *1929–30*

Soldered and painted iron, 206 x 117 x 85 cm (81 x 46 x 33.5 in). Musée Picasso, Paris

The two-metre high *Woman in a Garden* (see right) was probably Picasso's most ambitious and definitive welded metal construction to date. Both iron and bronze versions were first exhibited at the Galeries Georges Petit, Paris, in 1932, where the former was painted white and both works faced each other across the room of the gallery. Its great success derives from the sculpture's Ovidian transformations of flora and fauna, with female hair blowing in the breeze and waving philodendron leaves or branches suggesting a nymph, perhaps Daphne, hiding in a woody glade. Half-flame and half-leaf, with a skeleton of mechanical-looking parts representing her backbone and swollen mid-rift, this light-winged dryad breathes fertility, and appears a slightly comical creation from Vulcan's forge. The white-painted version is evocative of a bleached skeleton and the wedge of head, with its serrated teeth giving the impression of an animal trap or a *vagina dentata*, and nails hammered through the eye sockets, becomes a grimacing skull whose mouth is transformed into an orifice of horrible and painful-looking screams.

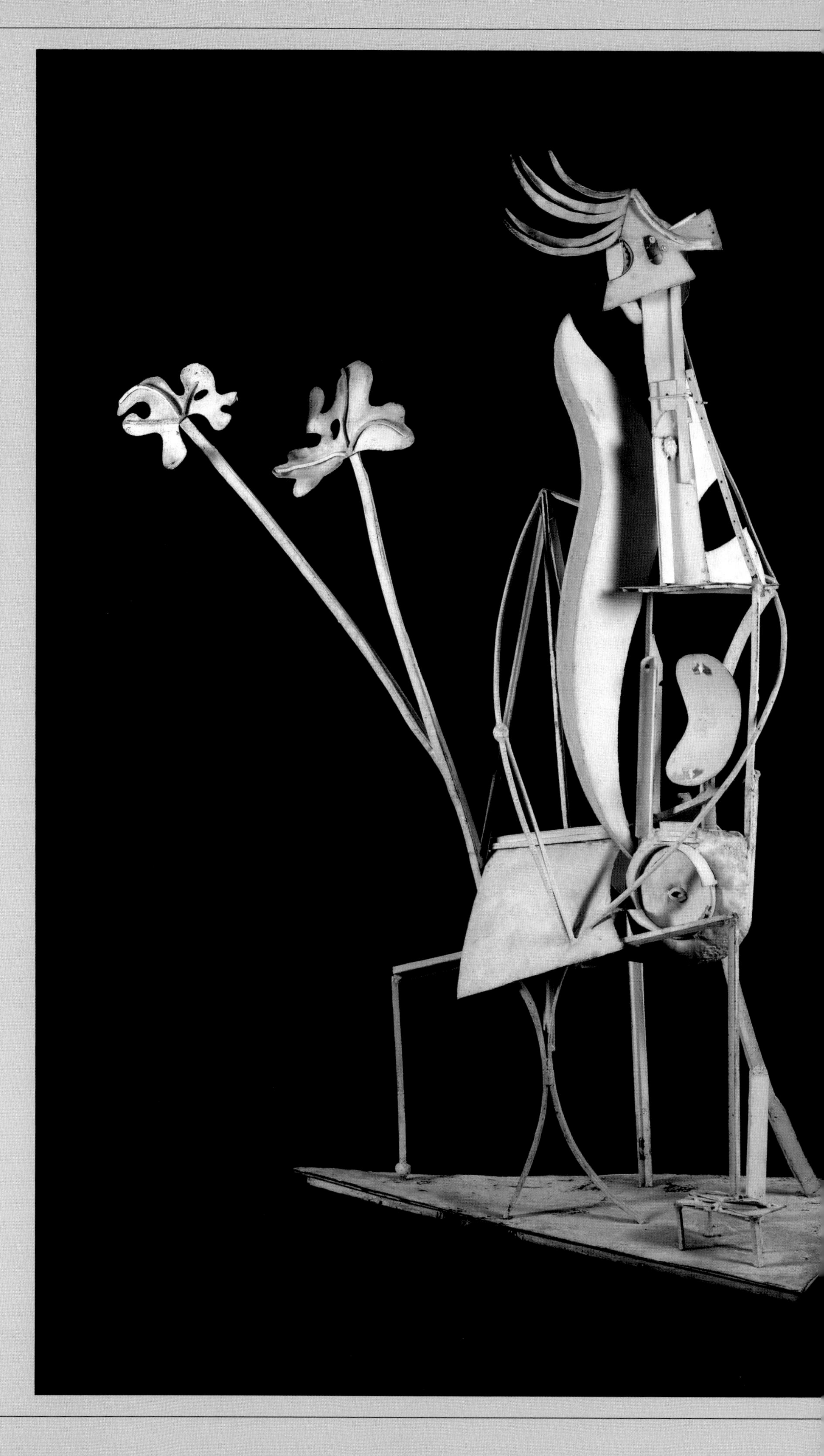

Above
Head, *1928*
Painted brass and iron, 18 x 11 x 7.5 cm (7 x 4.5 x 3 in).
Musée Picasso, Paris

This tiny brass and iron sculpture is one of three metal montages that Picasso created in connection with the Apollinaire monument. The sculpture suggest two figures (one black and one white) locked in a kiss, and an eternal motif that recalls Constantin Brancusi's stone sculpture *The Kiss* (1909).

Above
Woman Sitting in a Red Armchair, *1932*
Oil on canvas, 130 x 97.5 cm (51 x 38 in). Musée Picasso, Paris

Painted in January 1932, this work resembles dismembered and bleached bones, skulls, stones or ancient tools. Death and decay appear to be the main theme of Picasso's painting, as well as building a strange anatomy. The figure appears to have been made out of both human and animal remains.

Opposite, top left
Head of a Woman, *1929–30*
Iron, springs and colanders, 100 x 37 x 59 cm (39 x 14.5 x 23 in). Musée Picasso, Paris

The structural principle for this work derives from Picasso's 1924 dot-and-line drawings, particularly, a sketch from March (*Carnet* 215, folio 18, Musée Picasso, Paris) showing two globes surrounded by oval rings resembling the planet Saturn and supported by a similar diamond/tripod-shaped base.

Opposite, top right
Head of a Man, *1930*
Bronze, iron and brass, 83.5 x 40.5 x 36 cm (33 x 16 x 14 in). Musée Picasso, Paris

The cut and welded sections of the lozenge-shaped mouth in this work contrast with Picasso's roughly welded joints. The pin eyes and megaphone and moustachioed mouth also look back to the Cubist French and American Manager figure-costumes that Picasso created for the ballet *Parade* in 1917.

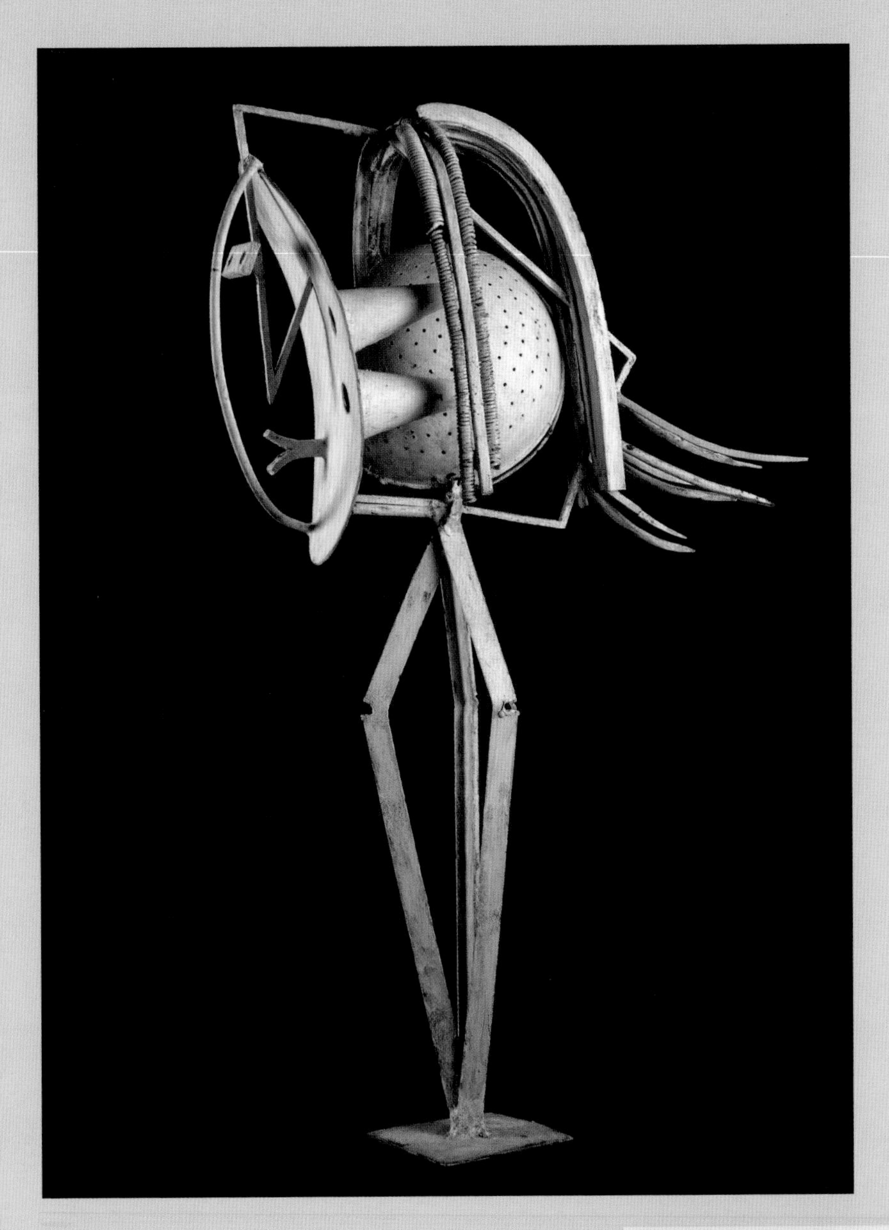

Right
The Crucifixion, *1932*
Ink on paper, 34 x 51 cm (13.5 x 20 in). Musée Picasso, Paris

This work is part of a series of ink drawings based on Matthias Grünewald's famous crucifixion panel of *The Temptation of Saint Anthony* from the Isenheim Altarpiece (Musée d'Unterlinden, Colmar, c. 1515), but metamorphosed into an eerie skeletal structure that demonstrates Picasso's obsession with bones.

Chapter 17

The Spectacle of Violence: Guernica and the Spanish *Corridas* of 1933-37

As an Andalusian born in Málaga – the ancient city of the *Corrida* – Picasso's images of bullfighting make ideal reference points to Spanish cultural identity in *Guernica*. In a letter to *The New York Times* in 1937, Picasso denounced General Francisco Franco's military insurrection by declaring that his most recent works "clearly express my abhorrence of the military caste, which has sunk Spain in an ocean of pain and death".[1] Picasso's most blatantly political work condemning Franco was a series of etchings *The Dream and Lie of Franco* (January–June 1937), in which the political tyrant is depicted as a monstrously ugly, vainglorious and cruel bigot. Here, Picasso expresses his outrage at the cruelties, chaos and calamities foisted upon ordinary Spanish citizens by using the iconography of the bullfight, as well as reaffirming the artist's belief in the power of art as an "instrument of war for attack and defence against the enemy".[2]

Despite expressing Picasso's "abhorrence of war and brutality", *Guernica* nevertheless treats ritualistic violence and death as omnipresent and natural spectacles, an approach seen in the proliferation of bullfighting images in his work between the years of 1933 and 1937. However, they become more persistent in 1934–35, following three successive trips to Spain with his wife Olga Koklova and his son Paulo to visit bullfights. They also coincide with the final dramatic collapse of Picasso's marriage. The cruel and emotional turmoil of Olga's discovery of Picasso's and Marie-Thérèse Walter's affair, and subsequent pregnancy, finally led to her leaving the artist and taking their son with her. The whole torrid affair appears to haunts *Bullfight: the Death of the Female Torero* (1933). The wounded yet magnificent beast collapses on its haunches through the sheer weight of exhaustion, accompanied by horse and female torero riding on the animal's back. With blood in its mouth and weapons piercing its hump, the bull is in its final death-throes. With her arms flung back, her limp, naked body suggests that she is not quite dead, but in a post-coital ecstasy. The stallion's whinnying neck, draped in the torero's crimson scarf, symbolizes that the *coup de grâce* has been dealt.

This confusion of identities would soon be annexed by the Surrealists and subsumed under the rubric of the bull-man of Greek legend in the Surrealist periodical *Minotaure* 1933. Man Ray's *Minotaur* represents this famous Surrealist incarnation, the head of a bull defined by the missing torso and arms of a woman. Earlier, in 1931–32, Picasso created a bronze *Head of a Bull* (see page 154), with dark, deep-pitted eyes, mouth and nostrils, as well as a massive skull with large protruding horns and ears. The head, cut from the body and designed to lie on the floor, becomes a sacrificial victim, and with its tragic, half-grinning physiognomy and countenance, is highly evocative of a Minotaur character. Bull's heads are also found in bars and bullfighting institutions all over Spain, and such objects are reminders of this ancient Mediterranean cult and culture.

Picasso was a frequent visitor to bullfights. He was great friends with the famous matador, Luis Miguel Dominguín, and undoubtedly knew and discussed the technical and symbolic character of the bullfight with his aficionados. Picasso and Dominguín were photographed together in 1955 (see page 137) with the artist playing bull for the camera, and practising or discussing the technical aspects of an attack. In *Bullfight: Death of the Torero* of 1933 (see page 154), Picasso's dark-haired hero is carried along on the back of a bull. With his eyes and mouth wide open, the matador is almost certainly dead or dying. His cape, used in a dance with death to court the bull, illustrates his undoing and has become a genuine river of blood, which cascades on to the sand below. Here, roles are reversed and the matador, symbolized by the undulating folds of his blood red cape, receives the *coup de grâce* in the form of a sexual climax. Most notable of all are the symbolic colours of flags flying in the breeze of the arena, and informing us that this is a Spaniards' painting depicting the Spanish national fiesta. It was in all likelihood Francisco José de Goya's disturbing Tauromaquia prints of 1816 and his painting *Death of the Picador* (1793) that seduced Picasso into depicting the violent themes based on the bullfight, and the artist may even have seen Goya's intricate oil painting when it was auctioned in Paris in December 1933. Goya's painting includes the same motifs and details, such as the sun-soaked arena, blue sky, the picadors' embroidered suits and an excited crowd hiding in the shade on the left.

These subjects also derive from the Cretan ritual and image of an acrobat leaping over a bull (see page 154) and ancient myths, rites and cults of Mithraism and the Minotaur. Picasso's collage of this ancient mythological beast even fronted Breton's Surrealist periodical *Minotaure* in 1933, playing with the animalistic side of man by using its Cretan relation. It was the virility, power and pathos of the Minotaur that interested Picasso the most. Picasso-the-Minotaur, the bull and bullfighter would often switch guises, with the artist portraying himself as a reveller, as a beast who dominates or subjugates others, and suffers himself. The bull's status as a mythological creature – as a sacrificial victim and a giver of life – is therefore crucial to the symbolism of the *corrida*. The cult of Mithras, Persian god of light, flourished in the late Roman Empire and had as its central ceremony the sacrifice of the bull. Altars such as that of the *Mithraic Altar* in San Clemente, Rome, illustrate the legend of Mithras, who, on the instruction of the sun god Apollo, thrust his sword into the spine of the bull to release a flow of blood, which became the wellspring of all life on Earth.

It is worth remembering that Picasso was born on shores close to Carthage, Phoenicia and Gilgamesh, home to ancient cultures with their bloody rites and rituals. Mithraism also shares the ritual of the consummation of flesh and blood with Christianity and Catholicism. Christian ceremonies reflect the custom in other religions of the ritual killing of a king, or at least, an animal substitute to act out symbolically the process of rebirth, regeneration and resurrection. Picasso certainly knew and understood this creation myth and its connection with the rituals of bullfighting and the Christian symbolism of sacrifice. In Picasso's painting *Crucifixion* of 1930 (see page 155), Christ becomes the sacrificial bull, whose side is pierced with a *pica* by a picador on horseback, in an image that suggests that he is the victim of animal brutality.

Of course all these cultural and religious references are present in *Guernica* by means of dramatic poses and expressive countenances, in particular those of the four wailing and despairing women who heighten the pathos of this tragedy. They also make allusions to cultural, religious and historical themes with which the spectator is usually familiar: "The Massacre of the Innocents" (the mother howling in despair over the body of her dead baby); traditional battles scenes (filled with armed soldiers, startled horses, corpses and broken lances); "The Crucifixion" (the dead matador/soldier lying in a cruciform pose on the ground and the grieving women wringing their hands); "The Last Judgement" (the burning woman falling into a hole at the right of the picture) and, in particular, the bullfight itself. Notably, sacrificial bulls were conventional illustrations on sarcophagi, and Picasso's main purpose was to honour the 1,600 people massacred in the bombing of Guernica, as well as those being slaughtered each day during the Spanish Civil War. *Guernica* has its roots in Spanish art, politics and culture; in mythological, historical or religious themes, such as wars, massacres, battles, rituals, crucifixion and pagan sacrifice, which were intrinsic to Picasso's identity as a Spaniard, and in the psychological or unconscious drives surrounding the events of his private life. A work of art such as *Guernica*, then, can never truly represent culture without drawing upon personal conflicts or interests of identity. These are inseparable from the artist's work.

---

1 Picasso, quoted in *The New York Times*, 19 December 1937.

2 Simone Téry, "Picasso n'est pas officier dans l'Armée française", *Les Lettres françaises*, 24 March 1945. In Dore Ashton, *Picasso on Art: A Selection of Views*, Thames and Hudson, London, 1972, p. 149.

Guernica, *1937*

Oil on canvas, 349.5 x 776 cm (137.5 x 305.5 in). Museo Nacional Centro de Arte Reina Sofia, Madrid

Picasso's monumental mural *Guernica* (see above), which was painted to mark the tragic events surrounding the saturation bombing of the town by a Nazi Condor Legion on 26 April 1937, does not conform entirely to ideas relating to the artist's opposition to fascism and war. Despite drawing Picasso ever closer towards heightened political engagement, *Guernica*'s central motif is, in part, derived from the Spanish *Corrida*. Some of the elements of the painting suggest a bullfighting scene symbolizing the brutal struggle between reason and chaotic animal passions, cruelty and violence. A mutilated and dying horse writhes in agony, a huge diamond-shaped gash in its flank and a lance piercing its mid-rift; a bull, standing apart from the battle, is victorious and perhaps a totem of the Spanish people; a soldier or matador lies floored and disembodied in the foreground, his hand clutching a broken sword. Picasso introduces three weeping, wounded and wailing women into his work: one cradles and laments the limp body of her dead child, another burns to death in a flaming building, while a lone female, who perhaps cannot find her child among all the chaos, drags an injured and flayed-looking leg across the foreground. *Guernica* reflects the horror of the bombing by using archetypal and symbolic motifs that express a wide range of human experiences and emotions. Picasso's *grisalle* colour scheme and

newsprint-like effects on the horse's flanks demonstrates that he had not forgotten his pre-war Cubism and that he had experienced the event from a distance, and through black-and-white photographs in newspapers and films.

Opposite, top left

Head of a Bull, *1931–32*

Bronze (unique cast), 35 x 55 x 53 cm (13.5 x 21.5 x 21 in).
Musée Picasso, Paris

Sculptural works like this bull's head had a much deeper significance for Picasso as sinister totems, emblems of death, or as powerful intercessionary accomplices. The bull appears to be smiling, but on closer inspection, the skin has started to decay and one senses bone beneath the flesh of the animal.

Opposite, top right

Bull and Acrobat, *1600–1450 BC*

Bronze, height 11 cm (4.5 in). British Museum, London

This tiny Cretan bronze was possibly a source of identity for the Andalusian and part of the inspiration for many of Picasso's bullfighting scenes. It is undoubtedly the ideal image of the bullfighter asserting his mastery, might and skill over the charging and terrifying mythical creature.

Opposite, bottom

Bullfight: the Death of the Female Torero, *1933*

Oil and pencil on wood, 30 x 40 cm (11.8 x 15.7 in).
Musée Picasso, Paris

Extreme violence often punctuates Picasso's work during the years 1933–37, and bullfighting scenes or cruel animal passions proliferate Picasso's painting. This beautiful and dreamy, but tragic-looking, image would be transposed into the subject of Picasso's famous painting *Guernica* in 1937.

Below

Crucifixion, *1930*

Oil on plywood, 51.5 x 66.5 cm (20.5 x 26 in).
Musée Picasso, Paris

This is one of the most intense and powerful religious images ever painted by the artist and recalls, once more, Grünewald's Isenheim Altarpiece as the ultimate image of suffering and cruelty. In this group the final death blow is issued by a picador on horseback.

Chapter 18

Classicism, Death and Magical Transformations, 1938–48

In 1937, Picasso took possession of an enormous new studio in the rues des Grands Augustines, and it soon began to fill up with earlier vestiges of his creative life at Boisgeloup. One of these was *Head of Dora Maar* (1941, see page 159), an 80 cm (30 in) tall sculpture, which would later be placed in the square of Saint Germain-des-Prés as a monument to his great friend Guillaume Apollinaire. Picasso had met Dora Maar (whose real name was Markovitch Henriette Dora) in 1936 when she was working as a professional photographer in Paris, and almost immediately she became his lover and muse. Dora is often identified as the image of a woman emerging from the window with a lamp in *Guernica* (see Chapter 17) and, unsurprisingly, Roland Penrose, a friend and witness to their romance recalled, "the variety of ways in which the presence and intelligence of Dora Maar nourished Picasso's inspiration".[1] The sculptor Alberto Giacometti recalled visiting Picasso during its creation and remarked on "all the extraordinary changes and transformations it went through".[2] *Head of Dora Maar* is something of an exception because Picasso produced few sculptures during 1933–1941. It was carved in Picasso's bathroom, a makeshift sculpture studio, because fuel shortages during the Second World War made heating difficult and, given the Occupation of Paris, death and oppression were probably very much on the artist's mind at the time. In Boisgeloup, Picasso had explored a similar approach in a series of heads (based on the countenance of Marie-Thérèse Walter), executed between 1930–31, and recalling a number of neo-classical paintings from the 1920s (see Chapter 13). Like many of Picasso's drawn, painted and sculpted heads of his lover, *Head of a Woman* (*Marie-Thérèse*, see page 160) has distinctly phallic properties: the protruding forehead and tumescent nose running down the face strongly recalls the fertility masks of which the artist owned, such as a Baga mask from Guinea, and idols like the Neolithic Venus of Lespugue, which he undoubtedly knew. The merging of tribal sources and classical serenity gives *Head of a Woman* a hieratic quality associated with fertility goddesses and supposed magical properties relating to *art nègre* by artists and intellectuals of Picasso's generation. Many other sculptures from this period, such as *Woman with a Vase* (1933, see page 161), are associated with commemorating Apollinaire. The massive sculpture, depicting a woman proffering a vase as a sacramental gesture, blends together youth, femininity, fertility, old age and death. Picasso gives his fertility goddess a pregnant, swelling body, and juxtaposes signs of youth with aged, battered, bony and withered limbs. Shortly after Picasso's death, a cast of *Woman with a Vase* was placed over his grave in the garden of Château de Vauvenargues, presumably in accordance with the artist's express wishes.

It may be significant then that Picasso's finest sculpture of the period, *Death's Head* (1943, see page 162), represents a skull that is partly flesh and bone, situated in between Picasso's living quarters and his studio, perhaps as a reminder of death's ever-present shadow. It is notable that a large number of the artist's paintings dating from the outbreak of the Second World War, including *Still life with Steer's Skull* (1942, see page 162) and *Monument to the Spanish Dead*, commemorating Picasso's fellow countrymen who died in the War, treat the subject of death in terms of a sombre *memento mori*. As Picasso told the photographer Brassaï, "It doesn't matter which bone you look at, you'll always find the trace of fingers".[3]

Picasso's preoccupation with the bony armature of the human or animal body, with bones, skulls and skeletons, appear in a number of sculptures where the interior armature of the constituent objects is like bone beneath flesh and, as such, becomes a symbol of death. In the sculptures *Woman in a Long Dress* (1943), *The Pregnant Woman* and *The Goat* (both 1950), and *Woman with a Key* (1954), the *bricolage* objects are on display through the exterior plaster, thus revealing the essential bones of the structure. *Woman with a Key* originally had the right arm hanging by interlocking rings from the shoulder of the figure (presumably so it could be extracted or moved backwards and forwards), whereas *Woman in a Long Dress* (see page 162) was cast from a dressmaker's dummy and a tribal artefact of a wooden arm and hand, apparently from the Easter Islands. These objects held magical and transformative properties for Picasso, as did many artefacts in the artist's possession, for he later re-used the Easter Islands arm, accompanied by the saddle of *Head of a Bull*, for a photograph by Brassaï in 1943–46 (see page 158) to create the image of death by means of a floored matador after a bullfight.

Magical and transformative themes are also intrinsic to Picasso's large painting *La Cuisine* (*The

1 Roland Penrose, *Picasso: His Life and Work*, p. 304.
2 Andre Forge interviewed by Cathy Courtney, in *Artists Lives Collection: National Life Story Project*, Hyman Kreitman Research Centre for the Tate Library, London, 1995, p. 347. Cited in Peter Read, Picasso and Apollinaire, Chapter 30, "Head of Dora Maar", p. 227.
3 Brassaï, *Picasso and Company*, Translated by Francis Price, Garden City, New York, Doubleday, 1966 [originally published, 1964], p. 74.

Kitchen) of 1948 (see page 163), the design of which appears striking when compared to a number of cabalistic diagrams used in the rituals of white and black magic. The rhythmical patterns, shapes and symbols, in particular the artist's use of lines, dots, circles and arrow-like formations, strongly evoke the strange calligraphy employed to cast spells or conjure-up demons in texts on ceremonial magic.

La Cuisine's schematization, a mass of lines and symbols in what is probably the most abstract painting that Picasso ever created, combines appropriately with his statement concerning the conjuring of an image "made out of nothing", which implies some kind of sorcery. The artist's inclusion of his pet birds, the owl and doves, which are often associated with Pagan and Christian magic, are coupled with the kitchen theme, and therefore frame it as a place of alchemy. Peter Read describes *La Cuisine* as a "pictorial monument" to the poet and the Holocaust.[4] Painted on 9 November 1948, the work appears to commemorate the poet Apollinaire, who had died 30 years to the day of its conception. Its highly schematic design and calligraphy, composed of sombre-looking black, white and grey lines, circles, dots and arrows, can also be compared to spell books, cabalistic diagrams and ceremonial magic of the kind beloved by Max Jacob who, like Apollinaire, dabbled in magic, mysticism and the occult. In this context, *La Cuisine* is possibly a *memento mori* to Max Jacob, who had died a few years earlier, a victim of the Nazi regime, in a concentration camp at Drancy on 5 March 1944. Evocative of Apollinaire's *Le poète assassiné* (1916), it too is a work "made out of nothing". Interestingly, Picasso was never actually able to fulfil the demands of a conventional tombstone monument for the Apollinaire committee, or place a sculpture on his friend's grave, and this unfinished project unexpectedly gave birth to a "phantom tomb". The Saint-Germain-des-Prés monument sat undisturbed in its square for 40 years. On the night of 30 March 1999, however, it vanished. It was later found, restored and returned to its plinth. "For three years, however, Apollinaire had been honoured in Saint-Germain-des-Prés, by a stone plinth, bearing, literally, a monument made of nothing".[5] The incident was, in the strangest way, a kind of fulfilment of the prestidigitation between the two friends, but also of the magical persona that Picasso and Apollinaire liked to transmit. If Picasso gave the impression of being a sorceror's apprentice, Apollinaire was "a magus and a prophet… Linked by a pact with all sacred animals, he knew all the gods and could make all the magic potions".[6]

---

4 Peter Read, *Picasso and Apollinaire*, p. 214
5 Ibid, p. 247.
6 Louis Aragon, "Oraison funèbre," SIC, January and February 15 1919, p. 283. Cited and translated in Peter Read, *Picasso and Apollinaire*, p. 135.

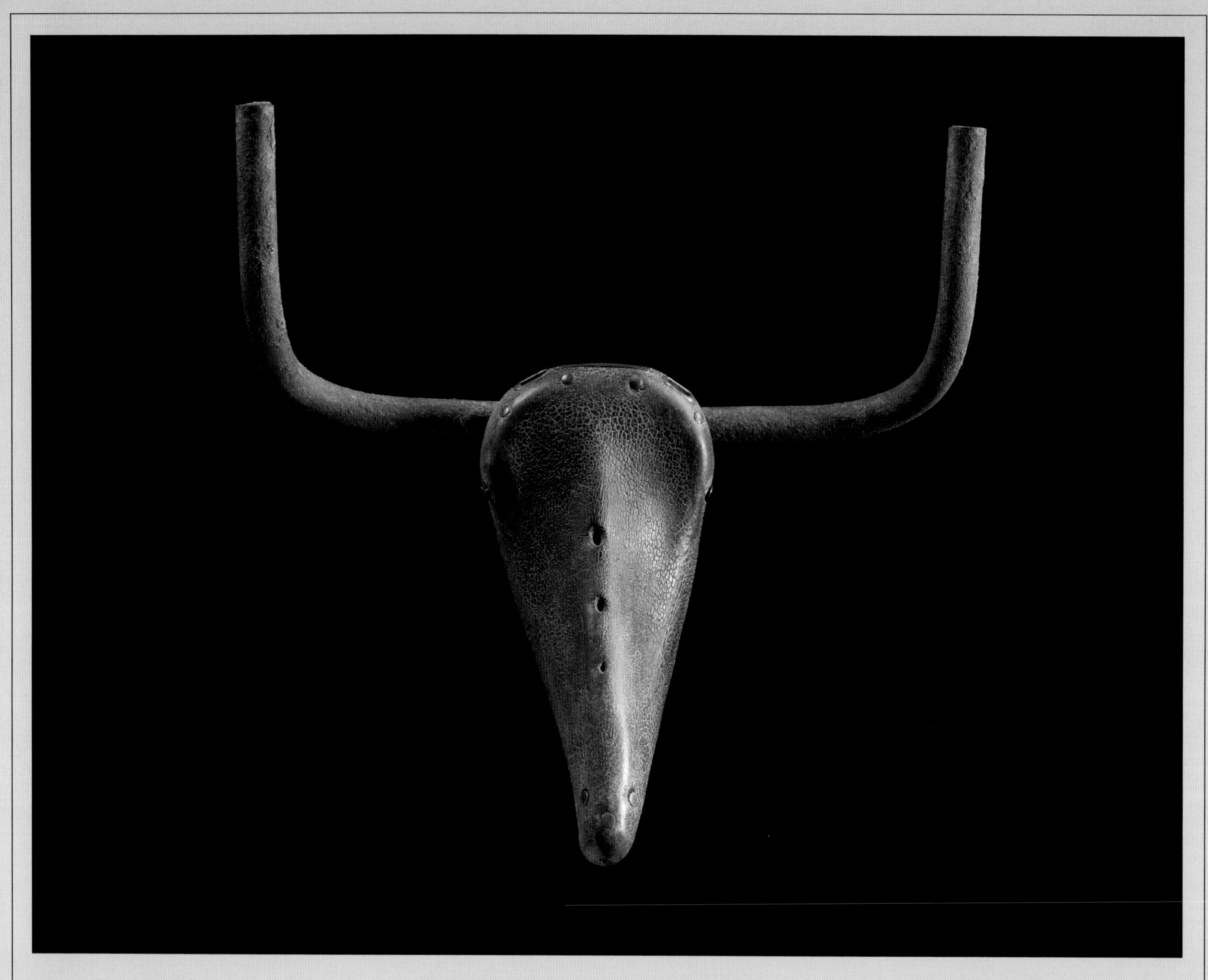

Head of a Bull, *1942*

Bicycle saddle and handlebars (leather and metal), 33.3 x 43.5 x 19 cm (13.1 x 17.1 x 7.4 in). Musée Picasso, Paris

Head of a Bull (see above) was created from a bicycle saddle and handlebars, roughly soldered together, and later cast in bronze. The bronze was published on the cover of *La Conquête du par Monde L'Image* in 1942, and was one of five sculptures exhibited at a retrospective of Picasso's work at the Liberation Salon in Paris in 1944. Picasso's somewhat inconsistent recollection of how the sculpture came into being is typical of his shamanistic attitude towards sculpture and art in his later years. The artist often recalled finding these objects by chance: one in a tip, another picked up on his way home from a funeral. Picasso was highly attached to this sculpture and his son, Claude Ruiz-Picasso, claimed that the artist saw the finished bronze as the true sculpture. Picasso often spoke about the role his work played in channelling things, forces and the surrounding elements when he asserted that "the artist is a receptacle for emotions that come from all over the place: from the sky, from the earth, from a scrap of paper, from a passing shape, from a spider's web".[7] Picasso's story about how the *Head of a Bull* magically came to be is no different, and his accounts vary quite considerably regarding its conception. On one occasion, much later in life, Picasso claimed that he immediately "imagined" its constituent objects as a bull's head, and stated that a cyclist would one day find his assemblage in a dump and alternatively see his work as a set of handlebars and a saddle. This, of course, is a prerequisite for magic, pseudo-magical ceremonies and magical thinking. The fact that the original bicycle parts were found in separate rooms during an inventory of his estate, and subsequently put back together using the bronze cast as a guide reinforces Picasso's "double metaphor" in framing his most cherished assemblage sculpture. Picasso also recounted how, having meditated on the two objects during the funeral service, Picasso returned later to pick them up and carry them home. The sculpture may therefore have been a fitting *memento mori* to his old friend Julio González, who died on 27 March 1942. Picasso was the principal mourner at his funeral and it is worth remembering that his fellow Spaniard taught him how to weld, aiding the artist with many of his most important sculptures during 1932. *Bull's Head* must surely be associated with González for Picasso painted three very Spanish-looking still lifes, recalling traditional *memento mori* themes of a steer's skull on a table (see page 62), shortly after his friend's sad demise on 6 April 1942.

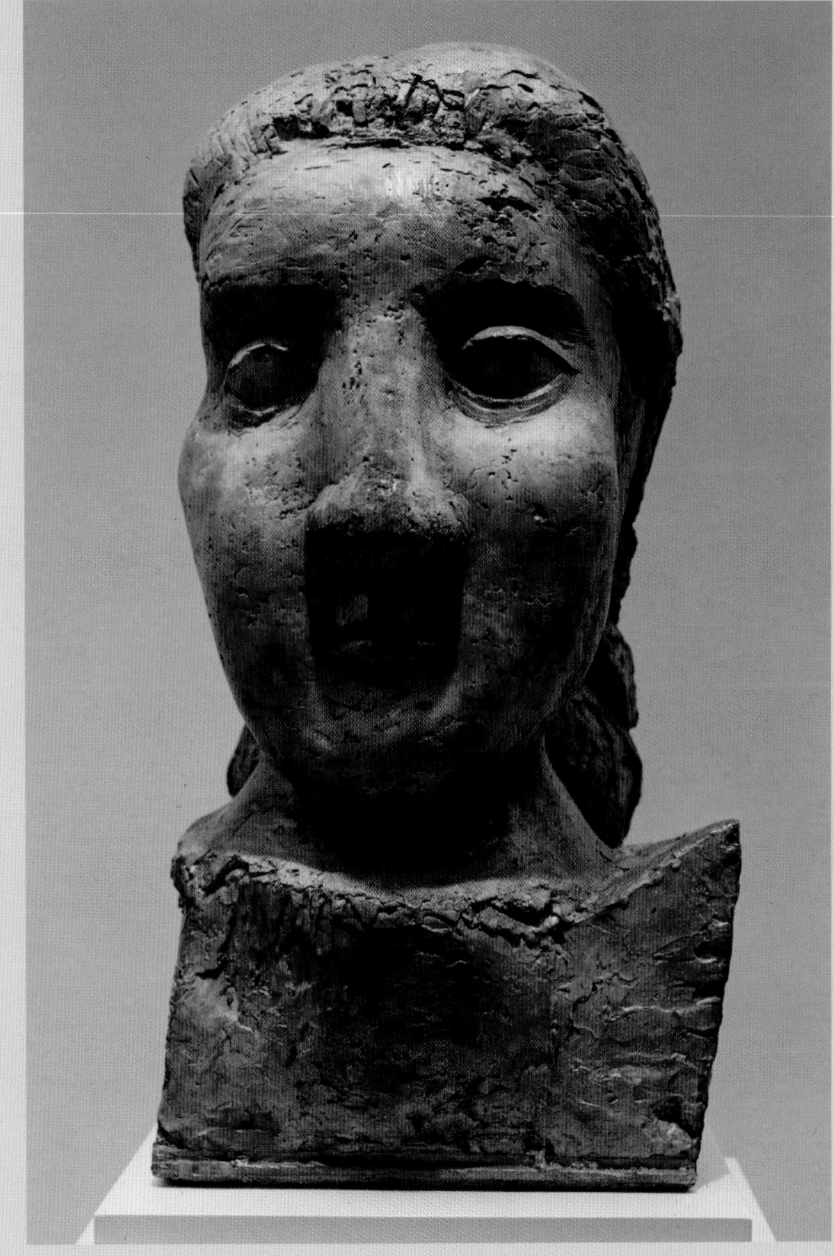

Above left
Monument for Apollinaire (Head of Dora Maar) in Saint-Germain-des-Prés, Paris

Friends and admirers (including Picasso) gather annually to commemorate the poet's death. The work finally came to symbolize the poetry, magic and mysticism of Picasso's work when, on 30 March 1999, it mysteriously disappeared and then reappeared after a number of years of gracing the picturesque Parisian square of Saint-Germain-des-Prés.

Above right
Head of Dora Maar, *1941*
Plaster, 80 x 42 x 55 cm (31.5 x 16.5 x 21.5 in).
Ludwig Museum Cologne

The work that was finally chosen for Apollinaire's tomb was this plaster sculpture of *Head of Dora Maar*, later cast in bronze, which was originally carved in Picasso's bathroom – the only room that the artist could heat during wartime in his Grands Augustine flat.

Opposite
Head of a Woman (Marie-Thérèse), *1930–31*
Cement, 78 x 44.5 x 50 cm (30.5 x 17.5 x 19.5 cm).
Musée Picasso, Paris

The highly phallic treatment of the head and tumescent nose of Picasso's female suggests that she is some kind of fertility goddess. The broken-looking shoulders and chipped sections around the breasts certainly give the work the hieratic dignity of an ancient temple statue.

Above
Woman with a Vase, *1933*
Bronze, 219 x 122 x 110 cm (86 x 48 x 43.5). Museo Nacional Centro de Arte Reina Sofia, Madrid

Picasso's masterpiece sculpture of the period is *Woman with a Vase*. Its relationship to the painting *Guernica*, and to death and mourning, is undeniable since the cement cast of this sculpture was actually placed outside (*Guernica* was inside) the Spanish pavilion at the Exposition Internationale in 1937.

Above left

Still life with Steer's Skull, *1942*

Oil on canvas, 117 x 89 cm (46 x 35 in). Pinacoteca di Brera, Milan, Donazione Emilio e Maria Jesi

The effect of this piece is one of gore and carnage, with the ram's flayed skull expressed by means of thickly modelled and streaked red paint. The black, deeply pitted eye sockets suggest brutality and suffering, while the wide-open mouth seems to utter hellish screams from the bloodstained tablecloth.

Top right

Death's Head, *1943*

Bronze, 25 x 21 x 32 cm (10 x 8.5 x 12.5 in). Musée Picasso, Paris

Skulls, skeletons and bones were of immense fascination to Picasso, as was his love of anatomy. Numerous drawings, paintings and sculptures are reminiscent of Vesalius's sixteenth-century anatomical engravings, which open up the human body so as to record its secret contents.

Above

Woman in a Long Dress, *1943*

Bronze, 161 x 50 x 36.5 cm (63.5 x 19.5 x 14.5 in). Estate of Mark Goodson, New York. Private Collection

With its assembled hand and arm, *Woman in a Long Dress* is one of a number of sculptures that explore the use of real objects in the casting process revealing Picasso's continued dependence upon *objects trouvé* (found objects) lying around the studio environment or the grounds of his home.

Above

La Cuisine (The Kitchen), *1948*

Oil on canvas, 175 x 252 cm (69 x 99 in). Musée Picasso, Paris

This work is clearly related to Picasso's *The Charnel House* (1945), depicting a family group's bodies massacred and piled up on the kitchen floor. The artist suggests absence, loss and sadness through near abstraction and the cat's cradle of lines, and by sombre, deeply symbolic, coloration.

Chapter 19

Picasso's Late Sculpture, 1942–61

Woman with a Key (*The Madame*) of 1954 stands apart from the works that Picasso created at Le Fournas, the large disused perfume factory in Vallauris, which gave the artist ample space to store, create and hoard numerous quantities of objects and materials that he needed to make sculpture. All the components of *Woman with a Key* were made from kiln furniture, arranged on the floor, cast in bronze and later welded together. The key, originally a leafy branch, was a rather late addition to the sculpture and, like the famous *Head of a Bull*, it was a classic case of using *objet trouvés* (found objects) to create the assemblage sculpture. To make the head, the artist pieced together fire bricks, originally intended to line the inside of an oven: a long curved, fire clay kiln prop (a *gazelle*) formed the body. Meanwhile, the limbs were composed of hollow, fired-clay sticks and a pierced, circular stand, usually designed to separate wares in the kiln. Thus the intervening spaces created by these objects signified the dress and fulsome bosom of this ancient-looking goddess. *Woman with a Key* has traditionally been described as the keeper of a brothel because her original title *La taulière* is a French colloquialism for "The Madame", as well as being seen as a priestess or goddess. Yet since she was born of fire (from the kiln), perhaps she may be seen as a protector of the fiery underworld? The key she holds so purposefully, her costume-armour and hammer-like arm do indeed suggest a sinister guardian, a jailer or some evil procuress. Furthermore, the key is reminiscent of the bather paintings that Picasso executed in 1928 of a figure holding a key to a cabin, and is perhaps a secret celebration of his passionate and highly illicit affair with the nineteen-year-old Marie-Thérèse Walter. Alternatively, Elizabeth Cowling claims that the sculpture is directly related to the artist's new muse Sylvette David. Whoever the sculpture portrays, it is clearly linked to the *bricolage* character of his other sculptures, created in the 1950s, and occupies a crucial position within Picasso's oeuvre, because it represents the long-standing subject of the interrelationships between the artist, his model and medium.

In 1954, Picasso began making folded sheet metal sculptures after meeting Tobias Jellinek and the young Sylvette David: the former became his temporary assistant, the latter his new muse and the subject of numerous drawings, paintings and planar iron sculptures. Many of the artist's works, such as *Sylvette* (1954), imitate folded-screen panels so as to illustrate multiple viewpoints, and combine feigned naivety with a complex, full representation of the human head. The creation of *Woman* (Cannes, 1961, see page 166) and Picasso's other crucial sheet-metal sculptures during this period originated when the sculptor met Lionel Prejger at Golfe-Juan in 1946. Prejger ran scrap dealership and metal tubing manufacturer businesses in Cannes and Vallauris. Picasso's creativity and sculptural output at this time was astounding, and conceived in great volumes, which he could only have previously achieved in sketches, paintings, or in his imagination. Working in three-dimensions as abundantly as he had done in two-dimensions must have pleased Picasso greatly, and the artist was jubilant because he could make sculptures in quantities that he had always imagined. Picasso could also continue to undermine conventional categories and processes in sculpture. He indulged in his much-loved *bricolage* techniques, and approached this new type of three-dimensional work with an entirely spontaneous and inventive spirit.

The cutting and folding of sheet metal for Picasso's *Woman* was supervised under the auspices of the skilled craftsman Joseph-Marius Tiola, who was well acquainted with Picasso, having worked with him in 1957. Created from a paper maquette, *Woman* was soon transformed into a sculpture through industrial processes, with the results of oxidization and spatial alignment clearly evident when viewing the work from different angles. From the front, *Woman* appears relaxed, as if the figure is resting an arm and pausing for someone. However, from the back, she seems restless, her expression troubled as if seeking answers to unknown questions, and her concertina arm looking less like a weapon, more like the shattered wing of a wounded creature. Picasso's dual design and doubling establishes an ever-recurring transmogrification that naturally relies on the asymmetry of the sculptor's three-panel composition.

The three-dimensional effects of *Woman* clearly show the latter's dependence on the Cubist idiom. The origins for creating sheet-metal sculpture lie in the cut-out silhouettes that Picasso made with scissors as a form of entertainment for his family from an early age, through the inventiveness, productivity and speed of his scissor techniques. Picasso's interest in this craft-based practice was intimately associated with childhood, and undoubtedly derived from observing the women in his family embroidering. Even the avant-garde character and logic of his synthetic collage work from this period, namely the famous cardboard *Guitar* of October 1912, depended on the skilful handicraft associated with tailoring patterns in dress-making. Other constructive forerunners for *Woman*, apart from his Cubist sculptures, were the theatrically inspired pop-up books from the mid to late nineteenth century, which Picasso would have seen and perhaps played with as a child. Naturally, then, the spaces and constructive language of *Woman* must have evoked childhood memories and, to a degree, gave new meaning to the concept of artistic play as a driving force behind Picasso's Synthetic Cubism. This is especially true of the playful characteristics of his Cubist *papiers collés* and *papiers épinglés*, which revolutionized the concept of materials in sculpture and the idea of *bricolage* as a sign of the artisan at play. Here we should also acknowledge the keen interest attracted by Henri Matisse's brightly coloured *papiers découpés* (see page 169). Matisse was Picasso's great artistic rival and the mercurial and highly competitive Spaniard was often jealous of the Frenchman's brilliantly inventive, vibrant and playfully spontaneous *découpage* techniques.

These fruitful relationships not only pre-empted Picasso's late folded sheet-metal sculpture, but forced the sculptor to pay closer attention to his contemporaries, as well as to re-examine his previous Cubist discoveries. Matisse's pasted paper cut-outs clearly left their mark on several of Picasso's late sheet-iron and steel sculptures on both a small and a monumental scale, especially on the gigantic *Head* for the Civic Centre Plaza in Chicago (1967) and *Head of a Woman* at Figaro Park in Halmstad, Sweden (1971), which reveal the organic process of making paper cut-outs and suggest the ancient art of origami. Gilot argues that many of the late pole sculptures and angled sheet-metal cut-outs, such as *Head of a Woman* (1957), *Standing Woman*, *Woman with Tray and Bowl*, *Woman and Child* and the famous *Seated Pierrot* (all 1961) should also be viewed within the context of Picasso's "longstanding identification with *l'art nègre*". The sculptures draw inspiration from the wooden totem poles of Pacific Northwest Coast tribes, African Fang masks, Pueblo Indian *Kachina* dolls and, in particular, the life-size Fon Statue of *Gu, God of War and Blacksmiths* from the Republic of Benin, which is highly evocative of Picasso's *Woman with a Key*.

After 1964, Picasso ceased making fresh maquettes or newly constructed works, although monumental versions of his sculptures continue to exist (notably those by Carl Nesjar, such as the large construction *Head of a Woman*, at Kristinehamn, Sweden, 1965). The 1960s thus signalled an end to Picasso's career as a sculptor, yet continue to be a fascinating subject of study. In the final analysis, the later works provided important evidence of the key interrelationships between Picasso's earlier drawing, painting and sculpture. How Picasso's sheet metal works were created is still a highly complex and fascinating subject and, up until recently, a little understood area of the artist's sculpture.

Assemblage sculptures

During the mid-1940s and early 1950s, Picasso continued to make use of miscellaneous items, metal pieces and *objets trouvés* (found objects) to create assemblage sculptures, such as *Head of a Bull* (1942), *The Venus of Gas* (1945), *The Goat* (1950), *Baboon and Young* (1951), *The Crane* (1951–52), *Little Owl* (1951), *The Glass* (1952–53) and *Woman with a Key* (1954, see page 169). These works were more or less akin to the facture and *bricolage* techniques used in his early Cubist sculptures, and a process defined by the anthropologist Claude-Lévi-Strauss as having to "make do with whatever is at hand".[1] For example, Picasso's *The Venus of Gas* is nothing more than a scavenged burner from a gas stove; *The Glass* is built with the aid of a procured nail and ring; *Baboon and Young* (see page 167) derives from pilfering his son Claude's toy cars to create the head of the animal; and *The Crane* uses a spade, forks and a gas valve for the tail, crested head and bony legs/feet. Meanwhile, *Little Owl* is an assemblage of screws, nails and various metal objects, including the blade of a garden hoe and a pair of pliers. All these assemblage sculptures exchange the anatomy for a *bricolage* of objects, in which the tools literally form the armature of the human or animal body. Of course, the way in which many of these sculptures were created suggests a degree of humour and playfulness regarding their assemblage characteristics, and the *Little Owl* is a case in point.

1 Claude Lévi-Srauss, *The Savage Mind* (previously cited).

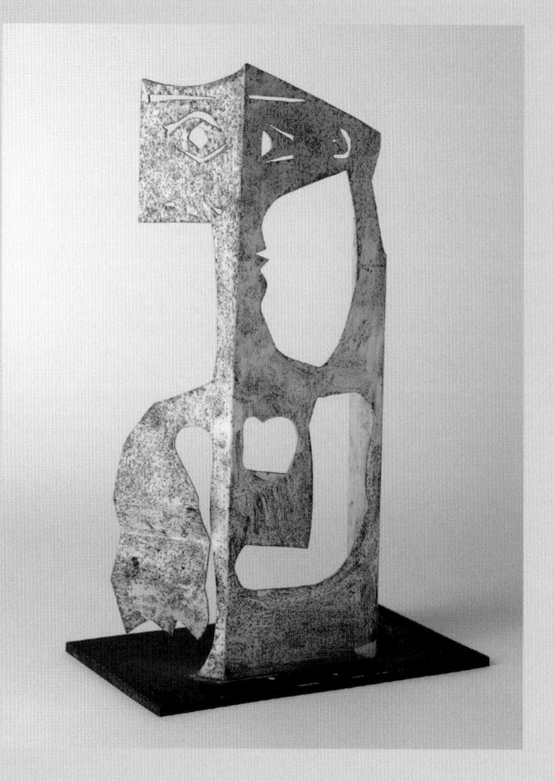

Left
Woman with a Key, *1954*
Bronze with stone base, 172 x 43 x 30 cm (67.5 x 17 x 12 in). Private Collection

This is one of the great sculptures Picasso created in the mid-1950s, and is typical of the *bricolage* nature of his late sculptures, which hinges together piecemeal components. Indeed, the work could not actually stand up and remained in fragments on the studio floor until it was cast and welded together.

Above
Woman, *1961*
Folded and painted sheet metal, 31 x 19.6 x 11.7 cm (12.2 x 7.7 x 4.6 in). Gift of Christine Ruiz-Picasso. Museo Picasso, Málaga

The magical transformation of a work of art constantly fascinated Picasso throughout his life and the child-like, toy paper cut-out characteristics of *Woman* are here exploited to disorientating effect in this sculpture. It uses Cubist spatial tricks to force the viewer to look through, around and at the work from various angles.

Opposite
Baboon and Young, *1951*
Bronze, 53 x 33 x 61 cm (21 x 13 x 24 in). Private Collection

This work incorporates *objets trouvés* (found objects). Toy cars form the baboon's head; a large pottery jar the vessel of the body. The ears are created out of two jar handles, the tail is formed from a car spring, and the rest is carved and modelled in plaster and wood.

Opposite
Head, *1967*
Steel, 15.2 m (15 ft). At the Chicago Civic Centre

When Picasso first envisioned sculpture on a giant scale in his painting *Monument: Head of a Woman*, in 1929, it was pure fantasy. And yet, the work was uncannily portentous in suggesting Picasso twenty-metre high Corten steel work, which, during the inauguration in August 1967, photographs showed swarms of tiny figures gazing in awe at Picasso's massive sculptural totem – *Head*.

Above left
Blue Nude, *1952*
Blue gouache on paper, cut and pasted on white paper, 112 x 73.5 cm (44 x 28.9 in). Musée National d'Art Moderne, Centre Georges Pompidou, Paris

Parallels can be drawn between Matisse's late *découpage* techniques and Picasso's sheet metal sculptures. In *Blue Nude*, Matisse allows the white background to act as space and recession, whilst the blue paper sections imply form and mass. Paper cutting was, for Matisse, like carving sculpture, and also characteristic of Picasso's late sheet metal works.

Above right

Seated Pierrot, *1961*
Cut-out, bent, assembled and painted sheet metal, 134.5 x 57 x 57 cm (53 x 22.5 x 22.5 in). Musée Picasso, Paris

A photograph of this sculpture in the process of execution, entitled *Picasso and Lionel Prejger with 'The Pierrot'*, shows the body in metal, but the arms still in paper and serving as a maquette. This records Picasso's methods of assembling the basic skeleton of a sculpture piece by piece.

Chapter 20

Painting the Old Masters: War and Peace, Life and Death, 1951–73

Picasso was in dialogue with some of the most celebrated Old Masters by 1957. Diego Velázquez's *Las Meninas* (1656, see page 173), depicting loyal subjects in the artist's studio at the court of King Philip IV in seventeenth-century Spain, inspired him to paint 45 variations in oil and 13 related works in around two months. Picasso was most probably drawn to the fascinating, beguiling and extraordinarily complex relationships created between the painter, the painted artist and the viewer in *Las Meninas*. As the art historian Jonathan Brown has suggested, "Critics, scholars, poets, playwrights, and philosophers all have tried to reach its essence, to provide a truly definitive explanation of its meaning, only to find that the picture has eluded the elaborate intellectual traps that they have set for it".[1] Picasso undoubtedly knew that the painting was not simply a factual document of courtly life, but an image about the representation, perception and engagement of the spectator. Picasso had known the painting as a young boy and paid it great attention in later life. The disquieting nature and arrested motion within Velázquez's interior, seen in the shadowy *aposentador* (Queen's chamberlain) standing on the backdoor steps and the Infanta Margarita transfixed by the moment, became something of a focus for Picasso in his many variations. In Picasso's version (see page 173), a giant Cubist figure represents Velázquez and the image of the shining Infanta perhaps pays tribute to his young sister, the blonde Conchita, who died tragically of diphtheria at the age of seven. Margarita and her retinue become the subject of the following 26 studies. The fact that the young girl is the chief protagonist of many of these canvases suggests that Picasso was meditating on both Conchita's death and his own mortality. In general, Picasso challenges the Spanish master on his own terms, by focusing, for example, on strange details such as the ceiling hooks, banishing Velázquez's murky interior and filling the room with light (by inventing shutters), or, switching historical characters for real-life ones. On one occasion, his own daughter Paloma is a stand-in for the young Margarita and his tiny dachshund "lump" replaces the family's huge mastiff. Picasso even changes the format of Velázquez's painting, opting for a landscape composition, a highly colourful palette and a level of complexity that recalls the painterly Cubist idioms used in his 1937 masterpiece *Guernica*.

Picasso's decision to invent such a challenging formula for his interpretation of Velázquez's painting was not a new idea, since the artist had long been in dialogue with the past. His 1928 paintings of *The Studio* and *Painter and Model*, depicting the paraphernalia-encumbered artist contemplating his subject, are comparable with both *Las Meninas* and Johannes Vermeer's *The Art of Painting*. *The Studio* and *Painter and Model* encapsulate many important characteristics of both masterworks, including: the iconography of the painter's brushes, the model and artist among the jumble of a studio filled with artistic accoutrements, light and shadow so as to become enigmatic variations on Vermeer and Velázquez's pictorial fancies. As Picasso famously stated, art is not necessarily bound up with reality but functions separately through various symbols, signs and abstractions: "Nature and art, being two different things cannot be the same thing. Through art we express our conception of what nature is not".[2]

Edouard Manet's *Le Déjeuner sur l'herbe* (*Luncheon on the Grass*, 1862–63, see page 174) was next in line to undergo a suite of variations during 1959–62, numbering around 27 paintings, 140 drawings, 18 cardboard sculptures (executed between 26 August and 31 August 1962) and three *linogravures*. Picasso knew Manet's painting well from his visits to Paris in the early years of the twentieth century, and would have without doubt been familiar with the work's role in the *succéss de scandale* at the Salon des Refusés of 1863, in which the naked and clothed figures, including the painter himself picnicking on the grass, parodied the theme of "sacred and profane love" in Titian's *Concert Champêtre* (c.1478–1510) in the Louvre with the intention of shocking audiences. Picasso explored the theme in a way that measured his own ability to lay claim to Old Master works by requisitioning, overlapping, melding and fashioning pictorial ideas relating to Titian's mysterious social gathering, Eugène Delacroix's odalisques in *Women of Algiers*, Paul Cézanne's large *Bather* paintings and, naturally, Manet's *Le Déjeuner sur l'herbe* itself. As the series evolved, it was clear that Picasso had not set out to create a finished work of art at all, but to explore the means by which an ongoing dialogue with Manet's painting would open out his work, slipping and sliding backward and forward with each new rendition as if fluidity and Terpsichorean shifts of intellect were his only real interest in transcribing the artist's picture. As Picasso explained to Françoise Gilot, "It's the movement of painting that interests me... the dramatic movement from one effort to the

---

1 Jonathan Brown, *Images and Ideal in Seventeenth-Century Spanish Art*, Princeton University Press, Princeton and New Jersey, 1978, Chapter 4, "On the Meaning of Las Meninas", p. 87.

2 Picasso, "Picasso Speaks: A Statement by the Artist", *The Arts*, New York, May 1923, Reprinted in Dore Ashton, *Picasso on Art: A Selection of Views*, London, Thames and Hudson, 1972, p. 3-6 [p. 3].

next… when the moment of my thought interests me more than the thought itself".[3]

Picasso's eulogies of great artists such as Manet, who himself paraphrased Old Master paintings, led him increasingly into a political arena. As we can see from studying Picasso's *Guernica* (1937, see Chapter 17), the *Charnel House* (1945), *Massacre in Korea* (1951, see pages 176–177), *War and Peace* (1952) and *Rape of the Sabine Women* (1962, see page 175), the artist adopted pacifist ideals and opposed Fascism, war and want. In particular, *Massacre in Korea* and *Rape of the Sabine Women* outline the Communist Party stance with regard to American involvement in the Korean War and, in the later years, the events surrounding the Cuban Missile Crisis. It was Manet who would again provide Picasso with the momentum for his futuristic aggressors, who appear as if they are about to execute a group of pregnant women and young children, and are derived in part from *The Execution of Maximillian* (1868) and Francisco de Goya's masterpiece *The 3rd of May 1808* (1814, see page 175), depicting the brutal slaughter of individuals by firing squad. Picasso's *Rape of the Sabine Women* clearly took its impetus from Nicolas Poussin's and Jacques-Louis David's well-known masterpieces by blending and conflating classical elements of both painters' works. Picasso also appears to make direct reference to the defiant indignation of the warmongers in Francisco Goya's *Dos Forasteros* (1821–22), as well as the hysterical compositional triangle of bodies in his earlier painting of *Bacchanal, after Poussin's "Triumph of Pan"* (1944).

Picasso therefore represents war in a much more encyclopaedic manner seen in a juxtaposition of Poussin's *Massacre of the Innocents* (c.1625), in which helpless mothers and children downtrodden by cruel, violent combatants, accompany the frenzied activity of the "*Triumph of Pan*", and a recollection of fighting between retreating German troops and Parisians during the Liberation of Paris in 1944. The warrior's giant knife in Picasso's *Rape of the Sabine Women* is more reminiscent of a ballistic missile than a simple stabbing weapon and perhaps illustrates the artist's response to a near nuclear catastrophe in the Cuban Missile Crisis. Malcolm H. Wiener's article on the Missile Crisis in *Apollo* cleverly observes that Picasso's first work in the "Rape" series, on 24 October 1962, coincided with the most difficult and tense stand-off between Soviet ships and submarines approaching the embargo lines. Picasso also explained to John Richardson that his work on this series, especially the final painting of January–February 1963, in which Picasso appeared as a combatant, had almost been the death of him. Picasso closely followed the Cuban Missile Crisis from his hilltop estate of Notre Dame de Vie near Mougins, and the troubled days of the Cold War obviously interrupted the peace, solitude and privacy of a home chosen to keep the outside world at bay.

Picasso's bid for isolation led to him becoming more reclusive and reliant on friends or the media to stimulate his interest enough to keep working. His work gradually began to show signs of deep self-reflection and an overt concern with voyeurism, pathos, old age and mortality. Fear of impotence and death – literally and artistically – in the final decade of his life, obsessed Picasso. Erotic fantasies of old men in the guise of past Masters (Balzac, Degas, Manet, Molière, Raphael, Rembrandt, Shakespeare and other costumed *dramatis personae*) lusting after or making love to beautiful young women in paintings and burlesque prints, such as *Venus and Love* (1968), are therefore numerous in quantity and artistic precedents.

Old Master predecessors are clearly visible in the figure paintings *Large Nude* (1964) and *Woman Playing with a Cat* (1969), relating to Picasso's favourite nude subjects, such as Titian's *Venus of Urbino* (1538), Goya's *The Nude Maja* (1797–1800), Ingres's *La Grande Odalisque* (1814) and Manet's *Olympia* (1863), all of which were appropriated to new interpretations of the theme of artist and model. In 1907, Picasso subjected the latter painting to the faceted language of a number of nude studies, as he had done for the infamous *Les Demoiselles d'Avignon*, which would lead to the new Cubist idiom. In June 1972, Pierre Daix, who had come to visit the artist to work on his book *The Cubist Years*, found Picasso more focused on present discoveries: "I did a drawing yesterday… and think maybe I touched on something. It's not like anything I've done before".[4] The drawing was the now famous 29 June *Self-portrait*, a hypnotic image of Picasso's own death-mask/head, in which every single feature – ears, lips, eyes, cheek bones – is sucked inwards to reveal a shrunken skull, etched out of a bold superstructure of black wax crayon. Death is the overriding human interest in Picasso's self-portrait: his cranium, created by a mass of jagged, graffiti-like marks, illustrates bone beneath flesh, a toothy rictus and a dark, physical presence that records life's ineffable ravages. Even the simian features of Picasso's self-portrait suggest an animalistic nature: the tragic and self-mocking character of old age grinning at Picasso's senescence. These "exorcism" drawings were his final act of introspection. In these works, he aimed at recording his physical frailty, his demise, as well as revealing the untouchable forces beyond corporeal being, thus performing a spiritual autopsy at the eleventh hour.

This was a typical shamanistic act by Picasso – projecting terror and vulnerability by using his image, nature and imagination to defy old age and to stave off a morbid fear of death. Defiant to the last, Picasso's intense productivity, emotional depth and wide-ranging creativity – often drawing upon the work of Old Masters – were to exert a lasting influence on subsequent generations of artists. As he later remarked, "We are heirs to Rembrandt, Velázquez, Cézanne, Matisse. A painter still has a father and a mother, he doesn't come out of nothingness".[5]

---

3 Françoise Gilot, *Life with Picasso*, p. 121.
4 Pierre Daix, *Picasso: Life and Art*, Translated by Olivia Emmet, New York, Harper Collins, Icon Editions, 1993, p. 368–69.
5 Picasso, "Picasso Speaks: A Statement by the Artist", in Ashton p. 4.

Women of Algiers, *1955*

Oil on canvas, 114 x 146 cm (44.8 x 57.4 in).
Collection of Mr. and Mrs. Victor Ganz, New York

During his long career as an artist, Picasso explored an astonishing variety of styles and media, often plundering the art of the past and present, not with any superficial intent, but to challenge the artistic masters he esteemed and envied so much. This was perhaps the longest and most fruitful part of his career and, confronted by the fear of death, he was astonishingly creative. Despite growing old, he was highly adept as a draftsman, painter, printmaker, theatre designer, ceramicist and sculptor. Faced by advancing age and by the fact that his work was no longer at the forefront of the avant-garde, as well as that of so many of the Old Masters he venerated – Velázquez, El Greco, Poussin, Vermeer, Rembrandt, Delacroix, Ingres, Courbet, Manet, to name but a few – he became increasingly concerned by his place within the "story" of art history. Picasso's desire to measure himself against the greatest masters came to fruition in 1947, when, at the behest of Georges Salles, director of the Museums of France, he placed a clutch of donated paintings alongside French and Spanish masters in the Louvre, including Eugène Delacroix's *Women of Algiers* (1834). The juxtaposition proved to him that his art was not only worthy of the French Pantheon, but that his greatest works had stood the test of time: "You see it's the same thing! It's the same thing!" Picasso repeatedly exclaimed.

In fact, until relatively recently, it was customary to think of Picasso's late work as somehow inferior to his previous oeuvre, but recent scholarship has demonstrated that his ingenuity, power and imagination had not floundered in the final years. Between 1954 and 1962, Picasso embarked on numerous variations of iconic paintings by Old Masters. In particular, he produced a cycle of 15 paintings, lithographs, aquatints and drawings of Delacroix's *Women of Algiers*, with odalisques relaxing and smoking hookah among the dark recesses of a room filled with decorative furnishings. *Women of Algiers* of 1955 (see above) was born of circumstances relating to the departure of Françoise Gilot, with their two children, in 1953; the death of Henri Matisse on 3 November 1954; the bloody struggles for Algerian independence from France, beginning with a revolt by the Front de Libération on 1 November 1954, and, typical of Picasso, the appearance of a younger woman (Jacqueline Roque) in his life. Inspired by Matisse's conversations, approaches and colour schemes, Picasso focus is on in on the semi-naked Jacqueline figure, exaggeratedly coiled in dreamy ecstasy around a rather phallic-looking hookah. Perhaps Picasso's version is a playful jibe at Western fantasies about the sexual liberation promised by the "gateway" of the Orient, a stereotypical notion in colonial France. As Picasso somewhat jokingly told his biographer Roland Penrose, "When Matisse died he left me his odalisques as a legacy, and this is my idea of the Orient, though I have never been there".[6]

6 Roland Penrose, *Picasso: His Life and Work*, p. 351–352

Above
Las Meninas, *1957*
Oil on canvas, 129 x 161 cm (50.7 x 63.3 in).
Museo Picasso, Barcelona

This is one of the 45 variations in oil that Picasso created of Velázquez's masterpiece. Here, the play of light and shade is represented by a series of geometric blocks and facets filled with coloured light.

Left
Las Meninas, *1656*
Diego Velázquez, 138 x 276 cm cm (54.3 x 108.7 in).
Museo Nacional del Prado, Madrid

The meaning of Diego Velázquez's painting has engaged art historians throughout the years. This was the reason Picasso was drawn to this mysterious work and, in his numerous studies of it, he focused mainly on the character of the young Infanta Margarita (whom Picasso associated with his dead sister Conchita).

Above
Seated Man resting on Elbow, *1962*
Cut-out cardboard and pencil on both sides, 25 x 26 cm (9.8 x 10.2 in). Musée Picasso, Paris

This sculpture is one of many in a series after Manet's famous painting *Le Déjeuner sur l'herbe (Luncheon on the Grass)*. These small cardboard figures were cut out, folded and had features drawn on to their surfaces with pencil.

Left
Le Déjeuner sur l'herbe, *1862–63, Edouard Manet*
Oil on canvas, 208 x 264.5 cm (82 x 104 in). Musée d'Orsay, Paris

Manet's painting had been much vilified by contemporary critics when exhibited at the Paris Salon des Réfuses in 1869. The artist was accused of painting "incomprehensible" works with arbitrary subject matter. Picasso was clearly fascinated by the hallowed and famously subversive work.

Above

Rape of the Sabine Women, *1962*

Oil on canvas, 90 x 130 cm (35.4 x 51.1 in). Centre Georges Pompidou, Paris, Musée National d'art Moderne, Paris

One of Picasso's many versions of Nicolas Poussin's *Rape of the Sabines*. Here, however, Picasso conflates and jumbles motifs and borrowings from artists such as Francisco de Goya and other art historical eras such as ancient Rome, the France of Louis XIII and even the Second World War.

Left

The 3rd of May 1808, *1814*

Oil on canvas, 268 x 347 cm (105.5 x 136.6 in). Museo Nacional del Prado, Madrid

Goya's painting had a great influence on many modern artists including Manet and Picasso. It commemorates Spanish resistance to Napoleon's armies during the occupation of 1808.

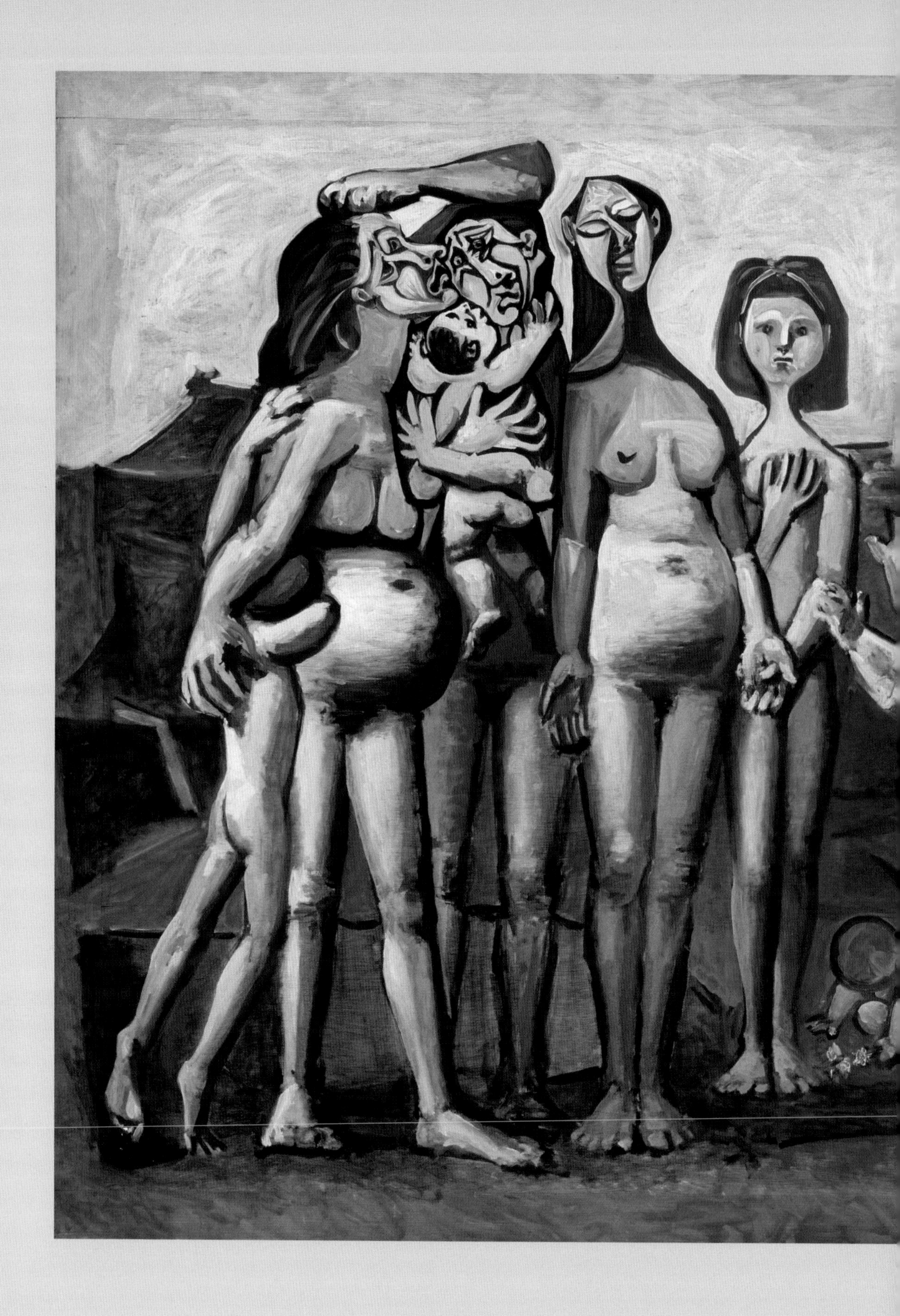

Right

Massacre in Korea, *1951*

110 x 210 cm (43.3 x 82.6 in). Musée Picasso, Paris

The suffering of the innocent and the victims of oppression and war eternally moved Picasso. In paintings such as *Guernica*, *Rape of the Sabines* and *Massacre in Korea*, any political content was eventually subsumed under a universal type of suffering.

INDEX

Page numbers in italic type refer to pictures or their captions.

CREDITS

The publishers would like to thank the following sources for their kind permission to reproduce the pictures in this book.

Akg-Images: 2tc, 2bc, 16-17, 20, 28, 34t, 64, 68-69, 72t, 98l, 98r, 104, 152-3, 159r; /Maurice Babey/© ADAGP, Paris and DACS, London 2011: 73 tl; /Cameraphoto: 118-9; /Electa: 73bl; /Erich Lessing: 23l, 29, 34b, 66l, 173b, 175b; /Nimatallah: 172; /© Succession H. Matisse/DACS 2011: 36; /Jean-Claude Varga: 27l

Art Gallery of Ontario: 73tc

Corbis: /© Burstein Collection: 63; /© Kin Cheung/Reuters: 96; /© The Gallery Collection: 9; /Vittoriano Rastelli: 142-3

Edward Quinn Archive: /© edwardquinn.com: 136-7

Getty Images: 58, 126-7; /Kim Karpeles: 168; /Time & Life Pictures: 133, 159l, 162br

Meadows Museum Dallas: /Michael Bodycomb: 91r

Museo Nacional Centro: /Archivo Fotogáfico Museo Nacional Centro de Arte Reina Sofía, Madrid: 161

Museo Picasso Malaga: /Rafael Lobato: 166r

Museu Picasso Barcelona: 6, 7l, 7r, 22r, 37, 40, 41, 42

National Gallery of Art, Washington: 26

Oskar Reinhart Collection: /Am Romerholz, Winterthur: 110br

RMN: 45, 48, 52-3, 72b, 73tr, 84, 103r, 134, 144; /Daniel Arnaudet: 135; /Christian Bahier / Philippe: 175t; /Michèle Bellot: 105, 121; /Jean-Gilles Berizzi: 57, 60, 109, 111tl, 111tr, 122t, 130, 138, 176-7; /Madeleine Coursaget: 44, 47 , 59, 128, 129; /Béatrice Hatala: 35r, 39, 51, 67, 85, 92l, 92r, 102, 103l, 110l, 115tl, 115bl, 115r, 120l, 120r 132, 146-7, 147,149tl, 149tr ,149b, 154tr, 160, 162tr, 169tr, 174t; /Jacques L'Hoir/ Jean Popovitch: 143; /Thierry Le Mage: 49, 53, 54, 55, 97, 122b,123, 136, 158; /Hervé Lewandowski: 22l, 65, 87, 174b; /René-Gabriel Ojéda: 38, 46, 50, 56, 81b, 90, 148, 154b, 155; /Jean-Claude Planchet: 74; /Franck Raux: 8, 15, 124r, 163

Scala Archives: 14t, 99l, 140, 166l; /BPK: 79; /Heritage Images: 47; /The Metropolitan Museum of Art: 23r, 32-33, 75; / The Museum of Modern Art, New York: 27r, 78, 80, 86r, 91l, 101, 108, 124l, 167

SuperStock: /© Peter Willi: 21

Tate Picture Library: 114

The Bridgeman Art Library: /Bacchus and Ariadne, 1520-23 (oil on canvas) (pre-restoration), Titian (Tiziano Vecellio) (c.1488-1576) / National Gallery, London, UK: 111b; /Blue Nude III, 1952 (gouache on paper), Matisse, Henri (1869-1954) / Musee National d'Art Moderne, Centre Pompidou, Paris, France / © 2011 Succession H. Matisse/DACS, London Giraudon: 169l; /Cover of the first issue of 'La Revolution Surrealiste' magazine, 1st December 1924 (litho), French School, (20th century) / Private Collection/ Archives Charmet: 125; /Dressage des Nouvelles, par Valentin le Desosse (Moulin-Rouge), 1890, Toulouse-Lautrec, Henri de (1864-1901) / Philadelphia Museum of Art, Pennsylvania, PA, USA / Peter Willi : 14b; /Guillaume Apollinaire (1880-1918) in Picasso's studio at the Bateau-Lavoir, early 20th century (b/w photo), French Photographer, (20th century) / Private Collection / Archives Charme: 43l; /Head, 1913 (papiers colles with black chalk on card), Picasso, Pablo (1881-1973) / © National Gallery of Scotland, Edinburgh, Scotland: 86l, /Homage to J.S. Bach, 1912 (oil on canvas), Braque, Georges (1882-1963) / Private Collection /©ADAGP, Paris and DACS, London 2011: 81t; /Las Meninas No.31, 1957 (oil on canvas), Picasso, Pablo (1881-1973) / Museu Picasso, Barcelona, Spain: 173t; /Man Leaning on a Table, 1916 (oil on canvas), Picasso, Pablo (1881-1973) / Private Collection: 93; /Nude, Green Leaves and Bust, 1932 (oil on canvas), Picasso, Pablo (1881-1973) / Private Collection / Photo © Christie's Images: 1; / Pablo Picasso (1881-1973) in his studio at Vallauris, 1950s (b/w photo), French Photographer, (20th century) / Private Collection / Roger-Viollet, Paris: 139; /Pablo Picasso (1881-1973) painting 'Guernica', 1937 (b/w photo), Maar, Dora (1907-97) / Private Collection / © DACS / Archives Charmet: 131; /Pablo Picasso (1881-1973) with Francoise Gilot (b.1922) and their son Claude (b.1947), c.1952 (b/w photo), / Private Collection / Roger-Viollet, Paris: 141; /Pablo Picasso (1881-1973), 1904 (b/w photo), French Photographer, (20th century) / Musee de Montmartre, Paris, France / Archives Charmet: 43r; /Portrait of Olga, 1922/23 (pastel), Picasso, Pablo (1881-1973) / Private Collection: 110tr; /Still Life with steer's skull, 1942 (oil on canvas), Picasso, Pablo (1881-1973) / Pinacoteca di Brera, Milan, Italy / Alinari: 2b, 162l; /The Absinthe
Drinker (Portrait of Angel Fernandez de Soto) 1903 (oil on canvas), Picasso, Pablo (1881-1973) /
Private Collection: 2t, 12; /The Toilet, 1906 (oil on canvas), Picasso, Pablo (1881-1973) /
Albright Knox Art Gallery, Buffalo, New York, USA / Giraudon: 35l; /Violin, Glass, Pipe and Anchor, Souvenir of Le Havre, 1912 (oil on canvas), Picasso, Pablo (1881-1973) / Narodni Galerie, Prague, Czech Republic: 99r; /Woman in Blue, 1901 (oil on canvas), Picasso, Pablo (1881-1973) / Museo Nacional Centro de Arte Reina Sofia, Madrid, Spain / Giraudon: 13

The British Museum: 154tr

Topfoto.co.uk: 66r

Every effort has been made to acknowledge correctly and contact the source and/or copyright holder of each picture and Carlton Books Limited apologises for any unintentional errors or omissions which will be corrected in future editions of this book.

Jacket images (front)
Photograph of Pablo Picasso, 1956

Mandolin and Guitar, 1924
Oil with sand on canvas, 140.7 x 200.3 cm (55 x 78 in)
Guggenheim Museum, New York

Editorial Manager: Vanessa Daubney
Project Editor: Victoria Marshallsay
Managing Art Director: Lucy Coley
Design: Grade Design Consultants Ltd
Picture Research: Jenny Meredith
Production: Maria Petalidou